PROJECTS with PEOPLE

The practice of participation in rural development

Peter Oakley et al.

*Prepared with the financial support
of FAO, UNIFEM and WHO*

International Labour Office, Geneva

Oakley, P.
Projects with people: The practice of participation in rural development
Geneva, International Labour Office, 1991

/Popular participation/, /Rural community/, /Rural development/, /Development project/s,
/Developing country/s. 05.03.3
ISBN 92-2-107282-7

ILO Cataloguing in Publication Data

Foreword

This study was carried out with the financial support of four United Nations agencies: the Food and Agriculture Organisation of the United Nations (FAO), the International Labour Organisation (ILO), the United Nations Development Fund for Women (UNIFEM), and the World Health Organization (WHO). These agencies are members of the Panel on People's Participation, an inter-agency body of the United Nations Task Force on Rural Development established in 1982 under the chairmanship of the ILO; its aim is specifically to promote the concept and the practice of people's participation in the rural development activities and programmes carried out by the United Nations specialised agencies.

The concern of the United Nations system with people's participation is to be seen in the light of its mandate to contribute to improving the living standards of the world's working population, especially the poor. It is by and large accepted that strategies and programmes to alleviate poverty cannot succeed unless the poor themselves are able to participate directly in such efforts. The Panel has attempted to enhance the understanding of people's participation in development through an earlier publication entitled *Approaches to participation in rural development*, by Peter Oakley and David Marsden (Geneva, ILO, 1984), and through various workshops and meetings organised around this issue.

As Peter Oakley of the University of Reading's Agricultural Extension and Rural Development Department recalls in this second study centred on the practice of participation, the challenge of participation is still very much with us. The growing acceptance of people's participation as a development objective has sharpened the demand for a clearer and more concrete interpretation of the methodology for promoting participation. This study addresses precisely this issue.

The author has sought to look at a wide range of experiences in which genuine attempts are being made to promote the participation of the people within the broad framework of rural development projects. The study presents a selection of case studies drawn from the three developing regions of the world, highlighting the methodological approach applied in promoting participation within a variety of sectoral, institutional and policy settings. Elements of a strategy and of a methodology for promoting people's participation are drawn from these case studies. This analysis contributes significantly to our understanding of the concrete steps and instruments needed to turn participation into a live momentum.

Naturally, interpretations of the concept of participation vary and the practice reflects this diversity. The author distinguishes between minimal participation in development where people are gradually involved in an activity designed and guided from outside, and participatory development where people are at the centre of the development activity. Participation has its own prerequisites, some of which may not be compatible with the orthodox yet widely used project framework. The author argues for a more flexible approach in which people, through their own resolve or through the intervention of an outside agent carrying out animation work, gradually work out an organisational base that becomes the instrument of their participation. Group activities in the form of discussions, meetings, group reflection, social and economic activities are the means by which people advance on the road of participation.

The challenge of participation is no less than a democratisation of the development process in which people would take precedence over economic or technological objectives. To this democratisation the members of the inter-agency Task Force on Rural Development are committed. It is our conviction that this study answers a plea, from persons with responsibilities for, and an interest in, furthering development, for concrete guidance on how to move in the promotion of people's participation. It is our hope that this study will stimulate further efforts throughout the Third World enabling its people to participate actively in their own development.

Samir Radwan,
Chief,
Rural Employment Policies Branch,
Employment and Development Department

Preface

It could be argued that, in terms of thinking and practice about development, we are currently in the age of "participation". For the past 30 years or so those concerned to begin a process of development in some of the less developed countries have continuously sought and experimented with alternative solutions to the poverty that is endemic in much of the world. The literature which has accompanied this search reflects the periodic emergence of new strategies that have greatly influenced thinking and practice. In the past major strategies of "community development", "integrated rural development" and "basic needs", for example, for a time predominated and received widespread support. All too often, however, disenchantment sets in, a temporary "crisis" in thinking emerges and the search for a more relevant strategy continues.

While it is historically impossible to pinpoint the emergence of these strategies with complete accuracy, it could be said that disenchantment with development strategies in the mid-1970s led to the emergence of "participation" as a major new force in development thinking. Interestingly, two broadly different schools of thought came to the same conclusion in arguing that "participation" was a critical element in tackling the problems of poor people in the Third World:

- One school saw "participation" as the key to the inclusion of human resources in development efforts; previously development planners had overlooked the contributions that people could make and the skills that they could bring to development projects. If, therefore, one could incorporate the human element in such projects and persuade people to participate in them, then there would be a stronger chance that these projects would be successful.

- The other school saw this "participation" in a very different light. It saw participation as more linked to tackling the structural causes of people's poverty rather than as yet another input into a development project. People are poor because they are excluded and have little influence upon the forces which affect their livelihoods. Participation is the process whereby such people seek to have some influence and to gain access to the resources which would help them sustain and improve their living standards.

Since the late 1960s there has been considerable support for the view that development in the Third World has for too long benefited the few and excluded the many. The means by which this trend would be reversed, it is argued, is a process of participation. In the past seven or eight years the literature on development has highlighted this increasing support for the concept of "participation", and the term is now commonly added to existing terminologies to suggest a major change of emphasis. Today we have "participatory planning", "participatory research and evaluation", "participation in communication", "participation in water supply", "participation in health development", and so on. Several of the major international agencies such as the FAO, the ILO, the United Nations Development Programme (UNDP) and the United Nations Research Institute for Social Development (UNRISD) have either launched substantial research programmes on participation or have sought to incorporate participation in their development practice; others, particularly the non-governmental organisations (NGOs), have strengthened existing commitments. Academic and research institutions have similarly explored the concept of participation, with the result that there is currently a large amount of literature on different dimensions of participation in development.

The purpose of this study is not merely to review and synthesise this vast corpus of literature. Several substantial reviews of the concept of participation have already been undertaken and there is less need for further theoretical analysis. Participation, however, has not remained on the drawing-board or in academic libraries but has begun to influence, in many areas substantially, the practice of development.

This study is concerned with that practice. It is, of course, possible to study "participation" in a range of different dimensions: participation as part of the process of political democracy; participation in an anthropological sense as communities extend their contacts with the wider environment; participation in organisations (e.g. trade unions or co-operatives), and so on. Here we consider the practice of participation in rural development projects that have been largely initiated and designed by an external agency and that seek to bring about some form of development. In this respect the term "external agency" is used in a very broad sense to encompass any form of structured or planned intervention. Development projects are a basic instrument of intervention to bring about some form of change and the means by which external assistance is brought to influence the development of a particular area or region. The majority of development agencies function on the basis of projects and it is by means of such projects that they seek to promote people's participation.

To date the literature on participation has been dominated by conceptual analyses, broad explanations of participatory strategies and arguments in support of them; but there is less literature on how this participation occurs. The study will therefore concentrate upon the issues of practice and methodology in order to examine how development projects go about promoting participation and what successes they have had. The aim is not to examine the details of one or two substantial examples of participation (and leave the reader to extrapolate his or her broader conclusions) but to cast the net widely and to include as many examples as possible for a better understanding of the nature and extent of participation as currently practised in rural development projects. The purpose is not to develop a single understanding of the practice or a single methodology of participation but to review the practice of participation widely across sectors, to draw this practice together and to see what methodologies are emerging from a range of projects to promote participation.

During a 20-year involvement in development I have visited or been in touch with a number of the projects reviewed; the study, however, is primarily a literature review, although the literature has not all been located in the conventional sense. There are few conventional texts on the practice of participation; but development agencies hold a vast reservoir of project literature, studies, evaluations and other documentation which illustrate the practice of participation. While this study has drawn upon available literature, it is also based to a large degree on written material in project files held by agencies such as FAO, ILO, UNDP, UNIFEM, WHO, OXFAM, Christian Aid, the Catholic Fund for Overseas Development (CAFOD), War on Want, NOVIB and CEBEMO. Staff of the above agencies made selected files available to me and provided me with a rich fund of material. I deliberately sought a balance between international agency and NGO project documentation in order to ensure a wide range of examples of participatory projects. In all I have reviewed file material from some 120 rural development projects across sectors, all of which were selected for me as projects which sought to promote and develop popular participation.

This study is not directed primarily at an academic audience but at the wide range of development practitioners working with development projects in different parts of the world. Many work with a commitment to "participation" but with only limited guidance on how to put it into practice. As I have said, this study is not intended to be a model, but rather a resource document that development practitioners in different sectors can consider and use as they confront the issue of participation in their own contexts. There is no one model or one way of implementing participation, but there are now a number of rich experiences which could help practitioners confronting a similar situation. The study sketches the broad dimensions of participation and encourages practitioners to explore the issue further in their own sectoral literature and documentation.

Chapter 1 briefly discusses the concept of participation and examines a number of key issues related to its practice. Chapter 2 reviews the practice of participation to date in the different sectors involved in rural development, while Chapter 3 brings together examples from a number of development projects. In this chapter contributors have not had to rely on a few already well-documented studies but present case studies drawn from their own direct involvement. Chapter 4 outlines and discusses the study's interpretation of participation as a strategy in rural development projects and examines in detail the key characteristics and elements of this strategy. Chapter 5 is a review of emerging methodologies of participation and a detailed examination of some of their more common elements. Finally, Chapter 6 examines the issue of the evaluation of participation in rural development projects.

This study should be read as a sequel to one I wrote with David Marsden in 1984,[1] which reviewed conceptually current interpretations of participation and which was sponsored by the Panel on People's Participation of the United Nations Task Force on Rural Development. I am particularly grateful to Philippe Egger and Anisur Rahman (ILO), Niko Newiger and John Rouse (FAO), Haile Mariam Kahssay (WHO) and Margaret Snyder (UNIFEM) for their organisations' support in the preparation of this study. I am also most grateful to Brian Pratt (OXFAM), Paul Spray (Christian Aid), John Cunnington (War on Want), Han de Grot (NOVIB), Stephen King (CAFOD) and Koenrad Verhagen (CEBEMO) for their willing collaboration with my researches and for allowing me to examine some of their agencies' project files. I trust that the end product does not betray their confidence.

Special thanks are due to Dharam Ghai (UNRISD), David Marsden (University College, Swansea), Norman Uphoff (Cornell University), Bernard Van Heck (Institute for the Promotion of Economic and Social Development – ISPES, Rome) and Koenrad Verhagen (CEBEMO, Netherlands) for reading the study in draft and for their most thoughtful and challenging comments. My thanks also to Charlotte Harland, Nick Leader and Wani Tombe Lako who worked with me at various stages of the book's preparation. Given the qualitative and essentially ideological nature of participation, it is impossible to write a text on this subject with which even a majority of readers would agree. Interpretation is critical and perspective fundamental. The final content and perspective of this study, therefore, are entirely my own responsibility.

Finally, more than a word of thanks to Diana McDowell for, as usual, taking full responsibility for typing and preparing the manuscript with her customary efficiency and to Jane Thompson for willingly throwing in her support whenever it was needed.

Peter Oakley,

Agricultural Extension and Rural Development Department, University of Reading

[1] Peter Oakley and David Marsden: *Approaches to participation in rural development* (Geneva, ILO, 1984).

Contents

Boxes

1

Understanding participation

The tragedy of underdevelopment is not that the ordinary people have remained poor or are becoming poor, but that they have been inhibited from developing as humans. Elites have taken over the right to develop society, and by this very act and claim have distorted the natural and profound popular notion of development. For no one can develop others – one can only stretch or diminish others by trying to develop them (A. Rahman).

While it is impossible to pinpoint changes in development thinking with any historical accuracy, there is no doubt that the mid-1970s saw the start of a fundamental shift away from the domination of the modernisation paradigm of development thinking and intervention and a move towards a systematic search for alternatives. The past 15 years have witnessed a searching re-examination of the nature and purpose of development, and this re-examination has correspondingly influenced practice.[1] The literature which has recorded this re-examination is prodigious, and many academics have immersed themselves in the new theoretical and conceptual horizons that have been provided. The re-examination threw up a whole new form of analysis – dependency theory – that has steadily influenced the different dimensions of development intervention.[2] The work of Haque and his colleagues (1977) was instrumental in giving structure to this re-thinking and their efforts have been built upon by successive researchers (Pearse and Stiefel, 1979; Galjart, 1981; Bhasin, 1985; Verhagen, 1985).

The central issue of this search for development alternatives was that development had become capital centred as opposed to people centred; it had by-passed or even marginalised people in its concern to build and construct. The counter-argument stated although physical development was important, it

---

[1] We still await a substantial text which pulls together the many strands of the different lines of thinking which have emerged since the early 1970s. More general texts include: R. Chambers: *Putting the last first* (London, Longman, 1983); G. Gran: *Development by people* (New York, Praeger, 1983); W. Haque et al: "Towards a theory of rural development", in *Development Dialogue* (Uppsala, Dag Hammarskjöld Foundation, No. 2, 1977, pp. 7-137).

[2] For a succinct review of dependency theory see A. Foster-Carter: "Neo-Marxist approaches to development and underdevelopment", in E. De Kadt (ed.): *Sociology and development* (London, Tavistock Press, 1976). A more recent study which examines historically the emergence of dependency theory in the Latin American context is C. Kay: *Latin American theories of development and underdevelopment* (London, Routledge, 1989).

must be approached in such a way that people had both a central role and some control over it. While it is, of course, possible to show that many of these capital-centred efforts improved the lives of some rural people, in most Third World countries the majority of them have benefited little or have even become worse off.[3] This capital-centred development helped to improve the material livelihoods of some and to develop their talents, skills and abilities, but it has been less successful in more widely promoting people's involvement in the development process. For too long development has been concerned largely with seeking to build national productive and physical capacities and measuring success with broad statistics and quantitative increases. Early in the debate Schumacher (1973, p. 141) was arguing that development did not start with these physical goods but "with people and their education, organisation and discipline. Without these three all resources remain latent, untapped potential". Development was seen as a process of humanisation and, it was argued, people should be central to any kind of development process. The following two early statements illustrate the contrasting views of development that have been debated over the past decade:

> Rural development is clearly designed to increase production and raise productivity. Rural development recognises, however, that improved food supplies and nutrition, together with basic services such as health and education, can not only directly improve the physical well-being and quality of life of the rural poor, but can also directly enhance their productivity and their ability to contribute to the national economy (World Bank, 1975).

> Rural development is the participation of people in a mutual learning experience involving themselves, their local resources, external change agents and outside resources. People cannot be developed, they can only develop themselves by participation in decision and co-operative activities which affect their well-being. People are not being developed when they are herded like animals into new ventures (Nyerere, 1968).

The latter quotation is a succinct statement of what is variously referred to in the literature as "another development", "alternative development", "people-centred development" "counter development", or "participatory development". Authors such as Rahman (1981), Galjart (1981), Bhasin (1985), Roling (1985), Gran (1985), Fuglesang and Chandler (1986) and Fals Borda (1987) have contributed to building up our theoretical understanding of alternative approaches to development. Such authors have not coalesced, however, around one single definition or model but have stressed the need to adapt the basis and approach of development to the social, political and

---

[3] See, for example, A. Pearse: *Seeds of plenty, seeds of hope* (Oxford, Clarendon Press, 1980), and K. Griffin: *The political economy of agrarian change* (London, Macmillan, 1974) for two of the more substantial studies of the differential impact of development interventions. Studies such as these gave rise to the proposals for "Growth with Equity", a strategy elaborated by the World Bank in the late 1970s.

economic context of the people involved. None of them argues that improvements in the physical environments of the rural poor (e.g. new crop varieties, better water supply or health facilities) are not necessary; indeed, many vividly depict the grinding poverty characteristic of the lives of millions of rural people in the Third World. Two arguments are put forward. First the poverty is structural and has its roots in the economic and political conditions which influence rural people's livelihoods. In order to begin to tackle this poverty, it is important to develop the abilities of rural people to have a say in, and to have some influence on, the forces which control their livelihoods. Second, development programmes and projects have largely by-passed the vast majority of rural people; there is a need, therefore, to re-think forms of development intervention to ensure that this neglected majority has a chance to benefit from development initiatives. The one single idea that has emerged from this major reappraisal of development is the need for a greater participation of rural people in development processes. This participation will not only change the nature and direction of development interventions but will lead to a type of development which is more respectful of poor people's position and interests.

The challenge of participation

Illich (1969) argued that underdevelopment, as well as being a function of physical impoverishment, was also a state of mind and that understanding it as a state of mind, or as a level of consciousness, was critical in bringing about change. In this respect broad, sweeping commitments to processes such as "participation" need to understand the powerful contextual barriers which perpetuate people's isolation or lack of involvement in development. These barriers entrench a state of mind which a process of participation seeks to reverse. In the early part of the search for alternatives, Freire (1972) wrote powerfully of the "culture of silence" and said that the rural poor had "no voice, no access and no participation" in development activities. Poverty is not just a lack of physical resources for development; it also implies powerlessness or the inability to exert influence upon the forces which shape one's livelihood. The literature and agency files vividly describe the lives of rural people, the grinding nature of their poverty and, in many instances, the oppression they suffer from other forces. The following is a typical example of the powerlessness of rural people:

> The majority of Alipuaton and Tinagaan residents have a miserable existence. Despite the rich natural resources and agricultural products the *barrios* can offer, 480 of the 580 households live in poverty and social injustice. Classified as small farmers, tenants and agricultural workers, they receive meagre pay from hillside farming or coconut gathering. Much of their poverty can be attributed

to the unjust and unequal distribution of wealth and power in an oppressive system and structure. With only a few rich landlords and businessmen virtually in control of the local agricultural economy, the peasants are almost always on the losing end. Buying prices for their produce are constantly low while the selling prices of basic commodities are staggeringly beyond the reach of the peasants (CAFOD, Philippines 16).

On one level, therefore, the challenge to a concept such as participation is to seek to make contact with and involve rural people whose lives are dominated by the issues described above. These reflect the reality of the majority of rural people's lives and must be the starting-point for development intervention. Participation, therefore, cannot merely be proclaimed or wished upon rural people in the Third World; it must begin by recognising the powerful, multi-dimensional and, in many instances, anti-participatory forces which dominate the lives of rural people. Centuries of domination and subservience will not disappear overnight just because we have "discovered" the concept of participation; this fact alone speaks volumes for the way participation must unfold.

On another level, the challenge to participation is also to reverse a style and an approach to development intervention that dominates so much practice (box 1). Classically, development interventions are undertaken by government or agency staff who use projects as the basic instrument of implementation. These projects are designed and managed by professional staff and, with varying degrees of sensitivity, are introduced into rural areas. The very style of such development projects is to suggest that the professional is the expert and knows, while rural people are inexperienced and do not know. Freire (1972), in his critical article on the practice of extension, concludes that this style of intervention results in rural people becoming the mere objects of development projects. Similarly, Chambers (1983) discusses in detail the consequences of this style of intervention and suggests the fundamental changes which will need to occur if it is to be reversed.

The increasing recognition of the inadequacies of total dependence upon a professionally dominant style of intervention has caused the search for alternative styles. This has led to the emergence of a number of new perspectives: bottom-up development, putting people first and putting the last first.

Whatever the individual merits of these new perspectives, they all essentially demand a pronounced shift in the style of development intervention. To date, however, there is more commitment than substance to these perspectives and Chambers' (1983) study is the only detailed analysis of the implications of a style of intervention which seeks to reverse decades of established practice. Participation similarly demands a reverse in practice and a radical shift in emphasis from the external professional to the local people.

Box 1.   Non-participatory development

■ The existing planning procedures for the project are not based on the understanding of the critical ingredients of participation; namely participation in decision-making, participation in implementation, participation in benefit sharing and participation in evaluation. When the villagers undertook projects on their own ... the participation of the local people in terms of all these dimensions was total. But when it came to the planning of activities under the World Bank project, their participation was only partial and limited to the need identification and subsequent implementation of a few rural works projects ... In most other sectoral activities the participation of the people at the village level was simply non-existent. Nepal (Uphoff, 1985).

■ In the traditional approach to development it is well known that the administrators of development projects and the beneficiaries do not sit on the same side of the table. In fact they sit at different levels, the former being always at a higher level. What follows, therefore, is quite inevitable. Each look at each other with suspicion. To the official, the villager is lazy, ignorant, unresourceful and irresponsible. To the villager, the official is conceited, unsympathetic, unconcerned and corrupt. Each does not take the other into his confidence. Instead of getting together they continue to stay apart. Sri Lanka (Talagune, 1985).

■ Community participation is non-existent. At times the people of a given area are not even informed of project implementation in their area. At other times, after plans are made, the community is informed through formal meetings where the officers justify their plans, but modification is not considered. Kenya (Lele, 1975).

■ Projects tend to be identified and designed by donors in consultation with central government officials, and the budgets and timetables are planned in a rigid way which make it difficult for the community to play a significant role. The emphasis upon the achievement of physical outputs within a limited period of time and with close supervision and accountability are added difficulties (Bamberger, 1986).

■ Overall, the principles guiding beneficiary participation in Bank-financed projects have been quite abstract and of limited operational impact. Beneficiaries were not assigned a role in the decision-making process, nor was their technological knowledge sought prior to designing project components (World Bank, 1988).

Interpreting participation

Participation defies any single attempt at definition or interpretation. Since the late 1970s an enormous amount of literature on participation has, on the one hand, broadened our understanding of the concept and, on the other, challenged all efforts to package it neatly within a single statement. In many ways it could be argued that participation has become an umbrella term for a supposedly new style of development intervention. It is now almost reactionary seriously to propose a development strategy which is not participatory and the major aspects of development intervention – research, planning, implementation and evaluation – have all been subject to reorientation in order to make them more participatory. There is, however, what Cernea (1985) calls a "cloud of rhetoric" surrounding this reorientation to participation, and a suggestion by several authors that participation in development projects is still more myth than reality (Midgeley, 1986; Fugelsang and Chandler, 1986; Ghai, 1988).

While this study does not concern itself primarily with the details of the debate concerning participation nor the content of its varying interpretations, it will be useful to review briefly some of the more important and contrasting statements on participation. Oakley and Marsden (1984) reviewed a whole range of interpretations of participation in development projects and presented them as a continuum to illustrate the direct relationship between interpretation and development analysis. In a more limited way, the following four statements summarise this range of interpretations:

(a) Participation is considered a voluntary contribution by the people in one or another of the public programmes supposed to contribute to national development, but the people are not expected to take part in shaping the programme or criticising its contents (Economic Commission for Latin America, 1973).

(b) With regard to rural development ... participation includes people's involvement in decision-making processes, in implementing programmes, their sharing in the benefits of development programmes and their involvement in efforts to evaluate such programmes (Cohen and Uphoff, 1977).

(c) Participation is concerned with ... the organised efforts to increase control over resources and regulative institutions in given social situations on the part of groups and movements of those hitherto excluded from such control (Pearse and Stiefel, 1979).

(d) Community participation [is] an active process by which beneficiary or client groups influence the direction and execution of a development project with a view to enhancing their well-being in terms of income, personal growth, self-reliance or other values they cherish (Paul, 1987).

Collectively the above statements capture the essence of the participation debate. Statement *(a)* is essentially an understanding of participation in terms of economic incentives to participate and be rewarded by some tangible economic benefit. Participation in this sense often occurs in the form of some kind of input or contribution to a project in order to enhance its chances of success and, correspondingly, personal economic benefit. Statement *(b)* has been widely influential, particularly among development projects supported by governments and international agencies. It helped launch a whole form of analysis which took decision-making, implementation, benefits and evaluation as the key elements in the process of participation. Statement *(c)* served as the working definition on participation for UNRISD's major research programme into the concept which began in 1979. It similarly launched a new form of analysis, particularly among NGOs whose approach to participation has been less tied to the notion of immediate economic benefit, and has been both widely influential and immensely productive in terms of research publications.[4] Statement *(d)* has emerged as a result of a review of participation in projects supported by the World Bank and suggests a balanced view in terms of the range of expectations that beneficiaries derive from participation. It is also an interpretation put forward with the benefit of hindsight and represents an ideal state which projects may hope to achieve.

It would be wrong, of course, to argue that the above statements are discrete and mutually exclusive and that all projects which promote participation must be located within one statement or the other. The statements are not presented to suggest universal models nor to show that there are clearly distinguishable dividing-lines between them. In essence, however, it could be argued that statement *(a)* appears to be different from statement *(c)* and would, therefore, imply different forms of participation. Experience generally suggests that the above statements do represent recognisably different forms of participation and that the general thrust of most development projects could be located within one statement or the other.

Apart from efforts to distinguish between definitions of participation, several other broader approaches can be used to help differentiate alternatives within such an all-embracing concept. One major form of differentiation is to distinguish between participation as a means or an end. Participation as a *means* implies the use of participation to achieve some predetermined goal or objective. In other words, participation is a way of harnessing the existing physical, economic and social resources of rural people in order to achieve the objectives of development programmes and projects. Participation as a means

---

[4] UNRISD launched its major People Participation Programme in 1979. The essential working document of the research programme was A. Pearse and M. Stiefel: *Inquiry into participation: A research approach* (Geneva, UNRISD, 1979). The research programme has produced a number of occasional papers, a publication entitled *Dialogue on participation* which encouraged debate between academics and practitioners, and a series of more substantial publications based on its researches in Latin America and Asia.

stresses the results of participation in that the achievement of predetermined targets is more important than the act of participation. Often government and development agencies see participation as the means to improving the delivery systems of the projects they seek to implement. In these cases participation is essentially a short-term exercise; the local population is mobilised, there is direct involvement in the task at hand but the participation evaporates once the task is completed. In many ways it could be argued that participation as a means is a passive form of participation. Participation as an *end* is an entirely different concept. Here we see participation essentially as a process which unfolds over time and whose purpose is to develop and strengthen the capabilities of rural people to intervene more directly in development initiatives. Such a process may not have predetermined measurable objectives or even direction. As an end in itself participation should be a permanent feature of any rural development project, an intrinsic part which grows and strengthens as the project develops. Participation as an end is an active and dynamic form of participation which enables rural people to play an increasing role in development activities.[5]

Other authors, such as Cohen and Uphoff (1977), Midgeley et al. (1986) and Paul (1987) have similarly sought to distinguish between the vast amount of interpretations and dimensions surrounding the concept of participation and, as such, have brought clarity to the inquiry. Cohen and Uphoff's state of the art review has been particularly influential in the way it has related participation to development projects and suggested the key stages in this process: decision-making, implementation, benefits and evaluation. Their analysis has launched a proverbial thousand projects which have sought to promote these four dimensions of participation. While all of the above have added richness to the inquiry and stretched wide the concept of participation, it could be argued that essentially there are three broad interpretations of participation:

Participation as contribution: The dominant interpretation of participation in development projects in the Third World sees participation as implying voluntary or other forms of contributions by rural people to predetermined programmes and projects. Health, water supply, forestry, infrastructural and natural resource conservation projects, for example, predominantly stress rural people's contributions as implicit in the participation and indeed fundamental to success. There are, of course, a whole variety of ways whereby these contributions are forthcoming and managed but, whatever the guise under which they are presented, they form the core of the participatory element in the project.[6]

---

[5] For a more detailed discussion of the distinction between participation as a means or an end see P. Oakley and D. Marsden: *Approaches to participation in rural development* (Geneva, ILO, 1984).

[6] The sectoral reviews of participation in Chapter 2 clearly illustrate the widespread practice of this understanding of participation. The word "contribution" is, of course, rarely explicitly used and the term is deliberately employed in this book to imply that the control and direction of the project does not pass to the local people; they are merely asked to contribute their different resources.

Participation as organisation: There has long been an argument across the range of development literature and practice that organisation is a fundamental instrument of participation. Few would dispute this contention, but would disagree on the nature and evolution of the organisation. The distinction lies between the origin of the organisational form which will serve as the vehicle for participation; either such organisations are externally conceived and introduced (co-operatives, farmers' associations, irrigation management committees, etc.) or else they emerge and take structure themselves as a result of the process of participation. The urge within development workers to suggest and structure appropriate organisations for rural people is at times uncontrollable; the alternative equally recognises the importance of organisation but seeks to encourage rural people to determine its nature and structure. In this respect Verhagen's (1987) work interestingly shows how even formal organisations like co-operatives can emerge as a result of a participatory process.[7]

Participation as empowering: Increasingly in the past five years or so the notion of participation as an exercise of empowering rural people has gained wider support. In 1979 the World Conference on Agrarian Reform and Rural Development (WCARRD) emphasised the importance of a transfer of power as implicit in participation. Since then "empowering" has become an accepted term in development vocabulary. It is, however, a term difficult to define and gives rise to alternative explanations. Some see empowering as the development of skills and abilities to enable rural people to manage better, have a say in or negotiate with existing development delivery systems; others see it as more fundamental and essentially concerned with enabling rural people to decide upon and to take the actions which they believe are essential to their development. Whatever the disagreements in perspective, the relationship between participation and power is now widely recognised.[8]

As with the earlier statements on participation, it is not possible to treat the above as discrete and inseparable categories. A development project might ostensibly contain elements of all three, although this is highly unlikely. A broad and recognisable distinction could be drawn, however, between participation as contribution on the one hand, and participation as organisation and empowering on the other. Certainly organisation is a fundamental ingredient of

---

[7] For two contrasting understandings of organisation in a process of participation see Y. Levi and H. Litwin (eds.): *Community and cooperatives in participatory development* (Aldershot, Hampshire, Gower, 1986); and K. Constantino-David: "Community organization and people's participation", in A. Fugelsang (ed.): *Methods and media in community participation* (Uppsala, Dag Hammarskjöld Foundation, 1985).

[8] For more detailed reviews of the concept of empowering see K. Bhasin: *Towards empowerment* (New Delhi, FAO, 1985); R. Lubett: *Non-government organizations as agents of empowerment*, Unpublished M.A. dissertation (Reading, University of Reading, 1987); J.B. Kronenburg: *Empowerment of the poor* (Amsterdam, Royal Dutch Tropical Institute, 1986).

a process of empowering; similarly it is often a prerequisite to local people's contributions. Practice suggests, however, that we can identify a dominant line of action in projects which promote participation, and contribution, organisation and empowering are those lines.

It could be argued that defining the nature of the participation which it is hoped to bring about is the essential first step of any participatory project. And yet the practice seems to suggest that this does not always happen. Indeed, it is not uncommon to review the detail and explanations of a particular project which supposedly has "participation" as an objective and to find little, if any, evidence of what the project understands by the term. For too many rural development projects participation is seen as yet another input to be programmed and managed along with other inputs. Not surprisingly, it is then often difficult to assess the outcome of the project in terms of participation. The overall conclusion must be that projects which seek to promote participation must be aware at the start of the project as to the likely nature of the participation they expect to promote. The nature of the participation might change, of course, as the project evolves but project staff should at least be conscious that they are dealing with an unfolding process. If nothing else, such an analysis will help projects determine the appropriate methodologies to promote participation.

Obstacles to participation

The practice of participation does not occur in a vacuum; on the contrary it is susceptible, in both a negative and a positive way, to a whole range of influences. Since the greater part of this study will deal with factors, elements and phenomena which can support and strengthen this practice, it would be useful to review here the kinds of factors which can affect it negatively. A number of studies are now emerging which suggest "problems" with the practice of participation or, more fundamentally, serious obstacles which can frustrate attempts at participatory development. In some instances these studies merely list the kinds of problems participation confronts and suggest appropriate solutions; in others it is clearly recognised that such problems cannot be isolated in the manner of other project inputs and, correspondingly, there are no instant remedies.[9] Reviewing the evidence before us, however, we can examine these obstacles to participation under a number of broad headings.

[9]Two examples of such lists of problems of implementing participation are found in Centre for Integrated Rural Development for Asia and the Pacific (CIRDAP): *People's participation in rural development* (Dhaka, 1984); and Pan-African Institute for Development: *Effective participation in IRD with special emphasis on the grass roots* (Douala, 1978).

Structural obstacles

The political environment within a particular country can in some circumstances be supportive of this process; equally, in different circumstances, it can constitute a fundamental obstacle. In countries where the prevailing ideology does not encourage openness or citizens' comments but prefers to maintain the direction and decision-making concerning state affairs in strictly controlled hands, the prevailing political environment will not be conducive to genuine participation. Furthermore, a centralised political system that lays less emphasis upon local mechanisms for administration and decision-making can greatly reduce the potential for authentic participation. Structural obstacles also include the tensions which can arise between the mechanisms promoted locally by the State in order to achieve centrally planned objectives and the spontaneous, informal development efforts at grass-roots level within development projects whose participants are excluded from these mechanisms. Similar tensions can arise between the policy of the State and development projects which seek to organise rural people in order to influence this policy in terms of a redistribution of political and economic power. In many instances there may be direct political influence on the direction of development projects or attempts to co-opt such projects for party political reasons. It can be seen, therefore, that the nature of the political environment within a particular State will have a strong influence on the potential for meaningful local-level participation.[10]

More specifically, the existing legal system within a country can seriously frustrate efforts to promote participation. This can function in two ways. On the one hand, the legal system often has an inherent *bias* both in the way it is conducted and in the way in which it maintains the status quo. On the other hand, many rural people are unaware of their legal rights and of the services legally available to them. Many legal systems do not overtly seek to impart this information to rural people, who thus remain largely ignorant and excluded from the effects of laws which are supposed to benefit them. In other instances the legal system acts as a direct constraint on the rural people's involvement in development activities. This is particularly the case in terms of legislation which governs the right of legal associations of different categories of rural workers. Studies undertaken by the ILO have highlighted how this right of association has been legally withheld from different groups of rural workers, which thus frustrated their efforts to build organisations to represent their interests. Similarly, legislation which gives sweeping powers to government to

---

[10] For a fuller discussion of the political context and its influence upon a process of participation see UNDP: *Report on an International Seminar on Popular Participation, Ljubljana, Yugoslavia* (New York, 1982); for a more detailed look at the influence of the political context in a particular country see B. Tsiane and F. Youngman (eds.): *The theory and practice of people's participation* (Gaborone, Ministry of Finance and Development Planning, 1985).

disperse "unlawful" assemblies can act as a powerful deterrent to the forming of organisations by rural people.

Administrative obstacles

Centralised governments encourage centralised administrative structures which, by their very nature, are major obstacles to people's participation. These administrative structures retain control over decision-making, resource allocation and the information and knowledge which rural people will require if they are to play an effective part in development activities. Administrators in such structures tend to have a negative attitude towards the whole notion of people's participation, which is often manifested as arrogance and a disbelief that rural people can ever assume responsibility for administrative matters. The result is that administrative procedures often become a minefield and an effective deterrent to rural people seeking direct involvement in or assistance from local administration. For people whose struggle for livelihood demands most of their time, such procedures cannot be afforded.[11]

Similarly, the planning of development programmes and projects is often centralised and planning procedures discourage local involvement. Government planners are invariably a professional group who do not concede their practice to the local level. Most rural development planning takes place in ministries in urban areas and there is rarely any genuine desire to devolve this responsibility effectively to the local level. Planning information and data are often complex in nature and rarely presented or interpreted in a way intelligible to most rural people. The costs, both in terms of finance and time, of encouraging effective local participation in planning are substantial and few governments are prepared to undertake such a commitment. Indeed it could be argued that in most Third World countries administrative structures are invariably centralised and, by definition, essentially anti-participatory. Korten (1981), however, sees the main obstacles to participation within the external donor agency where centralised decision-making, inappropriate attitudes and skills of project staff and frequent transfers of personnel render the implementation of a demanding and subtle process such as participation extremely difficult.

Social obstacles

Probably the most frequent and powerful social obstacle to the participation of rural people in development projects is a mentality of

---

[11] See D. Curtis et al.: *Popular participation in decision-making and the basic needs approach to development*, WEP working paper (Geneva, ILO, 1982).

dependence which is deeply and historically ingrained in their lives. In many Third World countries rural people for generations have been dominated by and dependent upon local élite groups. In practice this has meant that the rural poor have become accustomed to leaving decisions and initiatives to their "leaders". The lack of leadership and organisational skills, and consequent inexperience in running projects or organisations, leaves most rural people incapable of responding to the demands of participation. This state of affairs has been reinforced in many instances by handouts and actions which have not encouraged them to take initiatives themselves. The result is a widespread marginalisation of rural people from the activities of rural development, which in turn leads to a lack of confidence and ultimately to a psychology of despair. This dependent mentality is further reinforced by the fact that mere "survival" is for most rural people their greatest challenge and consumes much of their energies, leaving them precious little time to "participate". Many rural people, therefore, tend to accept the status quo and their position in a framework in which economic and social arrangements maintain the control of the few and the exclusion of the majority. In this context, therefore, the very notion of participation is far removed from reality and is almost unintelligible to rural people who have never before been invited to share in the activities and benefits previously dominated by others.[12]

Rural people do not necessarily constitute a homogeneous economic and social unit. Efforts to encourage participation which are directed at the "rural people", the "rural poor" or "farmers", as if these constituted distinct and homogeneous categories, fail to recognise the class, caste, religious and geographical differences that can exist in rural areas. Rural people may share their poverty, but there may be many other factors which divide them and can breed mutual distrust. Aggregating the rural people as one enormous mass is inadequate in seeking to promote participation. In this respect it is important to be aware of the economic and social differentiation that characterises the rural areas of many Third World countries and that, if misunderstood or inadequately managed, could severely frustrate efforts to promote participation. In many rural areas different groups compete for available resources and have very different access to development activities. The participation of one group may be very different from that of another.[13]

For most women in the Third World the male-dominated culture and society in which they live are the most formidable obstacles that they face in

---

[12] The enormous social and psychological obstacles which poor people need to confront in order to emerge from their isolation are vividly portrayed in United Nations: *Popular participation policies as methods for advancing social integration* (New York, 1987).

[13] The social, political and economic differentiation of rural areas is often overlooked by applied development literature which all too often refers to such aggregates as "communities", "villages" and "farmers". An interesting and vivid examination of this issue, in which the author sees rural differentation as a dynamic process of continual competition for resources, is C. Elliot: *Patterns of poverty in the Third World* (London, Praeger, 1975).

efforts to be included in development activities. Despite the advances of the past decade or so and the proliferation of projects directed exclusively at them, rural women confront an extra hurdle (i.e. existing cultural values, which assign women to prescribed roles and do not encourage their prominence in local activities) before they can join men in gaining greater access to development resources. Recognition of the fundamental socio-cultural obstacles which women face has given rise to two contrasting strategies: one prepares women through education to challenge and overcome these obstacles, and the other directs resources at women in the hope that their increasing economic power will lead to inevitable change. The latter strategy is more predominant and, according to UNIFEM, initial results are encouraging. Indeed, UNIFEM would argue that the two strategies are inseparable, and that efforts to develop the resource base of poor women will inevitably lead to their re-negotiating or even challenging the social and cultural practices which hinder their involvement in development.

The important issue to stress here is that participation, whatever form or direction it might take, cannot be regarded simply as some kind of physical or tangible input into a development project. Any form of participation occurs within a particular context and will be influenced by the economic and social forces that mould that context. Furthermore, simply to proclaim a commitment to participation will not ensure its unchallenged passage. Inevitably the deliberate encouragement of a process of participation will stimulate some kind of reaction; either on the part of rural people for whom it will be a "new idea" and contrary to their accustomed role in development, or on the part of official or other interests who may regard it as a threat to their positions. In either case participation will not be an effortless procedure.

The arguments for participation in development

Despite an apparent widespread recognition of the importance of participation in development, not everybody is convinced either that it is necessarily always a "good thing" or that to date it has clear practical advantages for development projects. Many planners would argue that there are potential risks and costs implicit in greater people's participation. These could include –

- project start-up delayed by negotiations with people;

- increases in staff required to support participation;

- the possibility that, when consulted, people might oppose a project;

- unpredictable participatory methodologies;

- over-involvement of less experienced people.

Indeed, a World Bank (1988) study even suggested that governments might prefer rural people to participate only in project implementation since their involvement in project identification and assessment might give rise to increased expectations.

Furthermore, there has been a tendency for some writers to be dismissive of many of the arguments for participation as being merely "lofty sentiments" or "popular faddishness". Midgeley (1986) refers to the "emotionally appealing case for participation" but argues that it is important to disentangle ethical issues from theoretical and practical considerations. There is an element of justification in these criticisms and it could also be argued that in many projects participation is more evident as an emotional commitment than a practical aspect of the project. Indeed Uphoff (1986b) refers to a state of "pseudo participation" and rightly argues that in many projects the participation is more illusory than real. Current practice suggests that undoubtedly in many rural development projects participation is stronger in rhetoric than in practical reality; that there is a good deal of lip-service to the notion of participation but less commitment to the changes in direction and style that would be required to implement it. It would be wrong, however, to assume that the arguments for greater people's participation in development are based purely on idealistic, humanitarian or egalitarian grounds. There are a number of substantive arguments for "participation" as an essential ingredient in development projects. Uphoff (1986b), for example, suggests a number of reasons why governments might gain some net benefit from promoting participation, despite political costs:

- more accurate and representative information about the needs, priorities and capabilities of local people; more reliable feedback on the impact of government initiatives and programmes;
- adaptation of programmes to meet local conditions so that scarce resources can be employed more efficiently;
- lower cost of access to the public for agricultural extension programmes, nutrition education, immunisation, supervised credit, etc., through local organisations and institutions;
- tapping local technical information that can otherwise be costly to obtain or to learn about the fact that rural people have more technical expertise than usually recognised;
- mobilisation of local resources to augment or even substitute for central government resources ...;
- improved utilisation and maintenance of government facilities and services ...; and
- co-operation in new programmes, which is more likely to occur when local organisations having the confidence of rural people share responsibility for the innovation (Uphoff, 1986, pp. 425-426).

On one level there are a number of general arguments that can be put forward in favour of participation. Castillo (1983), for example, has suggested that since previous essentially top-down strategies of rural development have clearly failed to make any substantial impact upon rural poverty, there is a case for reversing the direction and approaching development more from the bottom up. This argument is widespread and reflects an increasing tendency to turn development around and to see its impetus coming from below and not always directed from above. Castillo's is essentially a negative argument for participation and it should be noted that the converse is not always true. Another line of argument suggests that rural people are not ignorant, idle or apathetic, as they are often made out to be but, on the contrary, are resourceful, knowledgeable and hard-working. This line of argument has similarly begun to receive quite widespread attention and emphasis has started to be placed on indigenous knowledge, skills and practices as vital contributions to development. P. Richards' (1985) studies in West Africa revealed the tremendous depth and reservoir of indigenous agricultural knowledge which could be made available for development. In the health field the works of Werner and Bower (1982) have also shown the existence of indigenous knowledge on health prevention and cure, which should be the basis of health development activities. They and other writers have helped to forge a perspective which argues that rural people have so much indispensable knowledge to contribute to development that it would be a major loss if they were not involved.[14] Finally, there is the argument that rural people should actively participate in development in order for them to contribute a countervailing force to those élite groups who inevitably dominate development resources and activities. The dominant forces in many Third World countries seek to maintain the dependence and inequality which characterise the lives of many rural people, and at the same time to maintain the centralisation and bureaucratisation of the state administration. People's participation is a necessary counteracting force which should at least halt, if not seek to reverse, this progression. Since 1979, for example, the UNRISD inquiry has laid particular emphasis upon this dimension of participation.[15]

---

[14] The whole question of indigenous knowledge and its role in development is an emerging and important topic. P. Richards: *Indigenous agricultural revolution* (London, Hutchinson, 1985) is based upon a West African context but its analysis is widely applicable; see also Orlando Fals-Borda: *Knowledge and people's power* (Mexico, Siglo XXI Editores, 1985); D. Brookensha et al.: *Indigenous knowledge systems and development* (Washington, DC, University Press of America, 1980).

[15] Pearse and Stiefel, op. cit. This is the working document which launched the UNRISD's major research project into participation. This project has not only led to a series of studies but has also stimulated a debate between academics and practitioners in the field; B. Galjart: "Counterdevelopment", in *Community Development Journal* (Oxford), Vol. 16, No. 2, pp. 88-98, is a succinct statement upon a countervailing strategy of development; finally H. Sethi: *Refocussing practice* (New Delhi, Setu-Lokayan, 1987), is an account of participation as a countervailing strategy in an Indian context.

More specifically there are a series of arguments which see participation as extremely useful to the functioning of development projects. These arguments are much more fragmented, often extremely localised and are expressed in a range of at times quite different terms. If, however, we pull them together, then the following are the more substantive arguments:

Efficiency: Participation implies a greater chance that resources available to development projects will be used more efficiently. Participation can, for example, help minimise misunderstanding or possible disagreements and thus the time and energy, often spent by professional staff explaining or convincing people of a project's benefits, can be reduced. Participation is also cost-effective since, if rural people are taking responsibility for a project, then fewer costly outside resources will be required and highly paid professional staff will not get tied down in the detail of project administration. Participation, therefore, allows for more efficient use of the resources available to a project. There is, however, another side to the coin; arguments to justify the resource efficiency of participation in development projects can be met with accusations that this cost-effectiveness often results in governments and agencies making fewer funds available for development work and indeed transferring the burden of project costs on to local people.

Effectiveness: Participation will also make projects more effective as instruments of rural development. Projects are invariably external instruments which are supposed to benefit the rural people of a particular area. Participation which allows these people to have a voice in determining objectives, support project administration and make their local knowledge, skills and resources available must result in more effective projects. A major reason why many projects have not been effective in the past in achieving objectives is because local people were not involved. Effectiveness equals the successful completion of objectives, and participation can help to ensure this.

Self-reliance: This all-embracing term covers a wide range of benefits which participation can bring. Essentially, self-reliance refers to the positive effects on rural people of participating in development projects. Participation helps to break the mentality of dependence which characterises much development work and, as a result, promotes self-awareness and confidence and causes rural people to examine their problems and to think positively about solutions. Participation is concerned with human development and increases people's sense of control over issues which affect their lives, helps them to learn how to plan and implement and, on a broader front, prepares them for participation at regional or even national level. In essence, participation is a "good thing" in that it breaks people's isolation and lays the groundwork for them to have not only a more substantial influence on development, but also a greater independence and control over their lives.

Coverage: Most government and many agency-directed or supported development projects reach only a limited, and usually privileged, number of rural people. In many instances delivery services have contact with only a fraction of the rural population. Participation will extend this coverage in that it will bring more rural people within the direct influence of development activities. Participation will increase the numbers of rural people who potentially can benefit from development and could be the solution to broadening the mass appeal of such services.[16]

Sustainability: Experience suggests that externally motivated development projects frequently fail to sustain themselves once the initial level of project support or inputs either diminish or are withdrawn. Participation is seen as the antidote to this situation in that it can ensure that local people maintain the project's dynamic. Arguments which link sustainability with participation are largely economic ("the maintenance of an acceptable flow of benefits from the project's investment after its completion"), but others touch on issues of project ownership, political support and the maintenance of delivery systems. On a more general level, sustainability refers to continuity and sees participation as fundamental to developing a self-sustaining momentum of development in a particular area.[17]

The crucial question here is how far these arguments for people's participation in development projects constitute tangible benefits for the people themselves and suggest radically different ways of operating; or how far they merely represent the means whereby the old order of things can function a little more effectively. It is a fact that the majority of rural people have been by-passed by development, but now they are being invited to contribute and participate in development activities. It could be argued that strategies of participation which place the burden for development on rural people are shouldering them with unfair burdens. All argument for more participation in development must be scrutinised in terms of the tangible results and should be examined, not merely from the perspective of the agency involved, but in terms of the interests of the rural people themselves.

---

[16] The more substantive arguments presented here are a composite list drawn from a whole range of sources. Examples of these sources include: S. Paul: *Community participation in development projects*, World Bank Discussion Paper No. 6 (Washington, DC, 1987); J. Waddington: *Some participatory aspects of programmes to involve the poor in development* (Geneva, UNRISD, 1979); United Nations: *Popular participation policies as methods for advancing social integration* (New York, 1987); M. Bamberger (ed.): *Readings in community participation*, 2 vols. (Washington, DC, Economic Development Institute, 1986); E. R. Morss et al. (eds.): *Strategies for small farmer development*, Vols. 1 and 2 (Boulder, Colorado, Westview Press, 1976).

[17] See, in particular, M. Cernea: "Farmer organizations and institution building for sustainable development", in *Regional Development Dialogue* (Nagoya, Japan) Vol. 8, No. 2, 1987; and W. Stinson: *Creating sustainable community health projects: The PRICOR experience* (Maryland, Centre for Human Services, 1987).

Issues concerning participation

Participation in development is a complex phenomenon and cannot be presented in universally acceptable terms. Analyses of participation, therefore, throw up a whole range of issues and questions which different authors argue are crucial to the practice of participation. Uphoff (1985), for example, identifies what he calls the "key issues" relating to participation in project design and implementation: clarity; realistic objectives; introduction; investment; expectations; co-option; dependence; and bureaucratic reorientation. He discusses these key issues in relation to the Gal Oya Water Management Project in Sri Lanka and argues that attention to issues such as these is vital in strengthening participation at the project level. While few other authors have presented such a comprehensive list, many identify and comment upon a number of issues related to participation, and these are summarised below.

Who participates?

There is little general consensus as to who among the broad category of "rural people" is supposed or expected to participate in development. If we relate this question back, however, to the earlier discussion on the emergence of participation as a major new strategy in development, we can link this strategy with such broadly defined groups as "the rural poor", "the rural excluded", "small farmers", or "the last". The widespread conviction that previous development strategies had bypassed the majority of rural people has led to a concern that this majority should now "participate" in development. The more specific answer to the question "Who participates?" is, of course, linked to both the understanding of participation and the objectives of the intervention. In the first instance there is a strong identification of participation in many countries with the broad mass of poor, oppressed and marginalised urban and rural people, most of whom struggle to eke out an existence with paltry resources. Here the participation concerns a process whereby such people can begin to rise out of their poverty and seek some response to their demands. In this case the subjects of the participation are the broad mass of the rural poor. CEBEMO's work with the rural poor in Sri Lanka graphically characterises the subjects of the process and the forces they confront:

> The low level of the fishermen's income and their indebtedness are consequences of their economic exploitation. The fishermen do not get the maximum benefit from their labour; others own the fishing craft and so they only get a share of the catch. The fishermen are also exploited at the level of marketing. It is not they who fix the price for their produce, but middlemen who have the capital and transport facilities.
>
> The leadership in the fishermen's villages is based on a very pyramidical order. The poor have no opportunity to participate in exercising leadership. On the

contrary, the politicians always enforce their control on the masses by making use of the rich élite in the local communities. The poor are an unorganised sector. They hardly have a platform of their own to voice their problems. The people totally depend upon political leaders to find solutions to their problems. This attitude of total dependence on others on the part of the people has helped politicians to exploit them and use them for their own gain (CEBEMO, Sri Lanka 312).

The above eloquent statement is repeated many times in project files and attests to the commonality of structural problems facing the poor. It clearly identifies the forces which poor people confront and which will perhaps be challenged as their participation develops.

On the other hand, however, where there is a direct link between participation and the achieving of tangible project objectives, the client group becomes the beneficiaries. There is a very strong emphasis in certain types of projects on identifying the intended beneficiaries of a project; if, as a result of the project, these people do in fact materially benefit, then they are deemed to have participated. It goes without saying that the nature of the participatory exercise for beneficiaries and non-beneficiaries, will be, of course, quite different.

In the past decade or so, increasing concern has centred around strategies to encourage rural women to participate more in development. The emphasis upon women in development has mushroomed and a plethora of studies have examined problems concerning women's relative isolation and efforts to include them more in development activities.[18] This is not the place to review this extensive literature other than to note that efforts to involve women in development seem to fall into two categories. On the one hand, the dominant approach treats women as a separate category and seeks to improve their economic status by skill training or small income-generating activities. On the other hand, another approach seeks to get to the heart of women's isolation and sees women's participation in a more structural as opposed to a more limited economic sense. The two, of course, are not necessarily unrelated but they do suggest two broadly different strategies on women's participation.

Interestingly, UNIFEM recognises the value of both strategies and incorporates both in its work. UNIFEM's experience has demonstrated that support to projects directly benefiting women can provide the skills, experience, resources and confidence necessary for women to tackle the more fundamental causes of their isolation. Whilst UNIFEM's emphasis is upon the first strategy, this is clearly understood as a stepping-stone to more substantial women's involvement. The key is to develop an economic base from which women can begin to play a more prominent role in development activities generally.

[18] A classical text which has influenced much of the thinking and analysis of women's role in development is E. Boserup: *Women's role in economic development* (London, Allen and Unwin, 1970); see also B. Rogers: *The domestication of women: Discrimination in developing countries* (London, Tavistock, 1980); M. Mokhopadhyay: *Silver shackles: Women and development in India* (Oxford, Oxfam, 1984).

Participation and government

A major controversy around the practice of participation concerns the potential role of government and the extent to which it can facilitate or is an inevitable obstacle to a process of participation. The issue is controversial for two main reasons. First, in the analysis employed by some studies, government and its bureaucratic apparatus are seen as essentially hostile to the whole notion of reducing central control, devolving decisions to local level and supporting demands made by rural people for the kinds of radical changes that might be required to find lasting solutions for the poverty they suffer. Second, in many regions it could be argued that it is the government which is the basic instrument for maintaining the status quo and, correspondingly, for perpetuating the wretched quality of poor people's lives. Implicit in a genuine government concern for participation are such bureaucratic mechanisms as decentralisation and local-level planning structures; yet the evidence suggests that few governments have willingly devolved these bureaucratic controls to the local level. There is little in the practice to date to suggest that many governments have committed themselves to supporting moves to promote mass involvement in development processes. The reasons are not difficult to understand.[19]

It is a fact, however, that in several countries such as Ethiopia, the Philippines and the United Republic of Tanzania, national ideologies overtly encourage people's participation; other nation-wide programmes, such as Harambee in Kenya and Decentralisation in Nepal, seek to establish a basis for participation. Most Third World governments are similarly signatories to the 1979 WCARRD declaration on the central role of participation in rural development and few would declare publicly that they were opposed to participation. Midgeley (1987) argues that a major failing of the advocates of participation has been their assumption that the State has little positive role in promoting participation. On the contrary, he argues that:

> The role of the State has expanded enormously during this century and today state intervention in all spheres of contemporary life has reached a level that is historically unprecedented. The State is the prime initiator and promoter of development effort in most Third World nations and, in the field of social development, state provisions have grown rapidly. Accounts of popular participation should deal with these realities and incorporate them into a comprehensive approach that embraces the disparate elements of statist and participatory development (Midgeley, 1987, p. 6).

[19] A key dimension and litmus test of governments' concern to promote grass-roots participation can be found in calls for greater decentralisation of bureaucratic administration and decision-making. Indeed decentralisation has almost become synonymous with participation and seen as the essential first step to effective local-level involvement. See, for example, D. Conyers and R. Apthorpe: "Decentralisation, recentralisation and popular participation in developing countries", in *Development and Peace* (Budapest, Hungarian Peace Council), No. 3, 1982, pp. 47-59.

The issue of government's role in promoting or hindering participation arouses passionate debate and it is wise to put it on the agenda. Midgeley (1987) is right to point to the central position of government in development in terms of its control over resources; it is equally important, however, to see how efficiently and equally this control is exercised. Governments are inevitably the main protagonists of a top-down approach to development and the object of much critical comment on the effectiveness of big, donor-supported development projects. Most Third World governments have neither an unblemished record in project management nor a proven commitment to genuinely involving people in decisions and actions concerning their development. When, therefore, we consider the issue of government and participation, we must examine the nature of that participation. The main question is whether government's understanding of participation is essentially one of a means to control and mobilise local resources for development priorities; or whether it can genuinely promote participation which seeks to redress the imbalances of previous development strategies in favour of the masses of excluded rural people. Similarly, we can ask whether government officials can ever come to see rural people as having good minds and useful skills, and not just strong backs and deep pockets. Do in fact governments need rural people with their skills, innovativeness and resources to carry out necessary national improvements, and if so will this need eventually cause some genuine transfer of power?

Expectations and incentives

What kinds of expectations might arise in rural people as they begin to get involved in development and what incentives, if any, will be required to sustain this involvement? A sudden tide of enthusiasm and support for efforts to involve rural people cannot predict what aspirations it might raise or whether the impetus will need to be encouraged by appropriate incentives. It would appear that there are two divergent understandings of people's expectations. On the one hand, people's participation is often directly linked to some kind of immediate material benefit. As we have seen, there is a dominant element in the practice which equates participation solely with benefits. In this case, rural people who have previously received few tangible benefits from development projects are asked to participate in a variety of ways for their own benefit. On the other hand, the incentive may be linked not directly to immediate benefit but to a more long-term solution to people's poverty. Participation is seen as the process by which previously excluded people can begin to exert some influence, and this "emergence from exclusion" could be a more lasting solution. Neither perspective is mutually exclusive but they respectively suggest very different immediate and longer-term expectations on the part of the people involved.

There is evidence to suggest that where participation is linked to material benefits, readily available and dependable incentives are important in sustaining the participation. The Third World is littered with projects which had sought to obtain people's involvement by offering immediate incentives (e.g. inputs or credit) only to see the participation evaporate when the incentives failed to materialise. Buijs (1979, p. 11) quite rightly suggests that the easiest way to persuade people to participate is by "offering money or other material benefits". Where participation involves major contributions to big capital undertakings like irrigation schemes, then there often have to be substantial incentives to induce people to undertake the responsibilities demanded. Where, however, participation is not linked solely to immediate material benefits, incentives to sustain the participation revolve around other less tangible results. This form of participation often leads to a variety of political actions, e.g. pressure on local services or resistance to a large landholder, and the success of these actions is often the incentive to persist. Similarly, the linking up of actions on a district or regional basis builds up solidarity and greatly strengthens the resolve to continue.[20]

Practice to date has raised a whole range of other issues relating to participation. The role of NGOs is a major issue which we shall examine in later chapters, as is the nature of participatory projects and the more appropriate form of project design to promote participation. Of major concern also are the costs of participation, in both a financial and economic sense; the reactions on the part of established interests and the tensions which participation can provoke in established orders. In terms of practice, sufficient experience has been gained to date from several studies to produce lists of problems associated with participation, which confirms the conclusion that its practice is spreading and its force is being felt.

* * *

Even a limited review of the concept of participation in development must conclude that it is quite impossible to write anything that is universally meaningful about it. In the first instance, it must be emphasised that the focus of this study is participation in development projects. Many will argue that this is an impossible task, and that it is unrealistic to isolate the "project" as a distinct phenomenon and examine participation only in that context. Clearly the concept of participation knows no boundaries and its dynamic process cannot be contained within a project's framework. It is important to recognise that as rural people develop strength and cohesion they will inevitably forge links with other groups and interests within the project's context. This will surely happen and is an equally valid dimension of the process of study. We must not think of participation as some extremely localised activity which concerns only the

[20] Paul, op. cit.; United Nations: *Popular participation policies* ..., op. cit.

implementation of development projects. The central thrust of this study is to examine participation within the context of development projects, but in the clear understanding both that such projects are the products of the prevailing political context and that, as the process of participation unfolds, the people involved will inevitably interact with existing forces.

Whether participation is merely a passing fad or a plausible alternative strategy, its influence on development thinking and practice at all levels is now clearly evident. A review of the state of play must conclude that, whatever its meaning or direction, participation today is a major consideration at the development project level. References to participation are all-pervasive in both academic literature and project documentation, and the term "participation" is increasingly influencing development practice across the board. It is true, however, that to date the rhetoric far outweighs the substance of, as opposed to the commitment to, the practice. But this practice is expanding and can be examined to reveal its major approaches and content.

2

Sectoral project approaches
to participation

In practice, it is difficult to judge to what extent projects are participatory, just as it is difficult to distinguish between projects known as reformist and others which are more radical, because there are no pure projects (Gianotten, 1986, p. 19).

It is very difficult these days to pick up a book or document concerning rural development without some reference, substantial or otherwise, to the concept of participation. Participation has truly infiltrated the literature and, correspondingly, one assumes, the practice of development. Few sectors have avoided at least some acknowledgement of the importance of the concept and, while we could argue that much of this is rhetoric, individual sectoral approaches to implementing participation at the project level are now discernible. Indeed it could be further argued that participation has emerged as a single unifying principle across the breadth of rural development and, in theory at least, it would appear to be the single major influence on project implementation. Whereas up to ten years ago a review of project-based literature would probably highlight technological effectiveness, good planning and management, and resource efficiency as the key ingredients of project success, today participation figures prominently; some would say that it is the single most important ingredient.

The purpose of this chapter is to review briefly how participation is emerging and beginning to influence project approaches in the different sectors involved in rural development. There are, as yet, few even limited reviews of this sectoral practice, although there are now a number of substantial case studies across sectors. While Chapter 3 will look at a number of case studies from among the sectors, the purpose here is to analyse briefly how participation is interpreted in the different sectors, what broad strategies of implementation are being developed, what are the distinctive sectoral features in terms of participation and what important issues are emerging from the practice. While only fieldwork of global proportions would be able to state the exact extent and nature of the practice of participation across sectors, the documentation available allows us to make an assessment of the current situation.

Furthermore, a sectoral review is useful in terms of the differing backgrounds of development workers who may consult this text. It also serves as a kind of sectoral "state of the art" review of participation and allows us to contrast and compare the approaches and endeavours of the different sectors. Despite support given to such notions as "integrated" development, much rural development still takes place on a sectoral basis, and these different sectors appear now to be experimenting with the concept of participation. This chapter also presents a framework for the reading of the case studies in Chapter 3, many of which are based upon single-sector activities. If rural development projects are to maintain this sectoral approach, then it will be pertinent to examine the current meaning and practice of participation on a sectoral basis.

Agricultural development

Agricultural projects dominate programmes of rural development and agricultural services that seek to promote this development are widespread. Equally the technological component inevitably dominates agricultural projects and the professional training of project staff reflects this bias. Agriculture, of course, covers such areas as forestry, conservation and irrigation; our concern here is with agriculture in terms of agricultural production and approaches to increasing the levels of this production. While it could be argued that agricultural projects have always been participatory in that project staff have sought to involve farmers in discussions on their needs and problems and farmers have then participated in project benefits, more recent project documentation shows how such projects are beginning to tussle with the notion of more formal farmers' participation.[1] Agricultural projects have joined in the growing recognition of the need to develop farmers' participation more formally in order better to ensure project success. Apart from the more general issues of project efficiency and effectiveness, the following are the kinds of reasons put forward why agricultural projects should actively promote farmers' participation. Such participation can:

- increase coverage and extend agricultural services in situations where often only very few farmers have any kind of active contact with such services;
- help break down an inherent resistance to change which is characteristic of farming communities;
- ensure that projects meet the needs of farmers and do not merely depend on the ideas of outside professionals;

---

[1] Few texts, if any, in the fields of agricultural development or extension have ever suggested that agricultural extension agents should take no note of farmers' ideas or opinions. Indeed the earlier literature is full of calls to agents to listen to farmers, to become their friends and to be good teachers. In these earlier studies the notion of participation is evident, but under the guidance and control of the agent who is the representative of modern external ideas and technologies. See, for example, A.H. Savile: *Extension in rural communities* (Oxford, Oxford University Press, 1965); D.J. Bradfield: *Guide to extension training* (Rome, FAO, 1966); A.H. Maunder (ed.): *Agricultural extension: A reference manual* (Rome, FAO, 1973).

- ensure that projects do not benefit only better-off farmers but also smaller, more marginal farmers;

- help dispel any mistrust of outside ideas by ensuring that farmers' ideas are built into project objectives.

The very clear notion of participation that emerges in agricultural projects is that it is closely related to tangible project activities, involves some element of discussion with farmers, often demands some kind of farmers' organisation to facilitate the participation and results in farmers' participation in project benefits. It is a controlled and disciplined notion of participation that is easily manageable and permits relatively straightforward quantitative evaluation. The essence of the participation is economic benefit in terms of the increasing income derived from higher crop production; there is less emphasis upon any broader interpretation and the whole model is based upon the assumption that the benefits will provide the dynamic for future, more self-reliant farmers' development.

To examine further this issue of participation in agricultural develop-ment, we look at two major areas of practice: the activities of agricultural extension services and the role of major, donor-supported agricultural projects that seek to promote the massive participation of small farmers in agricultural development.

Participation and agricultural extension

The greater part of agricultural development takes place within the context of agricultural extension services. Most Third World countries have extension services and they are invariably centrally controlled, bureaucratically oriented and directed by professional staff. The major issue for these services in terms of participation is how to turn around decades of established practice. Extension services are predicated on the theory that the stimulus for change in farming communities must come from outside and that this change takes the form of externally generated knowledge and technologies that will modernise traditional ways of cultivation. The mission of extension services, therefore, is to bring this knowledge to farmers, break down attitudes and practices which might be dissonant with this new knowledge and persuade farmers to adopt new practices. The whole approach is essentially anti-participatory and, apart from some consultation with farmers or efforts to develop farmers' organisations, the farmers are regarded as the mechanism by which objectives and targets can be achieved. In this scenario, participation is almost seen as an extra burden on an already overworked extension agent. The FAO's *Agricultural extension manual* suggests that the extension workers' task of promoting farmer participation is not an easy one but offers the following recommendations on how it might be achieved:

■ Farmers are more willing to participate in activities which meet their felt needs. A quick needs assessment can determine farmers' needs and priorities. Again, the needs of all people should be taken into consideration, not just those who are accessible and co-operative.

■ If farmers are encouraged to express their needs and provide some input into the structure of a project, they should not be ignored. The price of widespread participation may be an additional burden on the extension worker, but if he or she wishes to sustain farmers' involvement, then the farmers' ideas must be taken into account.

■ Farmers are more likely to participate if actual benefits are directly tied to participation.

■ Farmers, especially those with low incomes, are more likely to participate and remain involved if the benefits are material, direct and immediate. There is evidence that in working with the uneducated, benefits have to be obvious and tangible. One of the best ways of getting farmers' interest is through the use of convincing and realistic demonstrations and trials (Swanson, 1984, p. 67).

Despite the efforts of such authors as Freire (1972), Jiggins and Roling (1982), Belloncle (1987) and Roling (1987) to fundamentally re-examine extension practice, it could be argued that the above is characteristic of current extension practice in terms of participation. In this practice participation is essentially functional and its implementation a mechanical exercise. Current extension practice reflects little of the issues we later examine in Chapter 4 despite, ironically, its solid grounding in non-formal education and its emphasis upon the farmer as an adult who has views and ideas. The rhetoric of extension is dramatically opposed by the practice which basically is still unable to treat the farmer as an equal. Jiggins and Roling (1982) confirmed this rhetoric but showed how emerging new approaches to extension, from a technical change to an institution-building approach, were beginning to come to grips with the issue of participation. They further suggested that a more participatory approach to extension must include such elements as user influence and control, group approaches to extension clientele, mobilisation and organisation of small producers and new styles of management.

In the past decade a major reorientation of agricultural extension has taken place in the form of the Training and Visit (T & V) system of extension. Currently the T & V system is the single most dominant influence in the practice of agricultural extension and its sponsors, the World Bank, have financed its dissemination throughout the Third World. Essentially the T & V system seeks to tackle a number of chronic problems associated with agricultural extension services – poor organisation, dilution of effort, poor coverage and mobility and limited training – with an approach that stresses a unified service, concentration on extension, regular farmer training and frequent agent-farmer contact (Benor and Harrison, 1982). With its emphasis upon externally generated technologies, hierarchical bureaucratic structure, and rigid framework of training and farm visits, and its obsession with quantitative results, in theory the T & V system is conspicuous for its lack of meaningful farmer participation. The frantic way in which the T & V system has been implemented in different countries has left little scope for processes such as participation. Indeed it could be argued that with the advent of the T & V system, efforts to promote participation in extension have taken a major step backwards. But a reaction has at last begun. Russell (1985) has argued that the T & V system must not be a one-way process and that village extension workers must be willing to learn from and work with the farmer in a participatory manner. The rigidity and the enforced external discipline of the system has come under attack and there has been a general call for a loosening and for allowing a more genuine two-way flow of ideas and decision-making within the system.[2]

A more positive reorientation of extension practice is the move towards involving farmers in agricultural research. The research-extension relationship is fundamental to extension practice and it is this relationship that participation is beginning to influence. Farmer Participatory Research (FPR) is an emerging trend which, if widely implemented, could help reorientate general extension practice. Farrington and Martin's (1987) review of this concept and its practice sees FPR as helping both to build farmers' knowledge into research activities and to ensure that new farming technologies are relevant to farmers' needs. FPR is, however, more than these two elements and implies a complete revamping of the conventional agricultural research approach; the usefulness of farmers' knowledge, the notion of partnership between farmer and researcher, a broader rather than a "model" approach to research and the emphasis placed upon identifying farmers' problems and constraints in agricultural development. Given the dominant research-centre, professional model of agricultural research, the notion of FPR is, at least, refreshing and potentially revolutionary. We should not, however, be too optimistic. The institutional constraints to FPR are enormous; similarly, FPR cannot emerge in isolation but can only be a product of a broader participatory process. FPR will flourish best where this broader process has already begun:

> The most striking cases of participation in problem definition (in agricultural research) are in contexts where features such as literacy or group

---

[2] The standard text on the Training and Visit system of Extension is D. Benor and J. Harrison: *Agricultural extension: The training and visit system* (Washington, DC, World Bank, 1977). For a discussion on the T & V system in practice see J. Howell: *Issues, non-issues and lessons from the T and V extension system* (Wageningen, Netherlands, University of Wageningen, 1984); also G.E. Jones (ed.): *Investing in rural extension: Strategies and goals* (London, Elsevier, 1986).

consciousness are most developed; or where project personnel have put a considerable time and commitment towards building these capacities (Farington and Martin, 1987, p. 33).

In the absence of other mould-breaking initiatives, FPR is a possible basis for establishing a more participatory approach to extension. If it could help redefine the relationship between the research station and extension practice, and give farmers a role in this relationship, then it might help reorient the basic anti-participatory nature of extension services. Greater farmers' participation in, for example, agricultural research design, control and evaluation could help shatter the dominant paradigm.

A recent and more substantial description of a strategy for people-centred agriculture in the Third World can be found in the work of Chambers (1988). Under the title *Farmer first*, Chambers explains what he calls a "complementary paradigm" of agricultural extension and research in the Third World, which would reverse the basic technology transfer paradigm with a strategy in which farm families would play a major role in technology development and choice. Chambers suggests that such a strategy is entirely realistic given the complex, diverse and risk-prone nature of Third World agriculture, for which the simple technology transfer model cannot be a universal panacea. The comparison between the "technology-transfer" and the "farmer-first" paradigms is shown in table 1.

Table 1.   The "technology-transfer" and "farmer-first" approaches

Indicator	"Technology transfer"	"Farmer first"
Main objective	Transfer technology	Empower farmers
Analysis of needs and priorities by	Outsiders	Farmers assisted by outsiders
Transferred by outsiders to farmers	Precepts	Principles
	Messages	Methods
	Package of practices	Basket of choices
The "menu"	Fixed	A la carte
Farmers' behaviour	Hear messages	Use methods
	Act on precepts	Apply principles
	Adopt, adapt or reject package	Choose from basket and experiment
Outsiders' desired outcomes emphasise	Widespread adoption of technology	Wider choices for farmers
		Farmers' enhanced adaptability
Main mode of extension	Agent-to-farmer	Farmer-to-farmer
Roles of extension agent	Teacher	Facilitator
	Trainer	Searcher for and provider of choice

While elaborating this alternative paradigm for Third World agriculture, Chambers is acutely aware of both the challenge it represents to existing professional delivery systems and the formidable obstacles to its widespread acceptance. He is right, however, to suggest that a "farmer-first" strategy must be seen as a priority if we are to provide the basis of a sustainable livelihood for many millions of poor rural people into the next century.[3]

Participation in agricultural credit and input programmes

In an institutional sense, participation in agriculture has been pioneered in the past decade by a number of major initiatives to extend agricultural services to rural people previously excluded from the benefits of such services. In this respect participation is defined in terms of access to these services. The essential argument behind this strategy is that the vast majority of rural people (and principally the "small farmers") are not involved in development activities because they lack the economic base from which to intervene; by directing resources at the small farmers, they will begin to develop this base and to intervene actively in local development processes. This strategy has emerged as a result of a widespread recognition that the resources available through agricultural projects have invariably reached only a select few. The small farmer has usually been excluded and thus is increasingly disadvantaged in relation to bigger farmers. This strategy is presented as participatory in the sense that it seeks to deliberately include small farmers within the framework of institutional services and to ensure that they can develop a base from which to maintain this inclusion. The strategy has received major institutional support through the FAO and the International Fund for Agricultural Development (IFAD) and constitutes a particular model designed to promote small farmers' participation. The common elements of this model include:

- the identification of a specific clientele, e.g. small farmers;

- the institutional provision of credit directed solely at small farmers;

- the organisation of small farmers into groups which serve as receiving mechanisms;

- the availability of a project agent to work exclusively on developing the small farmer base;

- an internal system of monitoring and evaluation in which the small farmers have a role and a voice.

---

[3] For the most recent and comprehensive review of the issue of farmers' involvement in agricultural research see R. Chambers, A. Pacey, and L.A. Thrupp (eds.): *Farmer first: Farmer innovation and agricultural research* (London, Intermediate Technology Publications, 1989).

The above strategy has, with local modifications, served as the basic participatory strategy of such major projects as the Small Farmer Development Programme (SFDP) in Nepal and other Asian countries, the Grameen Bank (GB) in Bangladesh (box 2) and the People's Participation Programme in Africa. It is a powerful strategy which has attracted substantial institutional support and constitutes a major effort to include previously excluded small farmers in the development process. The SFDP in particular has been extremely influential in mobilising institutional support for the strategy's approach.[4]

Both the SFDP and the GB have been exhaustively documented and periodically evaluated, and they are invariably cited in the context of how to achieve the participation of the rural masses in Third World agricultural development. Their statistics are impressive and few can deny that respectively they have helped to channel benefits to large sections of the rural poor. That they have brought resources which have noticeably improved the lives of rural people in Nepal and Bangladesh is undisputed and their approach is seen by some as a model of participatory development which can be replicated elsewhere. Both projects have broken new ground in terms of establishing, on a mass scale, links between existing services and resources and previously excluded rural people. Indeed this is the fundamental rationale of their operations: to begin a process of participation by providing previously assetless rural people with the means to establish an economic base.

But the approach of projects like the SFDP and the GB equally arouses controversy. Much of the assessment of both projects is quantitative and there is a need to look behind the figures and inquire into the nature of the participation that is occurring. Earlier studies of the SFDP concentrated on loan disbursement and recovery, economic activities and estimated economic impact, with less reference to social effects. More recent studies by Ghai (1984), for example, have begun to document the social impact of the SFDP, e.g. increased literacy, farmer training and improved sanitation facilities, as well as more intangible outcomes such as solidarity and self-reliance among participant families. Fuglesang and Chandler's (1986) recent study of the GB, however, similarly examines the GB strategy in terms of the broader process of participation, as opposed to more limited economic criteria, and shows how it has been successful in tackling some of the barriers of exclusion. For example, "It is not given that the local power structure is invincible. GB demonstrates that a participatory process among the poor themselves can disaggregate local power without confronting it" (Fuglesang and Chandler, 1986, p. 192).

---

[4] Both of these projects have been quite extensively studied, but more in terms of internal reports or project evaluations which find wider circulation; they have also led to a series of manuals and guides based upon their respective methodologies. Substantial SFDP texts include a range of evaluations undertaken by APROSC (Agricultural Projects Services Centre), Nepal, and evaluations for IFAD done by Ghai (1984). As for the Grameen Bank, the study by Fugelsang and Chandler (1986) is the most substantial and objective one to date. Ghai (1988) included both the SFDP and the Grameen Bank in his review of participatory projects.

Box 2.   The "small-farmer" strategy

Small Farmer Development Programme (SFDP), Nepal

This project started in 1976 initially in two districts and with FAO support. The basic objectives of the SFDP were to increase the incomes and living standards of the rural poor, promote participation and self-reliance and adapt government services to the needs of the rural poor. The SFDP's approach encouraged the rural poor to organise themselves into small groups, with the assistance of a group organiser, in order to gain access to credit for individual and group activities. The credit was provided on a group guarantee basis without any collateral.

The SFDP began with 440 small farmers in 1976; by 1984 this had grown to 25,000 and by 1988 to an estimated 50,000. The project groups use the credit for a wide range of economic and social activities, including livestock, horticulture, irrigation and cottage industries. Social activities have included health, education, family planning and village sanitation. The SFDP is managed by the Agricultural Development Bank of Nepal and group organisers are bank employees. Loan repayment has generally been good and many groups annually review their credit with the Bank. The SFDP is now a major operation in rural Nepal and it has clearly established durable links between small rural producers and institutional sources of credit.

Grameen Bank (GB), Bangladesh

The GB was begun in 1976 as an experiment to provide credit to poor landless men and women in rural Bangladesh. Initially supported as a project by funds from other commercial banks, it became an independent bank in 1983. The GB provides small, short-term loans to groups of five landless men or women who use the credit for individual or group activities. These include livestock rearing, domestic food processing, storage and marketing of input, and transport services. Ten groups are organised into a larger unit called a Centre and the loans are given for a one-year period during which the principal is repaid in weekly instalments.

The GB has expanded rapidly and its number of members has increased from 15,000 in 1980 to an estimated 250,000 in 1988. The repayment record of the loans is quite outstanding: in 1985 the loan recovery rate was 89 per cent. The GB is very similar to the SFDP in its use of local bank branches, group promoters and project groups as the basic mechanism of implementation. Group savings are encouraged and a number of social programmes such as family planning, nutrition classes, sports and music have been initiated. The GB is in fact the major source of credit for landless people in rural Bangladesh.

Critics of the GB approach point to the incorporation of poor people into capitalist banking systems, to the emphasis on credit as the mechanism for often hastily mobilising groups, to the apparently inevitable bureaucratisation of the group activities in response to the Bank's administrative demands and to the equally inevitable reduction of the group organiser's role to one of loan supervisor. They similarly question the outcome for other poor rural people of a programme that tends to concentrate upon a tiny fraction of the rural population of Bangladesh. If participation is defined in terms of organised access to inputs for development, then the SFDP and the GB are participatory; if, however, it is defined more in terms of building capacity to confront and tackle structural issues which enforce exclusion, then a more informed verdict is still awaited. Undoubtedly both the SFDP and the GB have brought about, under prescribed conditions, the participation of some small farmers in development assistance programmes; what is questioned are their strategies in terms of a more massive involvement of the rural poor in resources available for development.

Despite the efforts of projects like the SFDP and the GB to come to terms with the concept of participation in the context of the rural poor and at least to move towards participation as an objective, it is difficult to conclude that agricultural development projects in general have successfully negotiated the implementation of the concept. Few agricultural projects come to grips explicitly with the issue of access, which is fundamental to participation, but instead emphasise benefits and the better utilisation of available human resources. Primarily, however, agricultural projects are usually so dominated by the notions of technology transfer, innovation diffusion and quantifiable results, and by ideas of teaching, persuasion and resistance on the part of farmers, that it is difficult to imagine how a process of participation could take hold. Agricultural projects are still largely based on the belief that increased and better technological solutions will inexorably flood rural areas with universal benefits and that all rural people will participate in the fruits of modern science. Such a belief has undoubtedly benefited a considerable number of rural people; for the vast majority, however, it is still shrouded behind a series of economic and political barriers which they must first negotiate.

Resource conservation

There is an emerging school of thought which argues that development should be defined not only in political, economic or social terms, but also environmentally. Whatever understanding of development one may adopt, the development takes place within a set of environmental conditions. The protection of these conditions, therefore, should be a fundamental objective of development intervention since the resource base for development will inevitably decline if they are not maintained. International and bilateral aid agencies have taken a lead in creating public consciousness of resource conservation and are increasingly supporting programmes which seek to preserve national ecological resources for development. "Eco-development" has become a fashionable term and concern is widespread to protect and enhance countries' resource bases so as to ensure the livelihoods of the millions who depend on these resources.[5] All this is happening because the reality points to substantial deterioration of the natural resource base in many Third World countries. This base is essentially the land and the topsoil upon which millions cultivate crops for a livelihood. A recent FAO (1988) review pointed to land degradation in Africa on a massive scale and showed the probable future consequences of this degradation in terms of the terrible poverty it will inflict upon rural people.

Given the critical nature of land to rural people's livelihoods, various explanations have been put forward as to why rural people apparently seem less concerned with the protection of this basic resource. On a general level these explanations refer to the "ignorance" of rural people and their lack of "knowledge" to understand the issue of resource conservation. In many of these general explanations the blame is often placed on the rural poor for the destruction of their own livelihoods. While there might be evidence for such a statement in certain parts of the Third World, it is difficult to argue that as a whole rural people are ignorant of conservation issues. Indeed there are instances of traditional conservation methods which could form the basis of more substantial conservation work. More sympathetically, other explanations see the very day-to-day and hand-to-mouth existence of most of the world's rural people as the root cause of the degradation of their resources. A study undertaken by the University of Wageningen (1978) concluded that the increasing incorporation of small farmers into larger economic and political systems had resulted in the introduction of new species and methods, and a consequent deterioration in the natural environment. In a similar vein, another line of argument sees the increasingly sophisticated scientific and technological basis of development as ultimately detrimental to the natural resources which rural people have. In one major study of ecological patterns in the Himalayan region of India, for example, Rieger (1976) offered four possible explanations of increasing resource degradation:

- future-ignoring behaviour, or the emphasis on short-term survival over long-term investment;

- ecological practices which ignore social costs;

- lack of collective organisation that could be a basis for a common approach to resource conservation;

[5] See, for example, R. Riddell: *Eco-development* (London, Gower, 1981); also A. Gupta: *Ecology and development in the Third World* (London, Routledge, 1988).

–   lack of identification with public property, an attitude that sees national conservation schemes as alien or unwanted.

Whatever the explanations of resource degradation, there appears to be widespread agreement that in some countries appropriate action on a massive scale is now required. Equally, the prevailing view is that large-scale, top-down, government-managed conservation projects are not only ineffective, but also prohibitively expensive. Sanders (1988) critically examines the tightly controlled and centrally managed nature of these projects, their dominance by technical experts and the "well-known techniques" employed to jolt the local people into getting involved. Most conservation projects have been direct and unannounced interventions by government, or some other formally constituted body, in a region in order to improve or introduce conservation measures. Furthermore, there has been a common assumption in such conservation projects that rural people simply do not understand the issues relating to resource conservation and cannot therefore be entrusted with this responsibility. In a study of the characteristics of conservation projects and the ways in which they involve the local population, Oakley (1987) identified the following as their more common features:

External control: Conservation projects are normally externally planned and designed and then introduced into rural areas. Throughout the life of the project, control tends to stay with the external body.

Technology oriented: The emphasis is upon a technical solution to what is seen as a technical problem. Conservation projects are heavily dependent upon technological solutions which, if inappropriate, render the project ineffective.

Voluntary contributions: Conservation projects often seek voluntary contributions from the local people as a way supposedly of building up links between the people and the conservation practices. Indeed much conservation work is dependent upon these voluntary contributions, but it is not always certain whether the contributions are voluntary or not.

Education: A common objective of conservation projects is to educate rural people in the better conservation of the natural resources they have. The whole approach therefore is often very methodical, with the external agent teaching the local people how to do something better.

Limited task: Conservation projects are often limited to the task at hand, e.g. graded banks or contour ploughing, and cease to exist once the task is completed. Local involvement in the task disappears once the task is deemed to have been completed.

Extension agent: An extension agent is a common feature of conservation projects. The agent is trained in conservation measures and, therefore, has the knowledge. His or her task is then to teach this knowledge to the local people in order that they might also then have the knowledge to undertake conservation measures.

The FAO's (1988) review of conservation in Africa urged that the above approach needed to be changed. It linked success in halting the widespread resource degradation with motivating rural people to take responsibility for and manage better conservation practices: "The role of governments must change from that of the implementing agency for specific conservation projects to that of a facilitator – promoting, encouraging, guiding and making possible the wide-scale participation of rural people in developing and applying more productive and sustainable forms of land use" (FAO, 1988, p. 4).

While this call by the FAO has been widely echoed, there is as yet little evidence of any substantial change in practice. But the term "participation" has now begun to emerge in the project documentation on resource conservation and some initial ideas have been put forward on how this participation might be achieved (Tola, 1986; De Camino, 1987; Czech, 1987). In the first instance, an important issue is understanding; if rural people could be helped to understand better where their interests lie in terms of natural resources, then they would be more willing to collaborate and support conservation measures. Conservation projects, many of which are on a massive scale, can often appear to have a detrimental impact on the lives of rural people. While such projects in the long term are expected to be beneficial, in the short term such measures as reduced land use, limitations upon livestock numbers and reduction in fuelwood supplies can have profound consequences for those whose livelihoods are balanced on a fine edge. Similarly, if rural people could participate in the decisions about, for example, the use of communal resources, e.g. grazing land or forests, then they would be more likely to protect these resources and indeed bring pressure to bear on others to do likewise. In seeking to promote this understanding and to bring about greater participation, Tola (1986) suggests that four basic principles should guide conservation projects:

(*a*) rural people are more prepared to participate when they feel the need for conservation;

(*b*) rural people make rational economic decisions in the context of their own environment and circumstances rather than those prescribed by government and project staff;

(*c*) voluntary local commitment of labour, time, material and money to a conservation project is a necessary condition for breaking patterns of conservation paternalism which reinforce local passivity and indifference;

(d) local control of the amount, quality and especially the distribution of benefits from conservation activities is directly related to those activities becoming self-sustaining.

The above are certainly a broadly acceptable set of principles which could help develop participation within conservation projects. The principles also can be seen as a sequence; unless the need for conservation is internalised within a group of rural people, then the other stages might never occur. Equally, principle *(b)* is crucial; this implies a fairly radical re-thinking of the style of project intervention from that characterised above.

In terms of the practice, there is as yet little evidence of any substantial reorientation of the approach and content of conservation projects. Apart from individual studies in which the emergence of different approaches can now be noted, participation is still largely a commitment rather than a reality. De Camino's (1987) study has begun to fill this vacuum with his examination of the role of incentives in promoting community involvement in conservation projects. He distinguishes between *direct* (cash or in kind) and *indirect* (fiscal, service, social) incentives and details the ways in which both forms can be used in promoting people's involvement in conservation works. The use of incentives is based upon the assumption that some kind of initial stimulus is required in order to break the inertia that characterises rural people's attitudes towards resource conservation. Despite the detail of his study, however, De Camino concludes that incentives alone are not enough, but can only serve to bolster or encourage moves to great participation. Oakley's (1987) review of conservation projects is more comprehensive and suggests that there would be five important elements in promoting participation:

■ The developing of awareness among rural people of the importance of the conservation of their natural resources. This awareness creation becomes the important first task of the extension agent.

■ The complete involvement of the rural people in the planning stage of a conservation project.

■ Once the people have planned a conservation project in consultation with project staff, the next step should be maximum and voluntary contributions by the people to the proposed project. These contributions might be encouraged by the use of incentives.

■ Labour-intensive conservation methods, which utilise local resources and experience, should be used in place of capital-intensive techniques of conservation.

■ The maintenance of conservation works need to be ensured. Once external existence dwindles, the ability to maintain conservation practices locally will largely depend upon the level of participation which has been developed.

The above elements are complementary to Tola's (1986) principles and can similarly be seen as a kind of sequence. The implications of the above sequential approach is that awareness creation is the critical first stage and that, without a commitment to develop this awareness as a first step, conservation projects may fail to develop any form of sustained participation. They should therefore begin with this step and not seek immediately to implement technical solutions.

More recently, research undertaken at the Centre for Environmental Studies, Leiden, the Netherlands, has begun to examine more systematically the concept of participation in environmental projects. Drijver (1989) and de Groot (1989) have begun to establish a basis for the conduct of environmental projects which will ensure local people's involvement. Both authors confirm that "centralistic" environmental projects, whose objectives and modes of implementation are largely determined by a small professional group, are usually controlled by representatives of donor organisations, and local government and project staff. The contribution of the local population is inevitably restricted to the provision of labour. Drijver (1989) suggested a series of 12 lessons concerning participation which could be learnt from his study of conservation projects (e.g. motivation, avoiding reliance on local élites, project decentralisation, social control, project flexibility) and suggested that greater people's participation implied a radical change in behaviour for environmental scientists:

> The reality of participatory environmental projects requires a certain attitude and special skills from scientists who get involved in these projects. Environmental science for developing countries should place a strong emphasis on linking science and practice; in particular, field work that is designed and carried out together with the rural population. This kind of participatory environmental research forms a challenging new field of operations for environmental scientists (Drijver, 1989, p. 19).

Overall the approach to promoting participation in conservation projects would appear to depend upon two critical issues. First, the approach must be based upon persuasion and understanding and not simply on short-term incentives or even coercion. Resource conservation is inevitably seen as an urgent priority, and the urgency equally inevitably dictates the approach. While immediate action might be necessary in certain circumstances, a less immediate perspective often gives an opportunity better to develop local participation. Second, if rural people can share in explaining the causes of resource degradation, then they may more readily identify with the solutions. In this respect conservation projects have invariably seen resource degradation as a purely physical problem requiring technical solutions. Although these solutions may have been technically appropriate, they are in fact treating the symptoms rather than the causes. Rural people do not deliberately degrade the land which is the basis of their livelihood; economic, social or political factors, such as population pressures, the land tenure system and the level of locally available technologies might all contribute to the poor use of resources. Understanding the problem on the rural people's terms will provide a stronger basis for participation.[6]

Forestry development

Tropical forests and other woodlands are fundamental to the economic and social livelihoods of millions of rural people in the Third World. Forests supply people's energy needs and provide fodder for livestock which in turn produce manure for agriculture. Rural people also use forests for water supply, materials for house construction and for products like bamboo and medicinal herbs. Forests also absorb excess water during rainy seasons and release it later, thus performing the important function of re-allocating water over time. Forests and woodlands, therefore, constitute a vital resource for rural people and one for which careful husbandry is important. For poor rural people trees can be of direct and immediate use, a source of cash when required, a form of savings or a longer-term asset. The chance to derive benefit from this resource, however, is governed by existing land rights, access to tree lots, marketing facilities and the inherent risks involved in managing such a vulnerable crop. In countries such as India, Indonesia and Nepal, the forest and its products are critical to the livelihoods of millions.

But the forests and their resources are under threat and there is world-wide recognition of an alarming trend to deforestation. This is not the place to review the detail nor rehearse the arguments of this deforestation; there are ample publications which graphically describe the alarming deterioration of such a vital resource and its consequences for the livelihoods of rural people.[7] The World Resources Institute's *Tropical Forestry Action Plan* (1987), resulting from its high-level strategy meeting in Bellagio, Italy, quantitatively assessed the impact of this deforestation and proposed a ten-point strategy to begin to reverse forestry decline. This Plan was endorsed by such agencies as the FAO, the UNDP and the World Bank and has become the basis of a new world-wide strategy to halt the destruction of the world's tropical forests. Two central

---

[6]More recently, for example, an international conference held at Leiden University, the Netherlands, examined the issue of people's participation in the management and conservation of wetland areas. See H. A. Udo de Haes and M. Marchand (eds.): *Proceedings of an International Conference on People's Role in Wetland Management* (Leiden, University of Leiden, forthcoming).

[7]The most useful series of publications within this whole area of forestry development and conservation is the Overseas Development Institute's Social Forestry Network papers. This Network brings together academics and practitioners from all over the world and has proved fundamental in heightening concern for forestry renovation. Further details on the Network's activities can be obtained from ODI, Regent's College, Regent's Park, London, NW1 4NS, United Kingdom.

arguments have emerged: first, that the causes and consequences of deforestation are well understood and that political and institutional support and not lack of knowledge are now the major barriers to action; and second, that local communities must have a central role in managing and utilising forest resources and reforestation programmes. Indeed the Bellagio meeting concluded:

> Although political commitment and leadership is critical, it is widely recognised that governments and development assistance agencies alone cannot solve the deforestation crisis. Success will depend to a high degree on identifying measures to stimulate the active participation of the millions of small farmers and landless people who daily use forests and trees to meet their needs (World Resources Institute, 1987, p. 27).

The above Bellagio Statement is the culmination of a decade which has seen an increasing advocacy for greater people's participation in forestry development and deforestation control. In its regular programme review for 1986-87 the FAO, for example, argued that the central issue of forestry development was how to activate the involvement of local people in forestry activities. Although this principle has been widely accepted within forestry development and reforestation programmes, differences occur as to its exact nature and also in the terminology used. In the literature this new approach to forestry development is variously referred to as "social forestry", "community forestry" or "forestry extension". The debate mainly concerns the exact meaning of the first two terms, while the latter has emerged in the past five years as greater involvement of extension services in forestry development. The debate between "social forestry" and "community forestry" would appear to be inconclusive, with the main distinction being drawn between social forestry, based largely on individual or family enterprise, and community forestry, which is seen to be more concerned with community-based forestry activities. This would appear to be the chief difference since in the literature the terms are often interchangeable. Forestry extension, on the other hand, appears to imply merely the involvement of extension services in forestry development and, as a strategy, follows the broad lines of extension practice. The contentious issues revolve around the notions of "social" in social forestry and "community" in community forestry. The following is a typical set of objectives of forestry programmes designed on the basis of greater people's participation:

- to involve people in forestry activities and provide the basic needs for forestry resources by increasing the production of fuelwood, fodder, timber and poles;
- to promote self-reliance among hill communities through their active participation on the management of their forest resources;
- to reduce environmental degradation and conserve soil and water resources.

Social or community forestry, therefore, is different from previous approaches to forestry development and conservation principally because of the emphasis it puts upon involvement of local people. The approach is now widespread and, particularly in Asia, a number of nation-wide programmes have been started with international assistance. Mahoney (1987, p. 5) describes the difference as follows:

Social forestry	Traditional forestry
Stimulating, offering guidance and suggestions, imparting techniques and carrying out training for the general public	Supervising a workforce
Private ownership of trees	Government ownership of forests
Multi-purpose production of forest, fodder, shade, fuelwood and poles	Timber production
A varied and unpredictable work programme	A planned and structured work programme
Much contact with the public	Limited contact with the public
Bringing trees to the public	Keeping people out of the forests

The UNDP-supported social forestry projects, for example, stress the notion of "stewardship", or the assuming of responsibility by the people for the protection and development of local forestry resources. This stewardship is supported by the awarding of a certificate which gives the right to lease land and which can be used as collateral in business negotiations.

Box 3.   The social forestry approach

Social forestry locates the main thrust of forestry activities at village level, gives subsistence needs new weight and ushers in a new relationship between forests, forest users and forest. It leads, inconspicuously, but inevitably, to a complete reformulation of forestry policy (Shepherd, 1986, p. 26).

Local participation in social forestry projects extends beyond carrying out productive tasks such as planting and harvesting. Participation of farm family and other community members includes significant roles in planning and decision-making with regard to types of crops to raise; the pattern of crop integration; the timing and methods of planting and harvesting; the disposal of products; and the sharing of income and other benefits. To further increase farmers' involvement, governments sometimes afford local inhabitants access to, and control over, public lands as project sites either through outright transfer of ownership or long-term user rights arrangements (Vergara et al., 1986, p. 2).

From the literature it would appear that there is a wide range of social forestry (SF) practice with different emphases and elements according to the demands of the context (box 3). In his review of SF projects in southern Asia, Vergara (1986) distinguishes between two broad approaches; one where SF projects are planned and implemented by governments in a top-down fashion in which local people are reduced to minimal roles as hired workers who perform only specifically assigned tasks; and the other in which the forest and project activities, such as planning, implementation, management and distribution of benefits, are under the complete control of farmers. Inevitably Vergara concludes that most SF projects are now a cross between the above two extremes. Similarly, Chandrasekharan (1985) describes different approaches to SF largely in terms of the nature of the participation involved; in this respect he distinguishes between *private participation*, in which individuals receive state support to develop their own forestry activities, *passive community participation*, in which communities gain access to forest resources and may be allocated land but are not directly involved in the planning or decisions relating to forestry development, and *active community participation*, in which community members have a fuller role in reforestation initiatives and project management.

A review of this project-based literature reveals a number of key elements in strategies to promote greater people's participation in forestry. Whilst these elements do not constitute a model strategy, nor are they found in all projects, they do illustrate the general thrust of SF strategies:

- the use of incentives (seedlings, fertiliser) to encourage local participation, although caution is expressed concerning excessive dependence on incentives to sustain SF projects;

- an approach which emphasises co-operation between local people and their resources and technical knowledge and other inputs as provided by government;

- the importance of some form of organisation as the basic instrument for involvement, and the procedures and structure of this organisation;

- a forestry development package which includes the minimum technological requirements to be distributed at the community level to get the SF project moving;

- the selection of key foresters and/or families to take a lead in the use of the forestry package and in the diffusion process;

- the use of demonstration plots as the basic means to show and to teach the practices associated with social forestry;

- the employment of forestry agents whose task is to work alongside the people in developing social forestry activities.

SF projects appear to take a well-structured and carefully planned approach to involving local people. While in some instances they have been seen also in the broader process of participation as an exercise in empowering and while examples such as the Chipko Movement in India take an educational as opposed to a technological approach, SF projects' understanding of participation is essentially linked to encouraging people to become involved in externally designed programmes and in stressing the benefits that accrue from involvement. The emphasis in the educational component of SF projects would appear to be on technical information related to forestry activities and most forest agents are trained essentially for this task. Similarly, the whole thrust of SF projects seeks to involve people so as either to increase forestry production or to control degradation, rather than explaining to them the causes of deforestation. Falconer's (1987) review of forestry extension confirmed the still essentially top-down approach of SF projects and the emphasis upon production or other quantitative activities. Box 4 gives an example of social forestry in India.

The practice of participation in SF projects to date suggests a number of key issues which critically affect the process. This practice is now sufficiently mature for some tentative assessment to be made and this is greatly facilitated by the SF network managed by the Overseas Development Institute (ODI), London. This network has played an important role in promoting the concept of SF and the practice which it has documented suggests a number of key issues:

(1) Sen and Das (1987) suggest that crucially the biggest problem with SF projects lies in creating a "participative environment" (see box 4). Forestry Departments still seek to control SF projects; instead they should adopt a more catalytic and educational role. Gamser (1987) similarly sees institutional rigidity as one of the main obstacles to effective participation; indeed he further argues that in the Sudan too many SF projects are not participatory at all but merely tree propagation activities carried out within a centralised forestry programme.

(2) In consequence it would appear that the educational content of SF projects can often be quite low. SF implies that the people become aware and convinced of the importance of forestry conservation and development and are thus motivated to participate. The problem here, however, is between conservation and development; the former implies the need for a deliberate educational approach to involve local people in explanations of forestry degradation; the latter is closely linked to both perceived needs and expected benefits, and studies suggest that local people do not always rate forestry development as a high priority. On both counts, therefore, the need for a more explicit approach to establish a common understanding as a basis for participation is vital.

Box 4. Social forestry in India

The present practice of planning and management of community forestry in the states hardly fulfills the conditions of participatory programmes. Villagers are rarely consulted at the preplanting stage, and the preparation of a feasibility report, and selection of site and species is generally done by the local forest officials. The village *panchayat* or similar agencies offer the land (often with no or half information to their members) for plantation activities by the forest department. During the initial years till its hand-over to the *panchayat*, the villagers do not have any responsibility but to remain as passive watchers.

The situation, thus, leads to the basic questions: What kind of participation is expected from the people and what will be the role of government departments in creating a participative environment? Two possible alternatives for management of community forestry with people's participation emerge from the concept of social forestry.

One way is to look at the major operating tasks in community forestry and see at what stage people can participate in it. The operating tasks are *(a)* nursery raising; *(b)* land preparation (digging of pits); *(c)* watering; *(d)* weeding; *(e)* fertilisation; *(f)* protection; and *(g)* exploitation. The people's participation in these task dimensions is only in the form of wage labour with no scope of involvement in the decision making process relating to the management of the plantation. The forest department contributes the decision making and management of such plantations, while people's contribution is restricted only to diversion of their communal land and labour against wages.

Another way of looking at the creation of a participatory environment is to involve people in all the major management functions of community forestry right from the planning stage. These are *(a)* selection of land; *(b)* planning and deciding what to raise; *(c)* organising planting operations; *(d)* managing the plantation; *(e)* distributing the produce after exploitation; and *(f)* marketing of surplus, if any. These functions have to be carried out by the people themselves with forest department's contribution mainly in the form of technical assistance (Sen and Das, 1987, p. 4-5).

---

(3) Participation of certain sections of rural people in SF projects is frustrated by tendencies for officials to limit involvement to certain vested or élite interests. Shah and Weir (1987) raise the issue of equity in terms of access to SF projects and conclude that these projects are subject, like other development projects, to the pressures of vested interests. It is suggested that forestry officials manipulate SF projects to ensure that certain groups monopolise accruing benefits.

(4) There seems to be a noticeable link between more effective participation in SF projects and the presence of an NGO to support the project. Many SF projects are managed by NGOs, as opposed to forestry departments or bilateral aid agencies, and Dasgupta (1988), for example, argues that NGOs are

---

more effective in promoting a strong participatory base in SF projects. Indeed the Bellagio Statement (1987) confirmed the important role that NGOs have in SF and suggested that they were more able to promote the participatory element in SF projects.

(5) Many commentators point to a whole range of institutional and cultural constraints which can often limit either the desire or the ability of people to participate in SF projects. These constraints are identified in order to dispel simple notions that rural people are ready and willing to participate and, as long as the technology and inputs are available, they will do so. Land availability, legal rights of access to tree products, labour availability where farmers must seek off-farm employment to maintain family incomes and the inequalities of local social structures are major institutional constraints; differing incentives to develop woodland and negative attitudes towards forestry services are prominent social constraints (Falconer, 1987).

In his review of participation in forestry development, Chandrasekharan (1985) concluded that there was a trend towards developing effective participation but that progress was slow. He argued that active participation was rare and that there was little evidence of rural people playing major roles in SF. Social forestry projects are still essentially technical and directed by professional staff and project agents whose training is almost exclusively in the forestry or other agricultural sciences. There is, for example, little influence in the SF literature of the dimensions of participation which we will discuss in Chapter 4; but there is a dominant thrust which sees participation as linked to the benefits derived from better-managed or increased forestry stocks. Assuming that the SF delivery system functions reasonably well and that the necessary inputs are available, then undoubtedly rural people become involved in project activities; but their participation is linked to these two fundamental ingredients and would appear to have little life of its own.

Health development

The evidence is widespread that the majority of the world's people have no regular or dependable access, in the general sense, to health services. These people confront the diseases and illnesses which plague them with little, if any, formal support and in situations of scarce food and financial resources. In most countries of the Third World formal health services are simply unable to reach ever a fraction of the people whom they are supposed to attend. In terms of coping with the problems of basically staying alive and healthy, millions of people have little to support them but their own knowledge and efforts. In response to this situation the challenge of Health for all by the Year 2000, a declaration adopted in Alma-Ata in 1977, has been universally adopted by the

WHO and its constituent members and now serves as a basic direction and goal of health policy and development. An essential ingredient of this new world-wide strategy is the massive involvement of people themselves, not just in the support and functioning of health services, but more importantly in determining health priorities and the allocation of scarce health resources. Indeed it is argued that the strategy will be unattainable unless radically different forms of health care are put into practice to develop health services that are people's services and not those designed and maintained by external health professionals.[8]

The growing recognition of the central importance of people's close involvement in the development of health services has resulted from the limited or patchy successes of previous health strategies in making any massive or sustainable impact upon widespread ill health and resource-poor health services. Top-down curative health strategies have been widely successful in tackling diseases which had previously ravaged the world's population; they have, however, been less successful in achieving better and sustained good health for the majority of people. Alma-Ata triggered off an examination of previous health strategies which sought to identify why they had failed to develop people's involvement. This examination can be summarised under four main areas of criticism:

- Previous health strategies did not encourage people to think or act for themselves in terms of their health problems, but encouraged them to rely upon external professional sources for answers and action.

- Inadequate training meant that local people were unable to maintain a service which had been set up.

- Community involvement was limited to resource and manpower contributions to health programmes, but there was little active involvement in health programme design and implementation.

- The conflict between health-directed needs, as determined by the health professionals, and health-related needs (e.g. water and sanitation), as determined by the local people, often resulted in incompatibility and lack of community interest in externally promoted health programmes.

In response to the above and largely since the early 1980s, the concept of community involvement in health development (CIH) has emerged as a radically different strategy for health development designed to counter the

[8]The basic material for this section on health development is taken from a recent study commissioned by the WHO: P. Oakley: *Community involvement in health development – An examination of the critical issues* (Geneva, WHO, 1989). This book will also serve as a working document for a WHO Study Group to be held on the issue of CIH in Geneva in December 1989. It is expected that the report of that Study Group will be published as a major WHO statement on the issue of community involvement in health development.

kinds of failures noted above. CIH as a basic principle has already influenced the major sectors of health development – primary health care, tropical disease control, immunisation campaigns, family health and water supply and sanitation – as well as aspects such as the planning, management and evaluation of health programmes. As a strategy CIH has received widespread support and, theoretically at least, it has been accepted as the most important fundamental principle of health development. The arguments for CIH are substantial and are explained at length in the literature. They can be summarised as follows:

■ CIH is a basic right which all people should be able to enjoy. Involvement in the decisions and actions which affect people's health builds self-esteem and also encourages a sense of responsibility. CIH as a principle is of intrinsic value in the development of communities in a wider sense and should be promoted as the basic approach to health development.

■ Many health services, and especially those in developing countries, function on the basis of limited resources. In this respect CIH can be a means of making more resources available to health services by drawing upon local knowledge and resources to complement those provided by the formal health services. Furthermore, CIH can help to extend the coverage of health services and lower the overall cost of these services. Similarly, it can lead to the greater cost-effectiveness of health services and, in the long term, an adequate return on funds invested in the health sector.

■ CIH increases the possibility that health programmes and projects will be appropriate and successful in meeting health needs as defined by local people, as opposed to medical needs as defined by the health service. When health services can be linked to local perceptions of health needs and managed with the support of local people, there will be a better chance that the services' programmes will be successful.

■ CIH breaks the knot of dependence that characterises much health development work and, on a wider front, creates an awareness in the local people of their potential involvement in development in general. Ultimately it can help create a political consciousness among people that causes them to seek a voice and to be heard in development processes within their own country.

It may be said, therefore, that certainly at the level of the WHO and its member governments CIH is now a major strategy for health development, supported by a range of studies and other documentation which seek to explain it and suggest how it functions in practice. In this respect the following statement on CIH in primary health care illustrates the different efforts being made to define the concept:

Community involvement is a process by which partnership is established between government and local communities in planning, implementation and utilisation of health activities in order to benefit from increased local self-reliance and social control over the infrastructure and technology of primary health care.[9]

In a more general review of the health literature, we can conclude that there are currently two broad but distinct interpretations of CIH: *(a)* CIH as awareness and understanding of health and health problems; and *(b)* CIH as access to information and knowledge about health service programmes and projects. In the first, the strategy is to build up communities' awareness and understanding of the issues of health development and the causes of poor health as the basis for their future active involvement in health development. In the second, the strategy is to facilitate the direct access of communities to information about existing health service programmes and projects as a precondition to their involvement in health activities which have certainly been designed and may well be implemented by external health professionals. Given the current wide-ranging use of the notion of participation in health services and development, the above two interpretations help to give a focus to what could become an unmanageable concept and equally suggest the basic directions that CIH would take in practice (box 5).

Box 5. Interpretations of community involvement in health development (CIH)

Community participation means that the health programme will die without the support of the people. The people are the principle actors in running the programme whilst the programme staff are just facilitators. The staff initially plan during the early phase of the programme, but once the community develops its own community health workers, it is they who plan programme continuity (Christian Aid, Philippines Project 90).

Community involvement for health development is understood to refer to a *process* to establish participation between government and local communities in planning, implementation and use of health services in order to increase local self-reliance and social control over health care. Community involvement means that people, who have both the right and duty to participate in solving their own health problems, have greater responsibilities in assessing health needs, mobilising local resources and suggesting new solutions, as well as creating and maintaining local organisations (WHO: quoted in Oakley, 1989, p. 15).

---

[9] A. Fonaroff: *Community involvement in health systems for primary health care* (Geneva, WHO; doc. SHS/83.6).

While the literature has concentrated on arguing the case for CIH, presenting an interpretation or suggesting the more important aspects, there has been less attention to how CIH might be put into practice. Indeed in the earlier literature participation was simply added as an additional ingredient to existing practice in the expectation that practice would then change. The reality is that CIH is still largely at the level of commitment and enthusiastic support, and has yet to become a substantial influence on the practice of formal health services. Oakley's (1989) study for the WHO examined the current situation and suggested that a number of key dimensions of CIH would need to be addressed if the concept were to have a substantial impact. These are discussed in the following sections.

The community and CIH

An immediate critical issue is to determine the exact nature of the community which is to be the basic unit of CIH. In this respect the health sector lags behind other sectors in its use of geographically defined communities as the basic units for involvement in health development. As we shall see in more detail in Chapter 4, in the practice of participation there has been a concerted move towards breaking down geographical communities and instead identifying discrete, homogeneous socio-economic groups of rural people. Much of the current thinking on CIH, however, continues to see the community as a constant, static and uncomplicated unit and pays little attention to the inadequacies of this term. In this respect there is clearly a need for those involved in health development to recognise economic and social differentiation in rural areas and to define CIH more closely with this in mind. CIH talks of community contributions to health development; such contributions will need to be understood in terms of differential abilities to contribute, particularly if the level of contribution dictates access to health services. Communities are also often synonymous with organisation in CIH, but organisation is a complex issue and the nature and composition of local organisations demand careful study and understanding. Finally, there is the issue of a typology of communities and whether, when we talk of CIH, all communities are the same. In this respect a particularly interesting study from the Americas suggests certain characteristics of communities which are conducive to CIH (e.g. urban, internal health consensus, history of successful community action) as opposed to other communities where CIH is less easily applicable.[10]

---

[10] Pan American Health Organization (PAHO): *Community participation in health development in the Americas*, Scientific Publication No. 473 (Washington, DC, 1984).

Support mechanisms for CIH

There is common agreement in the literature that CIH cannot emerge and develop as a strategy without the support of appropriate mechanisms at different levels. CIH, in other words, cannot emerge on its own; it can only emerge and flourish in conditions which both facilitate its emergence and provide the means for it to develop. In this respect we can distinguish between certain preconditions that provide the indispensable climate in which CIH can emerge and those specific mechanisms which at the local level would support implementation. In terms of preconditions, CIH is not dissimilar to other sectors when it identifies the following, for example:

- political commitment to CIH and indeed to the notion of people's participation in general;
- bureaucratic reorientation in favour of devolution and delegation to local levels;
- the development of people's managerial capabilities to take responsibility for a process like CIH;
- the existence of a minimum health structure and coverage to serve as the basis for CIH.

The above, therefore, represent the indispensable broad framework within which CIH would begin to operate. When it is put into practice, however, a number of important mechanisms can facilitate CIH:

- decentralisation of health services and the corresponding strengthening of district health systems which would serve as the basic health unit for CIH;
- the development of local, community-based structures (e.g. health committees, traditional health groups) which would serve as vehicles through which people could participate;
- better local-level intersectoral co-ordination so that the underlying basis of poor health can be understood;
- the support of NGOs which can provide additional resources for health and equally play an important role in developing CIH.

There would appear to be a general consensus that the process of CIH needs support mechanisms if it is to develop and that it serves little purpose to proclaim CIH in contexts where such support is non-existent or unlikely to materialise in the short term. At the very least, there must be a minimum health structure in existence for CIH to begin to take hold. More importantly, however, CIH should not be seen in isolation but, where possible, should plug into other existing processes of participation and derive support from them.

Education and training for CIH

If it is argued that CIH is substantially different from conventional health development practice, then knowledge of the concept and the dimension of its practice will have to spread throughout health service personnel. Health services, therefore, will need to be "educated" in terms of understanding CIH and health staff "trained" in terms of its practical application. An inter-regional meeting on CIH in Brioni, Yugoslavia, in 1985 confirmed that progress to date in education and training was limited and there was still much to be done. The two important issues to be addressed are the appropriate levels for this education and training (e.g. professional staff, community-level health workers and community leaders) and the content, particularly in terms of the balance between the theoretical and the practical. J. MacDonald's (1989) study goes into some detail on the probable content of CIH training. He argues that for it to have an impact, CIH must become a basic characteristic of health care training and that similarly, in the first instance, the emphasis should be put upon training at the local level so that some meaningful involvement can begin.

In the past five years or so there has been a veritable flood of literature on CIH and the distinct impression is that its practice is widespread. This is not the case. Although the commitment appears widespread, the implementation of CIH is still in its infancy. Indeed a major WHO inter-regional meeting in Harare in 1987 on the issue of Strengthening District Health Systems issued a Declaration which identified the following critical issues concerning CIH:

- There are inherent contradictions between the orientation and structure of most government health systems and the conditions necessary for community participation.

- Methodologies for re-educating and re-orienting health staff towards community involvement have not been very effective. Although workers have been trained and can repeat the "right" words, their basic attitudes and resistance towards community participation remain unchanged.

- District medical officers and their teams often do not appreciate the value of community participation and are not sufficiently motivated or skilled to facilitate and support community involvement (WHO, 1987, p. 6).

The above is a powerful statement of the problems facing the implementation of CIH at the end of the decade. It is perhaps over-pessimistic in the sense that it is commenting on CIH in relation to formal health services; it would appear that CIH is more in evidence in health programmes and projects promoted by the NGO sector. Werner's (1988) examination of health development in the context of empowerment is an example of how the NGO sector is recognising the powerful implications of CIH and linking into the broader overall processes of people's participation.[11] CIH is a radical challenge to formal health practice and tremendous professional resistance will need to be overcome if it is to flourish. Oakley (1989) concluded that, if CIH is to be applied in the full sense of its meaning, then it would have profound implications for professional training and the control of health services; yet there existed the dominant belief that CIH could merely be plugged in as an additional resource to existing health practice. CIH, on the contrary, is a radical reorientation in the design and delivery of community health services and the time is now appropriate to spell out the content and direction of this reorientation.

CIH is unique in that it constitutes the only distinctive sectoral approach to promoting participation in project activities. It could be said that CIH is alive in medical practice in the Third World, but that the patient is making only limited progress. The future agenda of CIH is a major challenge but encouragingly declarations like that of Harare suggest that the challenge has been noted. CIH has a very long way to go before it constitutes a major influence in health sector practice; it needs the support of a political framework that encourage such approaches, it needs changes within the formal health service, it needs to be included in all levels of training with the medical profession and it needs to learn how best to put its philosophy into practice. Given the broad base of support, however, there appears an even chance that CIH might exert a substantial influence on health practice.

Irrigation and water supply

Irrigation

In reviewing the available literature it is difficult, in the first instance, to get a feel for participation as a dynamic or intrinsic factor in irrigation projects which are so dominated by professionals and governed by complex organisational and managerial arrangements for water distribution. Botterall's (1981) review, for example, of major irrigation schemes confirmed their highly technical and centrally co-ordinated styles; indeed Botterall concluded that, in the irrigation schemes he examined, efficiency deteriorated as people became more involved. More recently, however, the virtue of people's participation in irrigation has begun to be advocated and a more positive direction is emerging. It is important to recognise, in this respect, that rural people's willingness or wish to participate will depend basically upon their individual family needs for water and that participation in irrigation is, therefore, restricted to particular groups of rural people. Also it is important to note the two main dimensions

[11] An excellent example of the work of an NGO in promoting people's involvement in health development can be found in Lavon Tinklenberg: *Health indicators as a tool for community participation in programme planning*, Unpublished dissertation (Manchester, University of Manchester, 1988).

of this participation; one linked mainly to the building of the physical infrastructure of the irrigation system, and the other involving the development of the social capability for managing and sustaining the system.

Despite the dominance of the technical construction aspects of irrigation schemes and the cadres of associated professional staff, it is now widely recognised that irrigation schemes are as much social as they are technical processes. Hall (1981), for example, showed that the failure of many such schemes can be broadly attributed to insufficient attention to social aspects of project design and procedures for water control, problems which could have been avoided if local people had been consulted. In response Bagadion and Korten (1985) have argued that irrigation schemes should not be constrained by a specific, predetermined plan, but should be seen more as an overall process. This should be a learning process which brings together the professionals and the local people. In practice this process leads to greater people's participation in irrigation schemes which, they further argue, is critical to their smooth operation and maintenance. While not overwhelmingly apparent, arguments are beginning to emerge concerning the advantages of this participation. Patil (1987) sees these advantages in efficiency terms, particularly with regard to procedures and control of water distribution. Furthermore, in the laying out of the irrigation system, farmers' knowledge of the physical environment will be particularly useful. IFAD's experiences with irrigation suggests that participation is particularly critical in terms of sharing the costs of irrigation operation and maintenance. The question of costs is a dominant preoccupation concerning participation in irrigation schemes, but the authoritative view seems to argue that the additional costs incurred in extra non-technical staff to develop participation and the users' training required would be offset by the returns from a scheme which is successful because of effective participation.

Uphoff (1986b) suggests that when this commitment to participation in irrigation schemes is put into practice, it appears to have three main elements:

- participation in the procedures of water use within the system; the acquisition of the water, its allocation between participants, its distribution on an agreed basis and the tackling of any drainage problems;
- participation in the structures that develop the scheme; this includes participation in the design, construction, operation and maintenance of the actual irrigation system;
- participation in the organisation of effort, vital for the day-to-day functioning of the scheme, such as decision-making and local resource mobilisation.

He further suggests that farmers' participation in irrigation manage-ment is directly linked to the quantity of water available. In extremes of both drought and excess water, farmers' participation is less necessary; however, when just enough water is available and its distribution becomes a careful balance between conflicting demands, then farmers' participation reaches its peak.

The most common participatory characteristic of irrigation schemes is the Water Users' Association, or some other similar form of organisation, which is the basic means whereby participants can become involved (see the example in box 6). These associations are sometimes established on the basis of existing traditional water management practices on the farmers' initiative; more commonly in the bigger schemes they are formed with initial project assistance. Given the burgeoning bureaucracies of many of these schemes and the improbability of contact with each individual farmer, these associations are indispensable.

Box 6. The Water Users' Association and participation in the Philippines

Before the introduction of the participatory approach, National Irrigation Administration (NIA) field staff did not systematically consult the irrigators' association regarding the development of the physical system. Discussions were sometimes held with individual farmers or with the officers of the association, but full and regular interaction with the association on project planning and construction issues was rare. Achieving such regular interaction required a variety of co-ordination mechanisms. The community organisers encouraged the irrigators' association to develop task-specific committees to work with the NIA personnel on survey, design and construction of the project. Organisers needed to consult daily with the project-level engineer and bi-weekly with the provincial irrigation engineer to help link the technical decision-making with the issues the irrigators' association was facing (Bagadion and Korten, 1985, p. 64).

While the commitment on paper is clear enough, there is doubt whether irrigation schemes have begun substantially to adopt a more participatory approach. In his review Uphoff (1986) concluded that farmers' participation in irrigation schemes was "more often a potential than a reality". A major constraint appears to be the inability of highly technical and physically oriented schemes to adapt to the more subtle demands of participation. Irrigation schemes are invariably staffed by professionals whose qualifications reflect the dominant physical activities; few schemes maintain a permanent cadre of social scientists. Furthermore, participation in such schemes appears invariably linked to the demands of project success and farmers' involvement is limited to the extent necessary to ensure this success. Uphoff (1986) for example, concluded: "The orientation towards farmer participation is not one of maximising its extent, but rather of identifying and promoting kinds and degrees of participation which will further certain irrigation objectives."

Indeed Patil (1987) suggests that if the water distribution system can be managed by project staff, there will be less need for farmers' participation. In large irrigation schemes this participation is seen essentially as a cost and as a input that can be manipulated, and has yet to achieve the status of a broader, educational process.

Water supply

Van Wijk-Sijbesma's (1979) literature review of participation in community water supply and sanitation programmes first revealed the extent of participation in these fields. Since then studies by White (1981) and Whyte (1983) have built upon this earlier work and have offered guide-lines for the methodologies and planning involved in a participatory approach. Community participation in this type of project is very similar to the kinds of participation encouraged by more traditional community development programmes. In these programmes there is often genuine and active participation in the different stages of specific physical infrastructure projects which are of immediate benefit to the community. Community members participate directly in designing, planning, building and maintaining small physical improvements to their environment. With water supply projects there is also the notion that participation means good consultation. The technical aspects of the water supply are left to the external technician; the people are consulted on site location, resource availability and maintenance. Indeed Shepherd and El Neima (1983) concluded that successful participation in water supply could best be measured in terms of rate and length of breakdown; the greater the degree of participation, the greater the chances of continued water supply. Therkildsen (1986) suggests that this participation in water supply occurs over a series of stages:

Stage	Villagers' roles
Identification	None
Preparation of village scheme	Village approves or rejects proposal to construct scheme
Planning	Village approves or rejects water source; locates public standpipe subject to project approval
Construction	Village provides most unskilled labour
Operation	Village fully responsible (funds, labour, organisation)
Maintenance	As above
Monitoring and evaluation	Village provides project with information

While they clearly benefit from a successful outcome to the above process, at several stages the villages come under pressure. In some cases they are expected to produce cash down-payments before a scheme can begin: village labour and other resources are vital to keeping down costs, and finally villages are expected to assume an ongoing responsibility. There is active participation but it would appear to be linked closely to ensuring project objectives and to ultimate tangible benefits. The participation is concentrated upon the physical task at hand and there is less evidence that it is encouraged in a broader sense to help build up village-level skills to initiate and manage future projects.

Concluding comments

The above sectoral reviews are convincing evidence that participation has at least entered the vocabulary of project practice. In the past five years or so there has been a dramatic commitment in principle to a more participatory style of project implementation across the broad spectrum of rural development. The reviews above have been brief and limited to analysing each sector's basic approach to participation; in reality several sectors are already producing more detailed analysis and guides to project practice. The arguments for greater participation have been widely accepted, although we have to recognise that these arguments predominantly reflect a cost-benefit approach and see participation as a contribution of human resources and skills which might ensure the success of the project. There is a strong line of argument in the literature that projects have failed in the past for lack of people's participation; this participation should now be encouraged in order to better the chances of success.

On the basis of this review, what conclusions can we draw concerning the practice of participation within the different rural development sectors?

(1) Quite clearly there is very little co-ordination between the sectors in terms of their approaches to promoting participation. Indeed each sector lives within its own world and tackles the concept in a possessive and correspondingly limited way. This could well imply a substantial waste of resources. It could be argued that the basis and conditions for people's participation should be common to all the sectors, which could then develop their own individual project practice. But such an approach would demand a degree of project level co-ordination which, as we know, rarely existed even before calls for participation. It is perhaps not unexpected that the concept of participation should now be scattered to the different corners of un-coordinated project practice. It will take a lot of time before it is recognised that participation is a process independent of project structures and one which must be promoted in its own right and not just in conjunction with existing project strategies.

(2) It must be recognised that, while the different sectors have espoused the cause of participation and with varying degrees of commitment and sensitivity are seeking to put it into practice, there is little evidence of widespread and clear-cut people's participation in the key aspects of project practice, e.g. design, decision-making and management. This is largely because participation is not being seen as an educational process in which local people are helped to develop the capabilities and skills to assume greater responsibility. Predominantly sectoral projects still see participation as an input, which can be managed and planned at the project's convenience and which must be included in calculations concerning the costs of project implementation. This entrenched practice will be a formidable obstacle to overcome before projects can begin authentically to promote people's participation rather than merely seeking to involve people where useful in existing project operations.

(3) While sectoral projects have tried to adjust in terms of approach, sensitivity in their contacts with rural people and a less rigid project control, there has been little loosening of what Ghai (1988) calls the "conventional project style". Sectoral projects continue as external instruments, planned and budgeted from outside and managed within predetermined parameters of time and objectives; in such a rigid framework, it is difficult to imagine how rural people could meaningfully participate. Indeed it raises the valid question, if we understand participation as a process which enables people to assume greater responsibilities for their own development, whether such a process can flourish within the framework of the development project. Clearly such a question cannot be answered with an emphatic "yes" or "no", nor can we argue that development projects *sui generis* are hostile to people's participation. The evidence appears to suggest, however, that authentic people's participation is difficult within the framework of a development project, and both the explanations for and solutions to this situation need careful thought.

(4) There is little evidence to date that the commitment to participation has, in any substantial way, influenced the staffing of sectoral projects. Projects in agriculture and health, for example, are still dominated by staff with technical qualifications who must now include the promotion of participation within their ambit of duties. While anthropologists and rural sociologists continue to provide the non-technical support to the projects, there is precious little evidence of any systematic attempt to assess the skill requirements of staff on participatory projects and provide the corresponding training. Currently people's participation in sectoral projects is being promoted by staff with little, if any, preparation for the processes involved; the result is the persistence of participation as a manageable and quantitative input. If participation within development projects continues to be seen as yet another input, then little thought will be given to the skills required for its promotion. If, however, it is seen as a distinctive process, then projects will need to be staffed accordingly.

3

Case studies in the practice of participation*

Introduction

Participation has a powerful grip on the minds of many but a flimsy influence upon development practice. (Anon)

We have already seen in broad detail in Chapter 2 how the different sectors in rural development have begun to incorporate participation into their development practice. It is therefore time to look at this practice in more detail and to see how this apparent commitment is translated into action at the project level. Undoubtedly there is now a widespread endeavour to incorporate participation into development project practice. In some instances this endeavour is explicit in the sense that the major thrust of the project is participatory and a clear objective is to develop the project with the direct involvement of local people. In a majority of instances, however, participation is implicit in the project's activities but serious obstacles appear to frustrate its functioning in a genuinely participatory manner. There is often a yawning gap between proclamations of participation in initial project objectives and participation in practice in project activities.

In the light of the above, the case studies selected for this book fall exclusively within the earlier category of explicit participation. Indeed it would be impossible to write a meaningful set of case studies on projects where the participation is only implicit in project objectives but distinctly absent from the practice. The writing of the case studies has not involved any additional fieldwork and has been based upon documentation and experience existing to date. It was decided earlier on that the case studies would neither dominate nor be the main body of the book; instead they would be more limited and serve as illustrations of the issues discussed. A set of guide-lines was prepared and the authors encouraged to emphasise in their studies the practice and the methodology of the participation; the case studies were not to be seen as evaluations of the project concerned but were to serve as examples of participation in practice.

Edited by Peter Oakley. Please note that the references cited are listed at the end of the individual case studies rather than in the bibliography at the end of the book.

The selection of the case studies was inevitably heavily influenced by the availability of both writers and material. Furthermore, since no additional fieldwork was contemplated, adequate documentation had to be available, otherwise the study could not be written. Within these general constraints, however, a number of criteria were employed in case study selection and these included:

- a geographical mix of studies to include the three main continental areas of the Third World;

- an agency mix to include government, and non-governmental and international organisations supporting projects which promote participation;

- a functional mix to reflect both the different sectors and the emerging educational component of participation in development;

- where possible, case studies which could be written by somebody who had been directly involved in the project concerned.

In the final outcome the above criteria have been largely employed. It is probably impossible to be entirely happy with the eventual selection of case studies to reflect a process so difficult to define as participation. Some people will inevitably point to gaps and suggest alternatives. Collectively, however, it could be argued that the following selection of case studies is broadly representative of the current state of participation in rural development projects and, as such, amply illustrates the issues and the problems involved. Each of the case studies, of course, demands further explanation and is far more substantial than the limited review suggests. Rather than being judged individually, however, they should be read as a collective statement on the current state of participation in development projects.

The basic purpose of the studies is to provide evidence of participation in practice at the project level. They are purposefully short and intended to be illustrative, rather than evaluative, of the issues surrounding this practice. It was decided not to base this study entirely upon a small number of very detailed case studies and leave the reader to extract whatever could be learnt concerning methodology. Instead the case studies reflect the general approach of the study which is to cast the net as widely as possible and provide as much illustrative material as possible.

The following case studies are not meant to be read either as definitive statements or evaluations of the projects concerned. No judgements are offered as to whether the projects were successful or not. The whole purpose is to show how a number of projects, across the sectors, have tried to implement a process of participation and how this participation evolved methodologically. For this reason the case studies are short, concentrate upon the issue of methodology and range over a very broad spectrum. They are not intended to be studies in themselves, but more a range of illustrations to help capture the essential elements of a methodology of participation.

People's participation project: Ghana

Ellen Bortei-Doku *

The People's Participation Programme (PPP) as a basic strategy of rural development was launched by the FAO in 1980. The thinking behind the programme and its origins can be found in two principal sources. First, the World Conference on Agrarian Reform and Rural Development (WCARRD), organised by the FAO in Rome in 1979, identified participation as a key element in future strategies to tackle rural underdevelopment. Second, the successful implementation in the late 1970s of the Small Farmer Development Programme (SFDP) in Nepal, and its subsequent spread to other Asian countries, suggested a distinctive methodology of working with the rural poor which it was felt could be the basis of a new strategy of rural development. These two influences converged and in early 1980 the FAO launched its PPP with pilot projects in two African countries, Ghana and Sierra Leone. These had an immediate impact and the programme began to grow. Projects were begun in other African countries and subsequently extended to Asia and Latin America. By mid-1988 the FAO had 12 active PPP projects, nine of which were in Africa, two in Asia and one in Central America. This case study will illustrate the PPP approach by describing the Ghana project.

Basic principles and approach of the PPP

The basic philosophy of the PPP approach is in direct contrast to the more conventional top-down rural development where external planners design and implement projects and the rural poor are either passive collaborators or excluded onlookers. At the core of the PPP approach is the fact that the rural poor have inevitably been by-passed by previous rural development approaches and have neither benefited from nor been involved in development activities. The PPP reflects the spirit of WCARRD in its emphasis upon participation and its call to direct development initiatives at those who had

*Research Fellow, Institute of Statistical, Social and Economic Research, University of Ghana, Legon.

previously never benefited. In this sense, the PPP is a product of the development re-thinking of the mid-1970s in which concern for such issues as people and access in development became just as important as production targets and infrastructural development. The PPP took as its guiding principle this lack of access of the rural poor to the resources required for development and structured an approach which would establish this access and, as a result, develop the basis for the rural poor's sustained participation in development activities. The following statement summarises the PPP's understanding of participation:

> People's participation may be defined as the process by which the rural poor are able to organise themselves and through their own organisations are able to identify their own needs and share in the design, implementation and evaluation of the participatory action. Such action is self-generated, based on their access to productive resources and services other than their labour and the continued security of that access. It is also based on initial assistance and support to stimulate and sustain the development action programmes.

The PPP is different from many other rural development projects in that it explicitly seeks to promote participation. Whereas participation is frequently seen as another element, in the PPP it is central to the project's whole approach. As such, therefore, the PPP was launched with a distinctive strategy to develop this participation and with a number of key elements which would guide and structure the practice. These key elements, which have been applied as a model across all PPP projects, are as follows:

- *Focus on the rural poor:* PPP projects are designed to focus specifically on the rural poor; that is, on those people in rural areas who live at or below the subsistence level, e.g. smallholders, tenants, small fishermen and artisans. This deliberate focusing on the rural poor is to ensure that PPP resourcees reach those previously unable to gain access to development resources.

- *Self-organisation and self-reliance:* The fundamental principle in working with the rural poor is to develop structures and organisations which can help the poor become self-reliant. Such organisations would be of the people themselves, managed by them and structured in a way so as to avoid undue external dependence.

- *Income– and employment-generating activities:* A basic argument of the PPP is that participation is essentially a function of power which itself is linked to access to economic resources. A major emphasis within the PPP, therefore, is on promoting specific income-generating activities which would not only create economic benefits but equally would help bolster the rural poor's confidence. Increased economic activity by the rural poor would be the tangible basis of their empowerment and access to a greater share of available development resources and services.

■ *Small homogeneous groups:* A basic premise of the PPP is that the rural poor's participation can best be effected through the formation of small, informal and homogeneous groups of people who share common social and economic interests. The groups would serve as the organisation for undertaking income-generating activities and as useful channels for the delivery of development inputs and other services.

■ *Group promoter (GP):* The key person in the PPP approach is a new kind of project agent, known as the group promoter, who would work directly with the project groups. The major difference between the GP and other project agents is that the GP's role is directly involved with supporting and working with the project groups and not merely providing technical inputs. The GP is involved in the whole process of group development and has responsibility for approximately ten groups at any one time.

■ *Participatory monitoring and evaluation (PME):* In order to accompany and understand the development of a complex process such as participation, the PPP stresses the importance of PME. A PPP project cannot be evaluated simply in the conventional way by quantitative measurement carried out retrospectively; its qualitative approach demands a more continuous participative approach to evaluation in order to ensure that the full range of its outcomes are understood.

Within the framework of the above key elements, the major thrust of the PPP is to seek to strengthen the rural poor economically and financially, by the development of mechanisms whereby the rural poor can accumulate capital and thus acquire economic leverage – a critical factor in their ability to participate in a process of sustained development. Conventional development projects which provide financial resources, i.e. credit for rural development, have rarely reached the rural poor who universally are considered as a poor financial risk. Where such financial resources have been made available, this has often occurred in the context of large investment-oriented development projects in which the rural poor's lack of genuine participation has meant that they never accumulate sufficient resources to sustain their development. A major component in a PPP project, therefore, is to make immediately available to the rural poor several mechanisms whereby they could begin the process of building up their economic capital:

■ *Credit:* This could be made available via an existing commercial bank or other appropriate financial institution. A PPP project negotiates a line of credit to be made available to PPP groups; given the frequent reluctance of banks to lend to the rural poor, this line of credit is often supported by a guarantee-cum-risk fund which protects the bank against defaulters. While loans are made to individuals as group members, the group as a whole guarantees the loan.

- *Savings:* Credit and savings represent the PPP's balanced approach to the building up of group financial resources. The mobilisation of PPP group savings is a major emphasis for a variety of reasons: savings help group members accumulate capital; they can serve as financial collateral; when deposited they increase a group's involvement in the financial institution; and they can instil greater self-confidence.

- *Link-up:* Existing government and other services within a particular region can provide the services and support to help a PPP group sustain its development.

PPP literature is extremely detailed on how these different mechanisms operate to build up the financial and resources base of PPP groups. Implicit in their use, however, is the emphasis upon designing financial mechanisms within the context of existing savings and credit arrangements in a particular area. Emphasis is also placed on trying to make these existing arrangements more responsive to the needs of PPP groups. Finally, and crucially, financial arrangements must be within the capacity and competence of the PPP groups to understand, use, control and develop. Given the usual absolute lack of involvement of PPP group members with local financial institutions, this aspect of the PPP approach is clearly a major operational challenge.

The context of the PPP, Ghana

The Ghana project was the first PPP project to be established. Initial discussions took place in late 1980 and after several consultants' visits and agreements with the Government of the Netherlands to fund the project, Phase I began in May 1982, for a period of three years. As was to be expected with such a novel and pilot project, fieldwork did not really get under way until late 1983. The project then ran for a full three years before Phase II was agreed upon in early 1987. The Project is currently half way through Phase II.

Increasing concern in Ghana in the late 1970s at the lack of progress in rural development, coupled with the Provisional National Defence Council's (PNDC) stated priority in late 1981 of improving services in rural areas, provided the environment in which the PPP project was introduced. Ghana is largely an agricultural country, with agriculture accounting for over 50 per cent of GNP and nearly 80 per cent of export earnings; more than 60 per cent of the total population of 12.5 million gain a livelihood from agriculture. Cocoa cultivation is the mainstay of the agricultural economy, although both production and exports slumped in the early 1980s. The agricultural sector is dominated by peasant production, with the landholding size averaging 2.5 hectares and reliance upon simple tools such as hoes and machetes. Despite the contribution of agriculture to the national economy, development initiatives in the past

20 years have generally favoured the urban areas in Ghana. In 1985 only 14 per cent of the rural population had access to potable water, 21 per cent to health facilities and 2 per cent to electricity. Little impact had been made on these rural-urban disparities despite successive Governments' commitments to improving the provision of services to the rural areas. In response to the above the PNDC recognised the importance of the small farmer in future agricultural development in Ghana and pledged support for programmes which would seek to initiate development at that level.

From the beginning of Phase I, it was decided to implement the PPP project in two pilot areas. These were as follows:

- *Begoro Action Area:* situated 135 km north of the capital, Accra, in the Eastern Region of the country. In 1970 Begoro had a population of over 530,000 inhabitants scattered over more than 70 villages. Subsistence agriculture is the primary occupation but as productivity and income levels are low, most households supplement their income with petty trading, hunting, and the small-scale gathering and processing of forestry products. Primary education facilities are adequate but there is only one secondary school: health facilities are woefully inadequate. The subdistrict is connected by an all-weather road to Accra. The Begoro area is well located for the project as it can expand to the adjacent Afram plain as well as to other Volta lake settlement areas.

- *Wenchi Action Area:* Situated 420 km north-west of Accra in the forest/savannah transition zone. In Wenchi district there are over 100,000 inhabitants from five ethnic groups scattered throughout some 130 villages. While potentially Wenchi is a good agricultural area in which maize and yams are principally grown, the people are generally poor and cultivate on average 2-5 hectares per season. Due to migration and urban pull, however, labour is in short supply and females account for over 50 per cent of farm labour. Primary education services are adequate but there is generally a shortage of trained teachers. Medical facilities do not extend to most people; there is only one hospital and 22 health centres in the district. The district is also a Catholic Parish and the Church is an important influence for development. Otherwise there are few development initiatives in the district. The district has good market outlets to the Sunjani and Mumasi urban areas, as well as various bank branches.

The selection of an action area is one of the crucial first steps in the PPP approach. Early PPP guiding principles laid great emphasis upon the criteria to be considered in selecting the action area in order to ensure that the conditions there would be conducive to such a project. One of the more important criteria is the existence of government and other services to which the emerging PPP group could relate as they develop and thus begin the process of their participation. At the beginning of the PPP in Ghana there seemed little evidence of an existing structure in which the group could participate as and when they began to develop their own skills and abilities.

The PPP project approach

Within the context of the above two action areas, the PPP was officially launched in late 1982. Given the pilot nature of the project, however, the distance between the two action areas, the chronic shortage of supplies required to support the two areas and the inevitable structural teething problems, it took time for the PPP approach to emerge and to begin to have effect. Initially the project came under the direct control of the Ministry of Rural Development and Co-operatives; eventually, however, responsibility for its actual implementation was handed over to the Sanyani Diocesan Development Committee (Wenchi) and the Presbyterian Church of Ghana (Begoro). Similarly, the overall national co-ordinator was replaced by co-ordinators for each of the two project areas. By late 1985 the PPP project was organised as shown in figure 1.

This structure was intended to achieve overall national co-ordination within the fragmented PPP as well as ensuring the project's integration into national rural development strategy. The devolution of responsibility to the action area level was similarly expected to improve project performance and encourage each action area to develop its own dynamic.

The implementation of a PPP project involves a series of inter-linked stages, and we review these in the context of the Ghana PPP.

Base-line survey (BLS)

Most development projects seek to understand both the quantitative and qualitative dimensions of the context in which they expect to operate. A BLS, therefore, is an important initial step in the PPP approach and is concerned not just to detail the physical characteristics of the action areas but also to describe and interpret such aspects as the lack of participation and exclusion of the rural poor. A comprehensive BLS in this way provides the basis for later judgements on the results of the project. A BLS was undertaken in both of the two action areas although, for understandable reasons, its timing was not entirely appropriate and, at one time, GPs were trying to promote and support the emerging groups and collaborate with the BLS at the same time.

Selection and training of group promoters

A procedure to select and train GPs to work on the PPP project was established at the beginning of the project and was the responsibility of the National Programme Co-ordinator. GPs were recruited on a national basis;

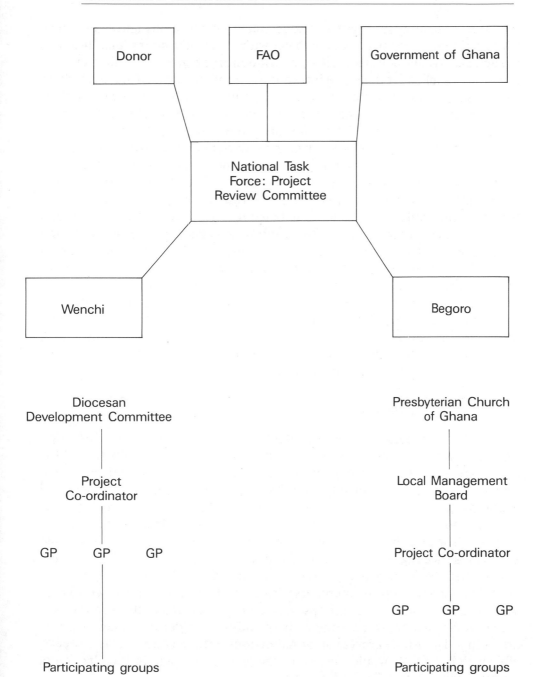

Figure 1. Organisation of the People's Participation Project, Ghana

selection criteria were essentially educational qualifications and experience, with preference given to those candidates with higher educational qualifications in such areas as agriculture, sociology, economics or regional planning. Over 60 candidates applied for the initial intake and eventually seven GPs, one of whom was a woman, were selected; all the successful candidates had degrees, their ages ranged from 26 to 43 years, three had no previous field experience whilst the other four had 12, 13, 16 and 20 years' experience respectively.

The original group of seven GPs received both inception training and a short period of in-service training some eight months after they took up their posts in September 1983. There were few models in existence at that time as to the most appropriate content of a GP training programme. In practice the content included such issues as detailed review of the PPP philosophy and approach, the methodology of the PPP, data collection and analysis, and techniques of participatory monitoring and evaluation. Given the pilot nature of the PPP, however, much of this initial training was conceptual and could not include the development of skills appropriate to participatory practice. Observations in 1984 and 1985 showed that the GPs were following procedures as established by the PPP but lacked understanding of such issues as group development and the evaluation of group processes. As the PPP developed, subsequent GPs have benefited from the cumulative experience, and training has been more in-service, informal and practical.

Formation of groups

In both action areas the identification of beneficiaries and their formation into homogeneous groups began with the GPs' examination of the action areas and their structuring of local villages into village clusters. Such issues as distance, road quality, population size, infrastructure, services and economic potential were used in structuring the clusters. GPs then visited the clusters and identified key people to whom they introduced the project and who in turn introduced them to the village chiefs and headmen. Village chiefs would then call a meeting to tell villagers about the PPP project. The villagers were encouraged to form groups, after which the GPs undertook brief socio-economic surveys of group members with a view to excluding those with a high socio-economic status. The groups were then encouraged to think in terms of some kind of income-generating activity and to consider how they might go about this. This whole process of formation took between three and four weeks, after which the GPs would meet with the groups and help in the election of Group Leaders and a Group Executive.

The above approach resulted in an immediate explosion of group formation and activities in each action area. Group formation began in the action areas in March 1984, and by the end of a three-month period some 70 groups had been formed. These became the basis of the first series of income-generating activities during the months of May to October 1984, after which the second generation of groups was formed. By the end of this second process a total of some 187 groups were recorded for both action areas in mid-1985. The GPs indeed quickly slipped into a cycle of activities: formation of a number of groups; support for groups; income-generating activities; group consolidation; next wave of group formations, and so on. A certain pattern quickly emerged and the GPs hoped to developed a dynamic of group formation, consolidation and expansion in which their overall role would be to guide and support the process.

Provision of credit

The key element in the above process was the provision of credit which would enable the groups to undertake income-generating activities. A series of discussions took place in 1983 with a number of financial institutions, but it was not until May 1984 that an arrangement was agreed between the PPP and the Ghana Commercial Bank (GCB) to make material inputs and credit available to group members. An initial agreement covered a total of over 2.6 million Cedis to be made available to 875 registered group members. Since that initial agreement the GCB has become the principal source of credit to PPP groups, although individual loan sizes have remained small. In Phase II of the PPP, the role of the GCB was reinforced and, in order to encourage it to expand significantly its loans to the PPP groups, a Guarantee-cum-Risk Fund of US$85,000 was made available. Also in Phase II, it was hoped to link up PPP groups with the Agricultural Development Banks and the network of Rural Banks. A key feature of the credit scheme is that loans are taken out on the basis of group liability in order to ensure overall group responsibility for loan repayments. The availability of credit to PPP members has been consolidated within the overall PPP process and there has been ready if limited access to funds for income-generating activities. In this respect the PPP was able to achieve this essential link between the groups and existing sources of credit.

Income-generating activities

On formation the PPP project groups would be immediately encouraged to identify and plan some form of income-generating activity for which appropriate inputs or credit would be made available by the GCB. These activities were seen as the essential outcome of the group process and had two broad purposes: first, in terms of quantitative impact and the likely increases in yields, incomes or savings that would result for group members; but second, and perhaps more importantly, in terms of the self-reliance, greater confidence and collective participation that successful activities would help develop.

The essential feature of these activities is that they are group based and are intended to strengthen group ties, as opposed to individual experience in building up economic assets. In the two action areas the majority of group income-generating activities have been agriculturally based, i.e. crop production, but other activities have included credit unions, timber processing, crop storage and marketing, and soap making.

Participatory monitoring and evaluation

Considerable importance was attached, at the beginning of the PPP project, to the need for regular, careful and detailed monitoring of the overall project and the project groups in order to understand the impact of the project in terms of PPP objectives. In the initial flurry of activities to get the PPP launched, this element of participatory monitoring and evaluation (PME) was largely overlooked. It was not until late 1984 that the BLS was undertaken and initially GPs had only a rudimentary system of keeping records of the groups. In late 1984 the first work was begun to define an appropriate PME system for the project; this was followed up in 1985 by a more detailed study and, in July 1986, a national-level workshop was held on the subject of PME in the PPP project. As a result a more formalised system of PME set up at both the action area and group level was expected both to generate information on the impact of the project and to serve as a tool to develop group project managerial and control skills. Inevitably, however, the implementation of this system has not been easy; problems have arisen related to the detailed nature of the system, its sophistication vis-à-vis the project groups and the time and resources required by GPs to implement it.

Action area methodology

Within the context of the above overall approach, it would be useful to examine in a little more detail how the GPs went about the process of group formation, the roles they assumed and what factors influenced their performance. A study in late 1984, after the first cycle of group formation, illustrated the methodology as explained by the GPs in the two action areas as follows:

Action area: Begora	Action area: Wenchi
Familiarisation with area	Establish rapport with village via use of influential persons
Make contact with villages using influential persons	Registration of villagers interested
Visit village chief / speak to whole village	Selection of beneficiaries in terms of PPP criteria
Village forms the groups	Inaugural meeting
GP makes contact with groups	Election of group leaders
Loan process begins	Process of group meetings and GP visits

It is not suggested that the above is the definitive methodology of the PPP project, merely the way the first group of GPs went about implementing the PPP approach. The above, however, does illustrate the process nature of group formation and development and how the GPs structured their work with the groups in a series of stages. Subsequent practice suggests that the above initial methodology has been somewhat modified; this has been brought about by increasing local knowledge of the PPP project (which has reduced the need for explanation), changes in GP personnel, the closer links between the groups and existing financial and other services and the consolidation of group numbers with the subsequent changes in the GPs' role. After the first cycle of groups in Ghana in 1984, many other groups immediately formed on their own and awaited their inclusion in the PPP project.

Understandably, GPs were at first unsure as to what their exact role with the groups should be. In a new project, there was little detailed guidance of how they should operate in terms of overall PPP objectives; their training had been at a general, overall level and none of them had had previous experience of the processes implicit in the PPP. The first batch of GPs began the initial cycle of group formation with great enthusiasm and, by the end of 1984, were contemplating the formation of the next generation of groups. At the end of this first cycle, a series of GP roles were beginning to emerge:

Adviser:　　　to the groups on the problems and issues they confront.

Organiser:　　of the groups and group activities.

Problem-solver: when problems arise and the group itself is not able to find a solution (i.e. transport for sale of group produce).

Instigator:　　of the group process and the central dynamic of the groups' development.

The GP's role with the group also raised a whole series of issues which the project formulators had not taken into consideration: the nature and content of the relationship between the GP and the group; the balance within the GP's role between developing the basis of the group or helping implement economic projects; and the distribution of the GP's time and resources between groups at different stages of development.

Project results

Despite being of a pilot nature and undertaken on the basis of limited resources, with a novel strategy and field staff who were still largely experimenting with project operations, the PPP Ghana project has grown steadily since it first became operational in early 1984. In quantitative terms, the three sets of figures show one dimension of the project's growth:

	No. of groups	No. of households
Nov. 1984	69	875
Nov. 1985	187	2 822
Nov. 1987	253	3 477

	No. of loans	Total amount (Cedis)
Oct. 1985	788	2 932 875
Feb. 1988	2 695[1]	17 623 185

[1] This figure represents the total number of loans in 1988 only for the Wenchi area ; the total amount, however, does include both Begoro and Wenchi.

	No. of savings accounts	Total savings (Cedis)
Aug. 1985	12[1]	2 147 00
Feb. 1988	165	495 680 00

[1] Wenchi only.

The above figures show the quantitative changes that have occurred as a result of the PPP project. They confirm that the operations of the PPP project have progressively increased over a three-year span and, in terms of making resources available to small farmers previously excluded from such services, it has had a major impact on the two project areas. The results of the project are not, however, merely quantitative and, while the data on other changes that have occurred are more tentative, there is no doubt that other more qualitative changes have resulted:

- the building up of local-level organisations which, for the first time, represent the interests of the rural poor and which can serve as a basis for their increasing involvement in development activities;

- establishing links between these organisations and existing government or other financial services;

- developing a small cadre of field workers experienced in working with the rural poor in a manner which promotes their interests;

- a general dynamic of development introduced into two areas where development initiatives are few;

- the perfecting of an approach or a methodology which might be applicable in other parts of Ghana;

- strengthening the activities of NGOs and giving them a more central role in development.

The above possible outcomes from the project, however, are more speculative than proven and reinforce the need in projects such as the PPP project for a more detailed and qualitatively oriented system for better understanding the range of outcomes from such projects.

Critical issues relating to PPP methodology

In terms of the overall approach and methodology, the PPP project in Ghana has come under quite intensive scrutiny. As a pilot project seeking to implement a methodology essentially derived from experiences in another country, it has been closely examined and voluminous comments written upon its performance. While we still await a substantial quantitative and qualitative evaluation of the approach, the group methodology and the Project's results, we can summarise what appear to be the main critical methodological issues which have arisen so far:

(1) The whole process of group formation and development was initially carried on at great speed when, it appears, emphasis was placed more upon the quantity of groups and their activities than on the quality of the process itself. The result has been a possible sacrifice of the development of such key group characteristics as self-reliance and sustainability in favour of an apparent immediate quantitative impact. In this concern for impact, less attention may have been given to the homogeneity of the groups or to internal mechanisms required to strengthen the groups' cohesion and solidarity. The statistics for the growth in the number of groups, for example, conceal the fact that in many instances the groups are dormant and lack the internal strength necessary for self-development.

(2) The use of credit or inputs as incentives to group formation has been a major influence upon the development of the project. On the one hand, there are those who would argue that the use of incentives can only distort the process and inevitably dominate the relationship between groups and project agent. On the other hand, the availability of such incentives undoubtedly provided an immediate dynamic for the project. It would appear, however, that the use of incentives has caused some intractable problems from a methodological point of view. The bureaucratic demands of setting up a credit or inputs system greatly affected the flow of the project and indeed dominated its methodology; once an incentive is made available, it is difficult to withdraw it and it causes dependence. There is evidence that the project's staff at times became bogged down in the sheer demands of credit management and that the availability or otherwise of this credit was the only motivation for some groups to continue to meet. Indeed one comment referred to the existence of "beggar groups" whose sole purpose of existence was to receive incentives from the

project. Incentives play an important role in group development; the issue methodologically is, however, the most appropriate timing and location of incentives.

(3) There has never been any dispute in PPP methodology that the Group Promoter is the key person in implementation; indeed the very term emphasises this crucial role. If this is so, then the most important issues relate to the exact role of the GPs and the training required for them to perform this role. Undoubtedly the GPs found it difficult to develop their role as facilitators or educators in the process of group development and, as a result of project pressure, became more involved in arranging loans and the technicalities of group structuring and maintenance. It is hard to avoid the conclusion that the groups see the GPs largely as sources of potential economic benefits and that their acceptance of the GPs' role is governed by the availability or non-availability of these benefits. The inability of GPs to develop a real educational role is highlighted further by the changes in personnel which have taken place in the project; by 1987 few of the original GPs were still attached to the project and thus valuable experience had been lost. Finally, there is little evidence as yet of GPs disengaging from certain groups which had already achieved some level of self-reliance; the notion that the GPs would change their relationship with the groups over time as a result of greater group confidence and internal organisational abilities has not yet materialised. Overall there is an increasing possibility that, if the project ceases after Phase II in late 1989, the GPs will be absorbed into the GCB as loan agents, as has happened with the SFDP in Nepal.

(4) Undoubtedly the PPP approach has been effective in beginning to link previously excluded groups with services which exist supposedly to assist them in their development. The involvement of these groups in an existing financial institution is something upon which emerging self-reliant groups should be able to build. The project has been less effective, however, in developing horizontal links between groups within each action area in order to provide a broader base for group solidarity and action. Such links might also be the basis of second-generation organisation which could emerge from the widespread group development process.

(5) The methodological difficulties suggested above influenced the project's ability successfully to establish an appropriate PME system at the action area level. Such a system is a function of the whole style of the project and, given the difficulties of emphasising the non-provider role of the GPs, the basis for such a system has been hard to establish. A lesson from the experience suggests that a PME system must be intrinsically built into the project from the beginning and that it must be a basic activity within the whole group process.

Bibliography

Bortei-Doku, E. 1988. *People's participation project*, Evaluation report. Rome, FAO.

Brown, C.K. 1983. *Report on PPP Ghana Workshop on Participatory Monitoring and On-going Evaluation.* Rome, FAO.

Dadson, J.A. 1983. *PPP Ghana: An operational manual.* Rome, FAO.

---. 1987. *A case study of the process of PPP replication in Ghana.* Rome, FAO.

FAO. 1984. *PPP in Africa: A review of implementation experiences in 7 African countries.* Rome.

FAP Project Files, including the Project Inception Report of 1982 and subsequent six-monthly reports from the two action areas.

Oakley, P. 1985. *The operationalization of the PPP approach to rural development.* Rome, FAO.

Uphoff, N. 1987. *Collective self-help: A strategy for rural development in Ghana.* Rome, FAO.

The desirable and the possible: Participation in a water supply project in the United Republic of Tanzania

Ole Therkildsen *

This case study presents an analysis of the practice of participation in a Danish-funded village water supply project in the southern part of the United Republic of Tanzania. The project was started in 1980 and by 1988 had reached approximately 450,000 people and invested some US$5-7 million per year. It will continue until at least 1993 and perhaps beyond.

Despite the unusually large and costly technical and socio-economic project preparations (three years, US$5 million, and 40 work-years of expatriate staff time), the formal project documents of 1983 on which large-scale implementation was based contained very few specific project objectives. In fact only one was explicitly stated: DANIDA would fund the implementation of water schemes in 300 high-priority villages in three regions over five years. With respect to participation, the formal project document stated only that recommendations made during the project preparations should be followed. This vagueness swept quite a few issues of importance to participation under the carpet. Its main advantage has been to give project implementators some room for manoeuvre. However, several unsettled issues have had a major effect on the long-term sustainability of the project.

From a participation point of view the most fundamental – but unsettled – issue concerns Tanzanian policies for development in general and for the water sector in particular. On the one hand, self-reliance has been emphasised as the key to development by the ruling party and the Government. On the other hand, these two institutions have established very ambitious targets for rural water sector expansion. The basic elements of the water sector policy were established in the 1960s when the principle of water as a free public service was introduced. Once the improvement of water supplies was no longer restricted by local willingness and ability to mobilise resources, they could be provided by the State according to need. This de-linking of service expansion from

*Research Fellow, Centre for Development Research, Copenhagen.

76

beneficiary resource mobilisation was followed, in 1971, by a declaration that all rural inhabitants should have access to an improved supply by 1991. Since then various donors have been willing to finance some 70 per cent of the investment costs of this service expansion. Consequently, the contradiction between the "self-reliance" and the "welfare" approaches to water supply development is only slowly being faced. Even today – when both the short- and long-term prospects for the Tanzanian economy are bleak – the Government and the donors keep planning for and investing in service expansions. Yet only one-quarter or less of the existing rural water supply capacity is presently being used. Non-sustainability of government- and donor-funded rural water sector activities in the United Republic of Tanzania therefore remain the sector's major issue.

Project statements on participation

The contradiction between the self-reliance and the welfare approaches to development was not resolved by the project planners and decision-makers involved with the water supply project. The project, therefore, did not develop an explicit, operational and accepted statement on participatory objectives. One attempt was made, however, prior to large-scale implementation. It is instructive to follow what happened to it. In 1983 the socio-economic planners involved in the preparation of water master plans for the three project regions recommended a basic approach to participation in which each village would be assisted to "plan, build, operate and maintain a water supply improvement with a minimum of external support. Ideally, the village is building and managing its own scheme assisted by the Government. Not the other way around."

This objective fitted the principle of self-reliance in Tanzania's stated ideology. Socio-economic planners on the project also regarded participation as a means to increase user benefits by ensuring that the project outputs corresponded to beneficiaries' needs, and that these needs would be so strongly felt that beneficiaries would contribute significantly in cash and kind to water improvement activities throughout the lifetime of the water project. Finally, participation was also seen as an integrated part of all project activities and not just as a component added to them. Thus the concept of participation as stated in the project preparation reports of 1983 contained both an efficiency and an empowerment dimension. However, in their write-up the socio-economic planners on the project clearly emphasised the self-reliance aspects.

Nevertheless, the Tanzanian authorities and the donor representatives emphasised the welfare as opposed to the self-reliance approach to participation. For them it was important to provide as many people as possible with access to improved water supply. This was in line with the United Republic of Tanzania's 1991 sector goal; the project planners had clearly established the need for improvements in rural water supplies and the donor had the funds.

Large and explicit production targets were therefore written into the formal project documents.

Clearly, both approaches to participation could not be pursued simultaneously. During the implementation of the project a major change in goals took place. The welfare approach predominated and a major emphasis was given to the production of new schemes at costs and speeds stipulated in the formal planning documents. It is important to note that this policy change was not the result of an explicit decision to change the participatory approach specified by the socio-economic planners. Rather it was the result of a lack of commitment to a self-reliance approach, combined with a positive decision to emphasise the construction of new schemes. Consequently, the main aim of participation since 1983 was to mobilise people to assist in building these schemes. The project was quite successful in developing methods for this mobilisation, as discussed below. Much less attention was given to the sustainability of completed schemes. The donor and the Tanzanian authorities justified this by assuming that –

- villages would by and large be solely responsible for the operation and maintenance of schemes. Only limited support from the authorities could be expected;

- villages which had participated intensively in the planning and construction of schemes would thereby develop a sense of ownership for them;

- villages that prior to the construction of schemes had signed contracts with the authorities which clearly stated that they were owners of the schemes and therefore responsible for their operation and maintenance, would actually honour such contracts.

As a consequence of these assumptions, and because of the focus on the production of new schemes, the project staff made only few and sporadic attempts at assisting and empowering villages to be able to operate and maintain the schemes.

The methodology of participation

The methodology used in the project evolved over a period of eight years. The basic elements were developed during an initial pilot testing in the early 1980s. Changes are still being made, although not uniformly in the three regions. Furthermore, participation has different implications and meanings in the various stages of a water supply project cycle. This makes a description difficult, since it is an evolving concept with many facets. A summary description of participation in the seven stages of the water project cycle can be seen in table 2. As can be seen from the table, participation focuses on soliciting

Table 2. Stages of participation in the Tanzanian water project

Stage	Key issues	Main beneficiary roles	Major assumptions/proposals/changes	Main participatory methods
Identification		None	Not feasible to involve villages in preliminary identification, because demand for water schemes far outstrips supply Candidate villages therefore identified on basis of physical criteria related to "need"	None
Preparation of village scheme	Acceptance	Village approves or rejects construction of scheme	It was originally proposed that village acceptance must be followed by payment of a cash deposit *prior* to the next step, so as to reveal real village priority for proposed scheme. This condition was not implemented. It requires sector policy changes that are still awaited	Village Water Committee (VWC) established to represent village vis-à-vis project authorities Village Participation Co-ordinator (VPC) staff explain village rights and duties Village Assembly approves/rejects proposals Contract between authorities and village signed
Planning	Acceptance, knowledge	Village approves or rejects water source; locates public stand-pipe subject to project approval	Source selection and design of distribution system made in dialogue with village to assure that water source is acceptable and that standpipes are properly located with respect to settlements and traditional sources	VPC staff explain basic issues in the location of taps VWC decides on location of taps. Negotiates for additional taps VPC staff and engineering staff approve
Construction	Acceptance, resources	Village provides most unskilled labour and organises this with assistance from the project	Village involvement important to reduce costs and to increase village commitment and skills for subsequent O & M tasks Village refusals at this stage stop project However, various pressures are put on villages when self-help activities slow down	VPC helps VWC to organise self-help labour for construction. Project Water Committee (PWC) co-ordinates work between village if needed VWC selects scheme attendants to work with technical staff On completion the scheme is handed over to village. A hand-over certificate is signed by village and authorities

Table 2   (continued)

Stage	Key issues	Main beneficiary roles	Major assumptions/proposals/changes	Main participatory methods
Operation	Knowledge, resources, control	Village fully responsible (funds, labour, organisation)	Village involvement in previous stages helps to ensure its willingness and capability to operate schemes. New O & M policies not yet approved. Both donor and Government find it difficult to abolish the principle of water as a "free" public good	VPC staff give ad hoc training to VWC and scheme attendants on operation and management of schemes. VWC identifies tap attendants at each tap. VPC staff brief tap attendants on their duties
Maintenance	Knowledge, resources, control	As above, but only with respect to distribution systems	As above; some outside assistance, funds, staff and material needed for maintenance of transmission system. So far only a few schemes handed over to villages. Too early for an assessment	Scheme attendant does minor repairs. VWC mobilises funds. Tap attendants clean around each tap. Mobile maintenance unit (includes VPC staff) does major repairs; sells spares; trains scheme attendants
Monitoring and evaluation (M & E)	Knowledge, resources, control	Village provides project with information and makes claims on it	Village involvement will help to ensure that it will make claims on government agencies to keep scheme running. Very little has happened so far but too early for an assessment	Mobile maintenance unit visits projects regularly; collects statistics; contacts VWC; and scheme attendants. Scheme attendant reports to it. VWC and PWV are the links between village and authorities. Raise complaints; disseminate information

acceptance from villages of various project proposals; obtaining and using local knowledge of the context on which specific plans can be based and post-construction activities carried out; resource commitments on the part of users to match external assistance; and a certain delegation to users of control over post-construction activities. Thus participation in the project has ranged from non-participation and manipulation over information and consultation to some degree of partnership and the delegation of power. The table also indicates some of the changes in actual implementation which have occurred, compared with what was originally planned. The methodology used consisted of four main elements: group formation and paraprofessionals; the use of outside agents; changes in old procedures and the establishment of new ones; and training.

Group formation and paraprofessionals

The project worked through various groups at the village level, some of which already existed, while others were formed with outside assistance. At the village level the project worked with the legally recognised Village Assembly (all adult villagers), the Village Council (25 members) and the ten-cell (a group of 20 to 40 adults) with a ten-cell leader. In addition to these bodies, the project assisted with the formation of two additional groups. The Village Council delegated the day-to-day responsibilities concerning water scheme activities to the Village Water Committee (VWC). On group schemes a Project Water Committee (PWC) was established, consisting of the chairmen of the VWCs. The PWC was expected to represent the interests of villages as a group vis-à-vis government agencies. The decision to add two committees to the already large number existing in the Tanzanian countryside was made in order to give women a more prominent role in project activities, since only few of them were members of existing formal organisations. It was also the intention to reduce project dependency on village councils, many of which did not function particularly well.

As table 2 shows, the VWC is involved in all but one of the seven project stages. The main role of the PWC is in the operation and maintenance phase, where villages must co-operate to clean the intake, prevent excessive use of water, especially in the upstream villages, and develop a common front vis-à-vis the authorities in case of problems for which outside assistance is needed.

Paraprofessionals were also involved. In each village the VWC selected one or two scheme attendants, including women, to be trained by the project during construction, so that later they could carry out organisation and methods (O & M) tasks on their own. For this they were supposed to be compensated by the village in cash and in kind, and terms were agreed between the two parties themselves. The VWC also selected tap attendants. Each of these looked after one public standpost, kept the standpost surroundings clean and reported to the scheme attendant or the VWC if breakdowns or vandalism occurred. Tap attendants were unpaid and only participated in a short orientation course run by the VPC assistant.

Outside agents

Although there was an ad hoc arrangement with the Community Development Department, the project employed its own extension staff for two reasons: the donor wished to control the implementation of the participatory activities because they were regarded as instrumental to the success of the project; and there was considerable doubt about the capacity and skills of the local community development staff. The project extension staff employed by the donor consisted of a Village Participation Co-ordinator (VPC) in each region (currently one Tanzanian and two Danes) and a number of VPC assistants (about 15 in each region). The VPC is an executive officer and presently has no local counterpart. VPC staff were located in and operated closely with the regional project implementation offices staffed by expatriate engineering advisers and their counterparts. These offices were attached to the Regional Water Engineer's Department. The primary role of the VPC staff has so far been to help the VWC to plan the distribution systems, and to assist in mobilising and organising self-help labour. The role of the staff in helping to build an organisational base which could empower villagers (especially women) to take a more active and assertive part in project activities was more limited.

The VPC assistants – of whom approximately half were women – were selected and trained on the job by the VPC. They were normally fourth-form leavers who had failed to be admitted to further education. They were fairly young and normally spoke one or more of the local languages in the region (apart from Swahili and English). The assistants needed skills in communication and analyses of village-level processes. However, no formal training material, other than a participation handbook, was available. The table shows that the VPC staff were important in all phases of the project, particularly in the maintenance and monitoring and evaluation (M & E) phases.

Procedures

A handbook on village participation was prepared for the project in 1983, and was revised on a continuous basis. The handbook laid out procedures in a series of 21 steps: from the introduction of the project in the priority villages selected by the donor and the regional authorities to the handing over of the scheme to the Village Council. Thus it covered all the stages shown in table 2. Each step involved a number of tasks. The handbook served several purposes. It helped to co-ordinate the field-level activities of the various agencies involved and it also helped the VPC to monitor activities in the ten to 15 villages where the VPC assistants were working simultaneously. The handbook assisted the individual, often inexperienced, VPC assistants to structure their fieldwork and it also made on-the-job training of the assistants easier. Some M & E procedures were also written into the handbook, but they were never implemented.

Training

In general, it can be said that the project had no strategy for, and did not place much emphasis on, training related to technical activities and participation. Training for participation consisted of on-the-job ad hoc training of the VPC assistants; informal training and awareness raising of VWCs and tap attendants; and some ad hoc information to expatriate and Tanzanian technical staff about the need for and approach to participation.

The training at village level started during the planning stage, as indicated in the table, and took place in all subsequent project stages. In the operation and maintenance stage it was supposed to be carried out by the donor-financed mobile maintenance units every time these visited a village. For that reason a VPC assistant was a member of the unit.

Project results in brief

In a series of studies a number of Tanzanian and foreign observers have concluded that participation in the Danish-funded rural water supply project in Tanzania has been fairly successful in the planning and construction stages. Their general assessment of participation in the project was as follows:

- The improvement of water supplies has received a high priority among both men and women in the priority villages.

- The VWCs and villagers in general have actively participated in the planning of the distribution systems of the schemes. This has led to significant improvements in user benefits from the completed schemes.

- Villagers have contributed significantly to the construction of schemes through self-help labour activities. Women tended to contribute more than men. In the group schemes the multi-village PWCs did not function once construction was completed.

- It appeared that many villages were well aware of their rights and duties with respect to operation and maintenance; there were, for example, many examples of VWCs and tap attendants who had carried out repairs of schemes, and found the necessary funds to do this. The main problem seemed to be that the project had failed to develop an operation and maintenance approach that would help villages to become more self-reliant when the schemes were completed.

■ Despite efforts to mobilise and empower women to take an active part in all project activities, this has only succeeded with respect to self-help labour contributions. Women have generally not had any significant influence on the village-level management of the water schemes.

Lessons regarding participation

Many lessons of relevance to the practice of participation can be drawn from this donor-funded water project. These fall in three distinct categories.

Policy space

Project-level staff often tended to regard the policy context as irrelevant or as given. Consequently, not much attention was paid to it. However, a much more differentiated approach is needed since policies have a significant influence on the scope and character of participatory activities. The methodological lesson of this project was that three types of policies could be distinguished from a project-level point of view.

Some project policies in the short term were already laid down and were unchangeable. At best they could only be influenced by project-level staff over the long term. In the short term the project had to adjust to them. The welfare approach to rural water supplies, on which the donor and the Tanzanian Government were in agreement, was a good example. It resulted in an external demand on the project to produce a specific number of new schemes each year. This stress on production resulted in participatory practices that emphasised the mobilisation of beneficiaries for construction activities. With respect to operation and maintenance, there was also a bias towards the welfare approach. The project established, for example, regional mobile maintenance units which visited completed schemes regularly, sold spare parts, undertook repairs, gave ad hoc training to scheme attendants and VWCs and monitored the schemes. These transport and foreign exchange intensive units were only sustainable with long-term donor support. The units also undercut village self-reliance efforts by resuscitating abandoned village schemes.

Other project policies, on the other hand, could be influenced by project-level staff. Visible results led to changes of policy relevant to participatory practices. The United Republic of Tanzania was well known for its policies on participation and self-help. In the rural water sector these were often not followed in practice by the regional and district authorities. In the water project area it was frequently argued that the basic Tanzanian self-help spirit was dead, that self-help was not cost-effective, and that it slowed down implementation. Such views were also reflected at the central level. After eight years of implementation, in which villages participated significantly in the planning and implementation of schemes in 270 villages, such attitudes have changed. During the past couple of years the Tanzanian Ministry of Water Supply has prepared a set of new policies which are fairly similar to those used in the project: village involvement in the planning of schemes; village ownership of completed schemes; village selection and employment of paraprofessionals to maintain schemes; and village responsibility for certain operation and maintenance costs. Thus an independent evaluation team made the following assessment: "Discussions with Tanzanian authorities and users showed that the DANIDA-supported water project has greatly contributed to the acceptance of full village participation at national, regional, and village level."

Finally, some project policies were controllable at the project level. These were typically policies on technical and administrative issues regarded as uncontroversial by the recipient and donor governments, as specified in the project handbook.

Methodologically, the policies which could be changed were the most interesting, precisely because they could be changed, reinvigorated or developed to be more appropriate for project-level participation activities. Three main factors accounted for the relative success of the project in this respect. First, advocacy of an increased emphasis upon participation was not done only by expatriate staff. Efforts by a Tanzanian socio-economist attached to the project, who had good connections at the central level, were important. Second, the advocacy was backed up by visible results in the field. Finally, the magnitude of the project in terms of funds and coverage, combined with strong donor support for mobilisation aspects of participation, was undoubtedly also important.

Institutional development

Institutional development refers to the process of strengthening the ability of institutions to reach their objectives effectively. This, however, was generally neglected by the project as exemplified by the low priority given to training. Moreover, with respect to participation, the focus in the project was on the village level (the VWC, and the scheme and tap attendants) and on the village participation field agents (VPC assistants). Experience over the past eight years has clearly shown that this focus was far too narrow. Participation did not just involve field agents and target groups. It also involved the institutions within which the agents worked. This was the first important methodological lesson of the project.

The second lesson was that the project's efforts to increase co-operation between different administrative sectors in order to promote participation created bureaucratic conflicts that remained unsolved and threatened the sustainability of the participatory activities. In the project the conflicts were between the technical and the community development staff. Traditionally, the Ministry of Water and water sector staff at regional and district level had a monopoly of water sector activities. This included a monopoly on donor funds to the sector. It also meant that technical staff were in charge of mobilising villagers for self-help activities and, if this failed, they could decide to pay villagers to do construction work. In the participatory methodology developed by the socio-economic planners on the project, the community development department and not the technical staff were expected to be the link between the authorities and the villages. As the technical staff would lose their dominant position, they resisted the proposal. Instead a compromise solution was agreed by establishing an extension wing within the water engineer's office headed by project VPCs (an expatriate in two of the three regions) and staffed by young Tanzanians directly employed, trained and supervised by the VPC. However, this set-up was never really officially approved; it was regarded as a temporary solution which gradually became permanent.

Although inter-organisational conflicts are common in development project implementation, the fact that this was a donor-funded project clearly aggravated the situation. Project staff were unaware of and unprepared for the potential for conflict of some of the organisational proposals. The project also favoured the water sector staff with funds, vehicles and administrative support, and it put much more effort into interaction with the water sector staff. Thus, while the concept of co-operation between community development and water sector staff was based on an idea of equal partnership, the donor and the expatriate project staff clearly treated the Community Development Department as the junior partner. The low profile and lack of interest in the project shown by the community development staff was a reflection of these mistakes.

A third lesson was related to the organisational set-up of the project itself. Inter-organisational conflicts were not the only reason why the role of community development staff on the project was rather limited. There were also justifiable doubts about the ability, capacity and willingness of these staff to carry out village participation work adequately. The project's emphasis on a high level of construction activities and the need for effective mobilisation which this entailed obviously amplified these doubts. The donor's control of the project's extension staff also reflected this. This contributed to the short-term successes of village-level mobilisation, but the project later faced the problem of how to get the local authorities to take over the implementation of the participation activities. It now became even more difficult to get the Community Development Department fully involved. The project experiences therefore confirmed the general consensus in the literature on project aid that by-passing of local institutions by the donor may produce short-term results but at the expense of long-term sustainability.

Participatory methods

Village-level groups and paraprofessionals did function fairly well during the periods of intense contacts with project staff, as for example in the planning and construction stages. Without contact with authorities during the operation and maintenance stages, however, many VWCs and scheme attendants stopped working. Under normal circumstances, such contacts were made twice a year through the mobile maintenance units. It is too early to say, however, if this frequency is of the right order of magnitude for the average village.

Most women in the VWCs kept a low profile, and this was a serious problem. It is possible that women would have become more involved if a stronger training effort had been made. However, differing issues of consciousness among both men and women, as well as structural factors, impeded these efforts. In the absence of women's own viable grass-roots groups in the country, efforts at strengthening the role of women in more formal groups will be slow for many years to come.

The village participation agents (VPC assistants) contributed significantly to the success of the project with respect to village participation in planning and construction. This showed that given adequate funding, regular supervision and a standardised approach to participation, it was possible within a short time to develop a fairly competent extension staff recruited from school leavers, who have no previous strong commitment to work in the rural areas, on the basis of only rudimentary training. However, the appointment of separate extension staff employed by the donor was problematic. The project's focus solely on VPC staff as extension agents was also questionable. Numerous and widely scattered VWCs and scheme attendants needed fairly regular contact with the authorities to be kept working. If government staff already stationed in the rural areas such as divisional and ward secretaries and school teachers could have been involved and trained in simple extension tasks of relevance to operation and maintenance, then the long-term sustainability of the water schemes would have been less dependent on the donor-funded, foreign exchange dependent mobile maintenance units.

The project clearly showed that established and agreed procedures to guide the implementation of participation were critical, and that continuous adjustments to these procedures was important. In its operations the project used a standard participation approach in all villages. As the number of villages covered by the project grew, the need to adjust procedures to specific types of villages became apparent. Differential procedures for user payments for operation and maintenance in rich and poor villages were especially needed. Moreover, the procedures needed to be written to fit the needs of the major user groups. These were the VWCs, who had to understand the basic procedures in order to be able to deal effectively with the authorities; the VPC assistants, who needed fairly detailed guide-lines to carry out their daily work; and finally the VPC and other project managers, who needed a special version of the procedures to help them to plan and co-ordinate project activities.

Unfortunately, little training was undertaken by the project and few lessons therefore were learned. However, given the scope of the project (five years and some 600 villages covered) and the large number of people in need of training from the village level and upwards, it was quite clear that training based on face-to-face contact between project trainers and trainees was not realistic. For village-level training mass communication approaches were more relevant, and a potential for letting villagers participate in training was never exploited.

Bibliography

The material upon which this case study is based is largely drawn from the author's own work with the water supply project. It has also included the following specific texts:

Clay, E.J.; Schaffer, B.B. (eds.). 1984. *Room for manoeuvre: An exploration of public policy planning in agricultural and rural development*. London, Heinemann Educational Books.

Cohen, J.M.; Grindle, M.S.; Tjip Walker, S. 1985. "Foreign aid and conditions precedent: Political and bureaucratic conditions", in *World Development* (Oxford and Elsmford, New York), Vol. 13, No. 12, pp. 1211-1230.

International Reference Centre. 1987. *The DANIDA financed rural water supply programme in Iringa, Mbeya and Ruvuma regions of Tanzania*, Report prepared by a Joint Evaluation Mission, 23 May to 20 June 1987. Copenhagen, DANIDA.

Msuya, M. 1987. "Status of the regional water master plans and implementation", in *Proceedings of the Arusha Seminar on implementation of rural water supply and sanitation in Tanzania, March 1986*. Ministry of Lands, Water, Housing and Urban Development and Norwegian National Committee for Hydrology.

Oakley, P.; Marsden, D. 1984. *Approaches to participation in rural development*. Geneva, ILO.

Taylor, E.; Moore, C. 1980. "Paraprofessionals in rural development: Reality and potential", in *Rural Development Participation Review* (Ithaca, New York), Vol. 2, No. 1.

Therkildsen, O. 1988. *Watering white elephants? Lessons from donor funded planning and implementation of rural water supply projects in Tanzania*. Uppsala, Scandinavian Institute of African Studies.

People's participation in soil conservation: Lesotho

*David Sanders**

The setting

Lesotho is a small mountainous country in southern Africa. As in most African countries, over 80 per cent of Lesotho's people – the Basotho – live in rural areas and are involved, in one way or another, in agriculture. But Lesotho's land resources are very limited and farming is not easy: most of the country is steep and rocky, and the rainfall is erratic while hail and frost make both livestock and crop production hazardous. There are only about 400,000 hectares of mostly poor cultivable land in the country to provide the staple food needs of a population which is now almost 1.5 million.

By tradition the Basotho are stock rearers and value their animals as a capital reserve, a status symbol and a means of meeting various social obligations, e.g. bridewealth is paid in cattle. But as the human population has increased in numbers so have the animals, and the country is now heavily overstocked. The result of this overstocking, combined with the intensive cultivation of poor, erodible soils and a rainfall that usually comes in high-intensity thunderstorms, is extensive and serious erosion. Hillsides are denuded and sheet-eroded; the flatter, cultivated land is dissected by gullies and has lost much of its topsoil. Soil erosion is therefore one of the major problems facing agricultural development in Lesotho.

Erosion has long been recognised as a problem in Lesotho and as far back as the mid-1930s the Colonial Administration started a soil conservation programme. This work was intensified in the 1940s and 1950s, and by the early 1960s most of the agriculturally important lowlands had been treated. The work consisted mainly of physical conservation works; earth contour banks were constructed on the flatter land, permanent grass strips were laid out on the steeper cultivated land, small earth dams were built in the watercourses and a limited amount of tree planting was done on badly eroded areas. But there was little follow-up. As all the work had been done by the Government with little or

*Senior Soil Conservation Officer, FAO Headquarters, Rome.

no involvement of the people, farmers felt little responsibility for the maintenance of the works and by the time Lesotho was granted independence in 1966 many of the works had broken down or were in a state of disrepair.

After independence and until the late 1970s Lesotho's approach to rural development centred on a number of relatively large area-based projects, i.e. those that concentrated their resources into particular areas of the country in an attempt rapidly to increase agricultural production and the general living conditions of the people concerned. As soil erosion was still seen as a major problem all over the country, soil conservation featured prominently in all of these projects. Typical of these projects was the Khomokhoana Project, assisted by the Swedish International Development Authority and the FAO, which ran from 1972 until 1980.

The Khomokhoana Project

The Khomokhoana Project was situated in north-western Lesotho and covered the catchments of the Khomokhoana and Likhetlane rivers, an area of approximately 26,000 hectares of which about 17,000 were cultivable, the rest being made up of rough ridges, roads, villages and streams. At the time of the project, the population of the project area was approximately 40,000 people, made up of some 8,000 farm families. As in other parts of Lesotho, most of the able-bodied men had left the area to work in the mines, farms and construction sites of South Africa, leaving behind the women and the old men to do most of the work in the fields and the young boys to care for the herds of cattle.

There were no towns in the project area and the people lived in approximately 50 villages which varied in population from nearly 2,000 down to 20. A main bitumen highway passed along the western boundary of the project joining the capital, Maseru, 180 kilometers to the south, with the town of Lerihe, 10 kilometers to the north. A gravel road ran from this highway into the lower catchment, then branched into dirt tracks to the different villages. The local administrative system for the project area was complex. A main district border ran through the middle so that the traditional administrative system came under two senior or Ward chiefs. The project area was then divided again into sections allocated to 12 subchiefs and minor chiefs who came under the jurisdiction of the two Ward chiefs. To complicate matters, the boundaries between some of the subchiefs and minor chiefs were not clearly defined and were the subject of constant arguments and litigation.

Objectives of the project

Although the long-term objectives of the project included a statement that it would "bring about a significant improvement in the standard and quality of living enjoyed by the farming community", the project was very much oriented towards increasing the agricultural production of the area while conserving and improving its soils. This was made clear in the project's plan of operation which set definite physical targets on what was to be achieved in the way of increased yields and area covered. However, little mention was made in the plan of how the people of the area were to be involved in planning and implementing the project; there was little, if any, concept of people's participation in the design of the project. Without a conceptual understanding, therefore, the project sought to involve the local people in soil conservation works, but with results which reflected this lack of understanding.

Project extension strategy and involvement of the people

The project was organised into sections which covered the subjects of agronomy, livestock, marketing and credit, farm economics, farm mechanisation, soil conservation and extension. The work of these different sections was supervised and co-ordinated by a National Project Director who was assisted by an expatriate adviser. Although the project was heavily oriented towards the achievement of physical outputs, the project's senior staff were aware of the fact that the project's goals could not be reached without the understanding and strong support of the local farming community. A considerable amount of time and effort was therefore spent in introducing the project into the area, presenting its aims and attempting to win the support of the farmers. The responsibility for this work was given to the project's small extension section. The extension approach followed the pattern normally used in Lesotho at that time. It was based on working down to individual farmers through the traditional administrative structure. The steps followed in seeking to make contact with and involve local farmers were as follows:

- *Meetings with Ward chiefs:* Project staff met the Ward chiefs and their advisers and explained the aims and provisional plans of the project. After discussions Ward chiefs promised their full support to the project and instructions were passed on to the subchiefs and minor chiefs that they were to assist the project staff. Follow-up meetings were held during the life of the project to keep these senior chiefs informed and to enlist their support whenever needed.

- *Meetings with subchiefs and minor chiefs:* Meetings were then arranged with all the subchiefs and minor chiefs in their villages. These meetings were held in the open and included the elders of the village who assisted and advised their chief. Again the general objectives and tentative plans of the project were explained and discussed and permission was sought to hold public meetings with the people of the village.

- Pitsos *or public meetings:* Once agreement was reached with the chief a public meeting or *pitso* would be arranged in each main village. At these meetings representatives from the project would be publicly introduced to the people by the chief and would then be invited to speak about the project. This presentation would usually be followed by a lengthy session in which the audience would question the project staff and express any views that they might have on the project.

■ *Individual contacts:* The public meetings would be followed by further discussions with the chief and senior villagers. At the same time the extension staff would try to identify and speak to influential farmers and would attempt to gain their support. All this took a considerable amount of time and effort by the project's small team as they sought to obtain the understanding, good will and participation of the people of the project area.

Despite a lack of any deep conceptual understanding of a process of participation and any implicit commitment in the project objectives, project staff did seek the involvement of local farmers in their work, albeit in a rather classical extension manner. The approach was traditional and hierarchical, and would have led to an involvement patronised by the local chiefs. Given the lack of training of project staff in this kind of work, the approach they took is understandable if extremely limited.

While these consultations were taking place a soil survey was made of the area and an overall soil conservation plan was developed. The conservation plan was based largely on the construction of physical erosion control structures such as contour banks, diversion works, silt traps and small earth dams. It provided for tree planting on badly eroded hillsides and also contained provision for the extension and improvement of the road system of the area. The intention was that this plan would be complemented by the introduction of improved agronomic and livestock practices that were to be developed by the other sections of the project.

Implementing the conservation plan

Physical soil conservation works can be expensive to instal and they usually do not lead to any direct increase in yields. Their main function is in keeping the soil in place and preventing further deterioration of the land: they usually do not provide any short-term benefits to the farmer. In the Khomokhoana Project a large proportion of the planned physical works were to be constructed on communal land and not just on the cultivated plots of the individual farmers. In view of this and in line with the prevailing policy of the Ministry of Agriculture, it was decided that the project would bear the full costs of installing the physical soil conservation measures. In return, the people of the area would be expected to maintain the works and co-operate with the project in introducing better agronomic and livestock management practices that would increase production and at the same time help to protect the land. This strategy characterised the essence of the people's involvement; it was the Ministry's project which, it was hoped, local farmers would be willing to maintain.

It was planned that mechanical equipment (tractors, bulldozers and graders) would be used to construct the major earthworks such as contour banks, dams and any main road works. Contractors would be employed to carry out difficult works such as those involving the use of concrete. But all the other, lighter work that could be done manually, such as tree planting, planting of grass on critically eroded areas, minor diversion works or silt-trap construction, would be done by the village people themselves. In return for their labour the people were to be paid in food rations under a sustained Food-for-Work Programme that was operating in the country at the time. It was reasoned that not only would the people in the villages welcome the chance for employment and food under the programme, but it would also offer them the opportunity to involve themselves physically in the activities of the project. In doing so they would gain a better understanding of what was being done and develop a pride in the works carried out in and around their own village.

As the whole project area could not be tackled at once, it was divided into 13 subcatchments. The idea was that the mechanical equipment would be concentrated in one or two of these subcatchments at a time and would systematically work through the whole project area. At the same time village work teams would be organised in any village which showed interest and would be put to work on the manually intensive tasks such as tree planting and building of silt traps.

Since the project area was severely eroded, the soil conservation plan called for a huge amount of work to be done. However, the resources of the soil conservation section were extremely limited. For most of the life of the project its staff consisted of two expatriate professionals assisted by not more than two young national officers who were considered as trainees. This was only about 40 per cent of the staff originally planned for. In addition, the national officers were changed from time to time so that more people could work with the project, gain experience and be trained. The idea was good in that it enabled the project to train a number of very good young professional officers, but it created problems of continuity, with new staff constantly having to learn about the project, get to know the people of the area and win their confidence. None the less, a good start was made. The extension officers, accompanied by the staff of the conservation section, visited the different villages and talked to the chiefs and farmers about what could be done on their lands. The tentative plans prepared by the project were explained and, once a general agreement had been obtained, work started.

In the project area the village people were organised into work teams. These were usually made up of either 25 or 50 people who would appoint their own foreman and a secretary who would keep records of attendance and hours worked. Project staff would discuss work with these teams, a programme would be agreed, hand tools issued and work would be started. Each team would be expected to work 15 five-hour days. At the end of this period the work and records of the team would be checked and, if everything was in order, arrangements would be made for the delivery of the food rations. Each work team would be visited at least once a week to check on progress and to make sure that the work was being done in the right way. During these visits the conservation officer would spend a few minutes talking about the work that was being done and in what way it would benefit the village. It was hoped that by doing this the people in each village would gradually learn more about conservation, appreciate what was being done and be prepared to look after and maintain the works in the future. At the end of the 15-day work period the team would disband and another team would be formed. In this way most people from each village who wanted to benefit from the Food-for-Work Programme were given an opportunity to take part. Through this system a large number of people were employed on the conservation programme and at times more than 20 work teams and up to 875 people were employed in this way.

Project problems

Through the use of the Food-for-Work teams and the project's equipment, a considerable amount of conservation work was completed. However, by the second year of the project it was becoming apparent that the conservation plan was too big and ambitious for such a small staff to handle. For example, completed works had to be inspected from time to time and, as more work was finished, this became very time-consuming. Maintenance of works had to be arranged and the village people showed little inclination to carry out repair work voluntarily. Since most of the able-bodied men were working away from home, women usually made up 80-90 per cent of the Food-for-Work teams while the men who did join were usually old and not very active. Not surprisingly, therefore, the output of the teams was generally very low as many of the tasks, such as carrying stones and digging banks in the hard soil, were physically strenuous.

There were also other problems. Other sections of the project were attempting to introduce a number of new and improved agronomic and livestock practices which would not only help overcome the soil erosion problems but would also increase farmers' yields and incomes. But this was proving more difficult than expected and progress was slow. Without the prospect of some immediate benefits it was difficult to maintain the interest of the farmers. At the same time, the project's small team of extension workers was becoming more and more involved with other aspects of the project's activities such as helping to establish farmers' associations, developing a marketing and credit system in the villages, introducing potatoes as a new crop to the area and training and organising local tractor contractors. This meant that less and less of their time could be devoted entirely to the soil conservation programme. Soil conservation staff therefore found themselves spending more time in contacting and talking to farmers, which resulted in insufficient time to devote to the planning and designing of conservation works and the supervision of the work itself. While this was not entirely a bad thing it did slow down the work and let the project slip more and more behind the very rigid timetable set in its Plan of Operations. Furthermore, project staff were becoming increasingly concerned that their extension efforts had been inadequate. A particular concern was whether or not the farmers would be prepared to maintain the conservation works without direct project support.

Over the last few months of the project more emphasis was therefore placed on extension work. Virtually all the conservation extension work was taken over by the soil conservation section itself and, in order to help with the work, existing village land allocation committees were enlisted to liaise between the chief, the people and the technicians during the planning and implementation of the conservation programme. With the help of these committees, more *pitsos* were held and seminars conducted for foremen of the Food-for-Work teams in an effort to explain more clearly to the people what was being done and what was expected of them. As the project drew to a close the project staff were still concerned, and so an independent consultant was hired to assess the impact on villagers' knowledge and opinions of the conservation activities carried out over the years of the project's life.

Project outcome

Disappointingly, the consultant found that in spite of the project's efforts, farmers' knowledge of conservation issues seemed no better than that of farmers previously interviewed in other projects in the lowlands of Lesotho. It would appear that the involvement of the people in the actual construction of conservation works had made little actual difference to what they knew or understood of the issues involved. On the positive side, the Food-for-Work teams had, over the years, raised awareness of the sort of work such teams could undertake and this knowledge seemed to have spread throughout the area and was not just limited to those villages where the work was concentrated. But, overall, the impact of the project on popular understanding of erosion and conservation was very limited.

In questions concerning the methodology of the project, the general opinion of the people was that the method of approach was right and there was overall approval of the way in which the project had consulted the chiefs, held *pitsos* and explained and discussed the proposals with the public. The innovative use of land allocation committees to help with this work was seen as an extension of, rather than a departure from, the traditional village system of government by discussion. Nevertheless, it was clear that the villagers' understanding of the project's aims and objectives in terms of soil conservation was far too low which led the consultant to conclude that:

> While it is not suggested that working through the chief and other existing organs of village government is an unsuitable approach, it must be concluded that too many villagers so far fail to understand how the conservation section has come to be working in their areas. The foundation for lasting popular involvement in conservation has yet to be built.

The consultant further commented that:

> ... the respondents' comments on what the project had done to counter erosion were based upon what they had seen rather than what had been explained to them. None of this offers a healthy prospect for long-term maintenance of the conservation work carried out, which as is known is the ultimate test of any such scheme's success in Lesotho. Although the project approached communities through the correct channels it did not involve the people sufficiently to make them understand what was happening, from either a technical or organisation point of view.

The consultant also pointed out that although many people had been physically involved in the scheme through the Food-for-Work teams, their main motivation was the food which they received in pay, and not the fact that they were controlling the erosion of their lands.

Conclusion

The Khomokhoana Project was designed with the overall objectives of increasing agricultural production and conserving the land resources of the area. The physical targets set were extremely ambitious considering the relatively short life of the project and, in practice, these targets proved to be unrealistic. Nevertheless, an impressive amount of physical conservation works, dams, fish ponds, roads and tracks were completed. These works did much, at least temporarily, to halt land degradation, improve access for village people and provide them with better water supplies. In addition, a team of young national officers were thoroughly trained in soil conservation. In retrospect, therefore, the soil conservation programme was far from a failure.

Unfortunately, when the project was designed the whole emphasis was given to the achievement of physical outputs and very little consideration was given as to how the people of the area were to be involved other than through traditional extension measures: no real concept of people's participation was built into the design of the project. In spite of this, a genuine attempt was made throughout the life of the project to inform, educate and involve the people and, in one way or another, hundreds of people did in fact participate in the activities of the project. Nevertheless, the approach used and the efforts made were not sufficient to bring about a clear understanding among the people of what the project was trying to do or to convince them that it was worth their while to continue the work, or even maintain what was there, once the project was over. Given the rigid, ambitious targets, and the limited time frame and resources available, it is difficult to see how the project could have done much more to improve the situation. Within the rigid framework of the project it is unlikely that much more could have been achieved merely by concentrating more of the project's resources in the same sort of extension, as suggested by the consultant who reviewed the project. The possibilities of success were limited by the way in which the project was designed and the approach that was followed.

Since the early 1970s when this project was planned and started, new approaches to people's involvement in soil conservation works have been developed and are being tried. These include designing projects so that they start with flexible timetables that can be adjusted as the requirements and constraints of the people become more clearly understood. These new approaches also promote the development and adoption of conservation techniques that can easily be fitted into existing farming systems. They concentrate on practices which not only conserve soil, but also lead to some immediate and obvious benefit to the individual farmer, perhaps by reducing the risk of crop failure or increasing yields. These approaches are still being tested but they do offer the opportunity for more effectively involving people in soil conservation programmes. Meanwhile, this case study is an accurate comment on the current state of affairs. It highlights the enormous problems that technologically based development projects have in adjusting to the demands of processes like participation. It confirms that participation cannot merely be incorporated into the design of a project like another input, but that it demands a major re-thinking of the methodology of projects which previously have merely informed and constructed. It is expected that these steps would be an adequate basis for local people's involvement.

Bibliography

Hendriksen, T.A.J. 1979. *Final soil conservation report*. Technical Document 56. Leribe, FAO.

Sanders, D.W. 1977. *Interim soil conservation report*. Technical Document 46. Leribe, FAO.

———; 1978. *The planning of rural development projects*, Unpublished M.Sc. dissertation, University of Reading.

———. 1988. *Environmental degradation and socio-economic impacts: Past, present and future approaches to soil conservation*, Keynote address presented at the Fifth International Soil Conservation Conference, Bangkok, Thailand, January 1988.

———; Leduma, T. J. 1972. *Watershed management plan for the Khomokhoana river catchment.* Vol. I. Technical Document 4. Leribe, FAO.

Smelcer, D. R. 1978. Interim conservation engineering report. Technical Document 57. Leribe, FAO.

Turner, S. D. 1979. "Khomokhoana project conservation impact survey", Produced as Appendix II of Hendriksen, op. cit.

West, Burnell, G. 1972. *Soil survey of the Khomokhoana catchment basin.* Technical Document 3. Leribe, FAO.

SARILAKAS: Grass-roots participation in the Philippines

*Charlotte Harland**

SARILAKAS was set up in 1981 as a reorientation of Project AID, which had been launched in 1979 by the Bureau of Rural Workers of the Philippines Government. Project AID had been intended to be a pilot folk research project for the rural landless, and its objectives were to promote a participatory approach to problem identification and analysis and to the formulation of solutions. The reality had been a paternalistic and delivery-oriented programme, which had not gone well and in which people did not participate beyond being given goods and services. There was some organisational development at the grass-roots level but this was entirely passive, and local people were little motivated to get involved other than to see their organisations as means of receiving government hand-outs.

In 1980 some of the senior members of the Project AID staff became involved in the ILO Technical Co-operation between Developing Countries (TCDC) Programme. This included visits to PROSHIKA in Bangladesh, the People's Institute for Development and Training in India, and the Change Agents Programme – PIDA – in Sri Lanka, all of which were considered to be established participatory programmes. Leaders from PROSHIKA and PIDA also visited Project AID. Through this experience, and their interaction with the staff and people of the other programmes, Project AID staff were able to identify important problems with their own methodology. Reflection on this experience led to the reshaping of Project Aid, and to the birth of SARILAKAS.

SARILAKAS was formed in February 1981, with the support of the Government of the Netherlands and under the ILO Programme on Organisations of the Rural Poor (PORP). In 1983 project staff established PROCESS, an NGO which took responsibility for the management of the project. The central philosophy of SARILAKAS was that people were truly

*Formerly Research Fellow, Overseas Development Institute, London; currently Monitoring and Evaluation Officer, District Development Support Programme, Mpika, Zambia.

empowered only when they gained access to and control of economic resources, reduced and overcame dependency on exploitative forces and managed their own economic activities. It was on the basis of this central philosophy that the SARILAKAS methodology emerged.

Project objectives

The primary objective of SARILAKAS was simply that the rural poor should increasingly participate in the development process. This was broken down more specifically into a number of immediate objectives. These were (i) to develop participatory, self-reliant organisations of ten to 20 people, engaging in collective work for economic and social co-operation; (ii) to train agents in catalytic methods of promoting these organisations; and (iii) to increase incomes and employment on a sustainable and equal basis.

Understanding or participation

The philosophy of SARILAKAS was reflected in its name: "Sariling Lakas" means "own strength". The objectives further showed that the focus of SARILAKAS was on promoting poor people's organisations, and on raising their awareness of their social and economic rights. The basis of the project was that through collective assertion, people could gain rights to forest land, fair tenancy, collective bank loans and fishing rights. This could be achieved by a process of animation and awareness creation in which a continuous action-reflection dynamic was established in a local organisation. The organisations were based on livelihood sectors, and concentrate on these rather than on community issues. This had implications for the nature of external inputs into the village-level organisations. SARILAKAS was intended to "focus on providing external inputs of a catalytic nature only toward the generation and development of participatory people's processes and self-reliant organisations of rural workers". The intention was specifically to avoid the major focus becoming the passive receiving by the people of goods and services, as occurred under Project AID; instead the aim was to build up people's capacities to generate change from within. The SARILAKAS approach, therefore, was based on a dual educational strategy; firstly to develop awareness and secondly to gain knowledge. The latter component focuses particularly upon knowledge of legal processes and rights.

The methodology

Elements and instruments of participation

The organisation

The fundamental unit of operation in SARILAKAS was the local-level organisation. Membership of these groups was usually between ten and 20 people, both male and female, and was based on sectors of livelihood – farmers, fishermen and women or hacienda workers, for example. Livelihood as a basis for group membership ensured a degree of economic homogeneity within the group.

The precise structure of the groups varied according to the wishes of the members. The common underlying pattern was of a body of actively involved members, who formed the basic decision-making unit, the general assembly. During the process of establishing the group, SARILAKAS provided training on the nature of organisations and leadership. This was to enable the members to reflect upon what leadership would be likely to mean in the context of their organisation, and therefore elect those who could best fulfil the role, rather than immediately choosing those who seemed the obvious candidates. The elected leaders formed a committee or executive, whose size and role was dependent upon the size and activities of the organisation. In some cases there was a devolution of responsibility to committees of both elected representatives and general assembly members. The committees and executives were not intended to be the locus of power in the organisation, but rather implementation bodies, acting on the will of the general assembly. Maintaining this and enhancing the dynamic involvement of the ordinary members was an important element of the approach that SARILAKAS adopted.

Education and training

The training activities of SARILAKAS reflected the project's approach to participation; this emphasised strength, organisation and awareness of people's social, political and economic situation, and also knowledge which could facilitate and enhance group activities. Thus the training and education component of the project reflected these elements. The training involved (i) a continuing process of awareness raising; (ii) regular training on organisational and management issues relevant to local organisations, in order to retain responsibility and involvement in the running of the organisation and a critical capacity amongst the ordinary members towards the way in which their leaders act; and (iii) technical training according to the activities of a parti-cular group.

One particular SARILAKAS local organisation began "pre-membership training" for prospective members. It involved a workshop on the aims of a participatory organisation, and the responsibilities of members. It was established on the initiative of members, who recognised the strength of an active membership body, the commitment required for this to work, and the potential effect of even a small group of members whose participation was passive or destructive, rather than active and creative.

Activities

SARILAKAS organisations established activities relevant to their members' livelihood sector. These were often economic, but were also concerned with campaigning and pressure activities. The decision on what kinds of activities to undertake was made by the general assembly. SARILAKAS saw the value of economic activities both in terms of their immediate effect, and in their potential for generating increased access to resources through local organisations. However, problems arose from involvement in economic activities. The technicalities of economic projects (such as marketing or accounting) could quickly become major issues when they did not run smoothly. They could even become a divisive factor, splitting a collective organisation. SARILAKAS' experience was that economic activities could be counterproductive and diversionary, although they were very common in the local organisations. The possible drawbacks were recognised, and preventive steps taken during implementation. These included collective management, rotating responsibilities for collective activities, frequent meetings and an active role for members. The issues surrounding economic activities were included in the members' training as appropriate.

Other activities of SARILAKAS local organisations were largely associated with undertaking political activity for the acquisition of rights or the abolition of unfair practices. These included acquiring rights to land and forests, stopping the illegal system of levying a concessioner's fee for fishing, and gaining better working conditions for sugar plantation workers. These activities were supported by educational activities which raised the level of awareness of a particular situation and provided a forum in which to analyse problems and formulate strategies for action. Acquiring knowledge of the law and forming links with other SARILAKAS organisations were two very important aspects of this work, and are discussed further below.

The change agent

The underlying dynamic element of SARILAKAS local organisations was intended to spring from the ordinary, general assembly members. Through this, organisations made themselves fully self-sustaining. The question therefore arose of how an external agent could initiate and facilitate a process which essentially came from the people. In the context of SARILAKAS, we can examine this issue by looking at the pattern of involvement of the change agents, at who became a change agent and at the generation of cadres, or "folk catalysts".

In development practice, local organisations or groups can easily become dependent upon external change agents. This dependence upon the agent was a problem which SARILAKAS recognised and sought to avoid. From the beginning, the development of the local organisation was built on the objectives of independence and self-reliance. One of the ways in which the will to reduce dependence was acknowledged was through the gradual withdrawal of the agent from a group. This generally occurred after two or three years, although the emphasis was upon pulling out when the organisation was ready, not simply after a measured period of time. The agent was then available to the newly independent group on a consultancy basis, at regular intervals or on demand. In his evaluation report of SARILAKAS, Rahman (1983) cited some members' opinions on the gradual phasing out of a full-time change agent (box 7). The members quoted were all from groups quite close to this process. What was notable was the specificity with which they viewed the change agent's task, which showed that their training in organisation and management functions had equipped them to analyse and break down the tasks and associated skills required for their organisation, and the capabilities available within the organisation.

Soon after the local organisation was started the change agent identified possible local counterparts, who were approached and invited to become "folk catalysts". These people were trained, together with others from different villages. The intention was that these cadres would gradually take over the role of the change agent within their area, and would be left in that position when the agent moved on. This role was not clearly defined or analysed in the literature on SARILAKAS, but it appeared that the folk catalysts were not necessarily the leaders of the local organisation. Their role was that of a cadre worker for SARILAKAS, rather than as an officer of the local organisation. They were often involved in initiating organisations in nearby villages, which enabled potential participants to find out what SARILAKAS was offering from a person they might perhaps have trusted more than a total outsider.

People who became change agents were generally young (aged 24-28), middle class and recruited through newspapers or personal contact. They were not development or technical specialists, and there was a deliberate attempt to avoid any similarities with "expert" change agents. Their training reflected the methodology of SARILAKAS, and the dual educational strategy which it adopted; new recruits underwent both an awareness-building process, in which their consciousness of the situation of the poor and their potential for participatory action was raised, and also a knowledge-acquisition process, which

Box 7.   SARILAKAS change agents

Malabor Group

"The facilitators need not stay with us continuously any longer. They may leave, provided they visit us at least once a month, and are available up to twice a month for consultation when we need them. They may perhaps work in nearby *barangays* so that we can consult them when we have a problem we cannot solve ourselves. We do not yet have enough knowledge of the various bye-laws and about how to run our organisation in all matters. But we do not want the facilitators permanently because people in other areas also need them."

"Even tomorrow they can leave and work in other *barangays*. But we need more legal education. In a month, perhaps, the folk catalysts and officials of our organisation can discuss these with the facilitators and acquire the necessary knowledge. We want them to be of service to other *barangays* also. I dream of such organisation as ours in each *barangay*."

"There are still weak points in our organisation, so that we still need the advice of the facilitators. But an arrangement for consultation with them once a month should normally be sufficient."

Amar Group

"We do not need the facilitators always, but we need them when we have special problems that we cannot solve ourselves. We still need technical help in matters like how to apply for loans. But the facilitators may leave tomorrow and visit us once in three months or so for consultation."

"I think we need the facilitators more frequently. The folk catalysts are not yet ready; they have to develop the sensitising and motivating skills further, and also knowledge of bookkeeping and accounting. We need the facilitators twice a week for six more months."

Importante Group

"We need the facilitators once a month only for consultation. We can carry on with most of our activities on our own, but we need some help for communicating with other government agencies, writing petitions, and for assessing whether some action we want to take is legal or not" (Rahman, 1983, pp. 24-25).

involved strategies and means by which catalytic approaches to development could be implemented.

Thus the role of the change agent in SARILAKAS was very much one of facilitator; the agent generated and nurtured the dynamic which came from the people, and subsequently acted as a resource person. A local cadre was formed, which gradually took over this process, as the change agent moved on to new villages.

Evaluation of SARILAKAS

SARILAKAS was evaluated in 1983 by Md. Anisur Rahman of the ILO. The methodology of that evaluation reflected the nature of the project, and did not lead to a quantified, concrete conclusion, but to a qualitative insight, which included both the tangible and the intangible aspects of SARILAKAS.

The evaluation began with village-level workshops, which explained the purpose of Rahman's visit and led to preliminary discussions about the nature of organisational development. This was followed by individual discussions with one-third of the members of each local organisation about their personal opinions and experiences of their group. This material was used to build up a picture of each organisation, and was such as to shed light upon it from a personal, rather than a mechanical, point of view. This emerging picture was fed back to the whole organisation for discussion and reaction. The members then considered various issues which had been raised, and others contributed by the evaluator, in small groups. In their final plenary members also questioned the evaluator.

The evaluation also involved discussions with the folk catalysts, the local change agents, SARILAKAS staff in Manila and the law centre which acted as an important resource for SARILAKAS local groups. The SARILAKAS staff prepared a separate report, as did a representative of the Government of the Netherlands. Local-level members did not come up with a report, and there is no evidence that their self-evaluation was any more formalised than the regular reflection process which was part of the process of creating and maintaining a self-reliant local organisation.

Problems and practice of methodology

The methodology of SARILAKAS included a strong element of anticipating and averting potential problems. This may be because of the level of interaction with established and experienced projects, and their staff, before SARILAKAS was launched. Mechanisms were designed to avoid problems such as the election of inappropriate village-level leaders, economic activities which dominated and diverted the focus of local organisations, and the creation of dependence on change agents. The explicit identification and conscious attempts to overcome these and other problems which arose from the methodology of a project such as SARILAKAS appeared to go some way towards overcoming them. Certainly, in the studies reporting on SARILAKAS, these potential problems were not reported as occurring at a significant level.

The problem of conflict, and the ways in which it can be handled, inevitably arose in SARILAKAS. The methodology was not geared to avoiding any conflict of interest between the poorest people who belonged to

SARILAKAS local organisations. However, there were processes built into the methodology which attempted to help groups to overcome internal problems and situations of conflict. These included the links created between various local organisations before any potential causes of conflict manifested themselves, and the legal component of all SARILAKAS training. It would be misleading, however, to present the presence of conflict as a problem, since the fulfilment of the objectives of SARILAKAS inevitably involved a certain amount, and the identification of the necessity of conflict management was a strength of the SARILAKAS methodology.

The SARILAKAS approach contains several important lessons for the methodology of participation. In particular, one can point to the level of attention paid to the selection, training and role of local leaders, and to the detailed analysis of the change agents' role. This dual strategy is important in maintaining the fully active participation of ordinary members, and preventing the emergence of a leadership élite. The SARILAKAS methodology also confirmed two other essential elements in a process of participation: the central importance of organisation to provide a structure for the process, and the critical value of educational work as a first step in this process. SARILAKAS saw participation not in terms of involvement or some immediately available development programme but as something far more fundamental, and its methodology reflected this analysis. It did not seek hastily to construct the means for local people to make contact with existing development initiatives, but to build and strengthen the basis for their more permanent access to these initiatives.

Bibliography

Espiritu, Rafael S. 1986. *The unfolding of the Sarilakas experience.* Geneva, ILO.

ILO. n.d. *Employment promotion through participatory initiatives.* Geneva.

Rahman, Md. Anisur. n.d. *Catalytic action to promote participatory rural development: A review of methodology and experience.* Geneva, ILO.

———. 1983. *Sarilakas: A pilot project for stimulating grass-roots participation in the Philippines.* Rural Employment Policies Branch. Geneva, ILO.

de Silva, G.V.S. et al. *Cadre creation and action research in self-reliant rural development.* Geneva, ILO.

From passive to active participatory forestry: Nepal

Mary Hobley *

Introduction

The oil crisis of the early 1970s and changing patterns of development theory led to the realisation that many Third World countries were facing an energy crisis of enormous proportions. In Nepal by the late 1970s prophecies of impending disaster abounded as it was seen that the rapidly diminishing forest resource could not meet the demands of a growing population for firewood, fodder and other forest products. The World Bank spoke of the complete disappearance of all accessible forest in the Middle Hills over the next 15 years; it wrote of massive soil erosion and increasing populations of both humans and animals to levels that the environment could not sustain. The solution proposed by development agencies and government was community forestry, or as it is increasingly referred to, social forestry: the creation of new forest resources by and for the local community, which would stabilise the environment; the supply of basic needs in fuelwood and fodder; and steps to ensure that there was forest left to meet the interests of the State. This community approach to forestry was expected to promote rural development and eradicate poverty. In 1980 the FAO declared in support that "governments of both developed and developing countries should lend support to institutionalising self-reliant mechanisms by which forestry activities will be increasingly based on endogenous decision-making and the full participation of the rural poor" (FAO, 1980, p. 7).

Forestry and participation

The past decade of forestry practice has seen a shift from large-scale industrial plantation projects to small-scale community and individual-based programmes. However, one form of forestry did not eclipse the other; industrial forestry and community forestry are the two faces of the forestry coin. Although the types of forestry intervention diversified, the profession continued to

*Social Forestry Research Fellow, Overseas Development Institute, London.

embrace those traditional practices which propelled forestry in its doctrines of "timber primacy and sustained yield". The profession was not ready to accept people first and trees second, and thus community forestry remained a top-down technical programme for forestation. The technical and élitist orientation of both the expatriate and local forests staff helped to skew project actions at the local level in favour of the rural élite. The skills and knowledge needed by foresters to draw the rural poor, both men and women, into community forestry were absent; and furthermore the absence of these skills remained unnoticed and unquestioned by the forestry profession.

The notion of community subsumed within the new doctrine of community forestry promoted policies which were directed towards the community as an undifferentiated entity and united for common action by its need for firewood and fodder. These policies ignored the differential access to both natural and political resources within a village and assumed that all individuals would benefit equally from tree-planting programmes. Although the emphasis of forestry intervention had changed from support of plantations for the forest department to plantations for the village, the rural poor, who had been identified as the group to benefit from the new initiatives, remained excluded from access to the new resources.

Current debates within and outside the forestry world are directed towards understanding "community" and "social" in the new forms of forestry. The implicit assumptions originally made about a community of beneficiaries are now questioned, and have led to new initiatives focused on the participation of the forest users in the management of their forest resources. However, the degree to which users actually participate in decision-making varies according to the ideology of the organisation. For some organisations community forestry means the empowerment of poor men and women through giving them control over access to the forests and decision-making; for other organisations community forestry is a top-down intervention where community participation is limited to the use of local labour in the creation of forests for the State. In Nepal the forms of community forestry followed by projects lay in between these two extremes; they were neither exclusively top down nor bottom up. Project initiatives were based on the active involvement of forest users in the management of forest resources but with continued technical support from the state forest department. In the following sections we describe the evolution of a form of participatory community forestry in one forestry aid project in Nepal.

The Nepal-Australia Forestry Project (NAFP) is a bilateral aid project funded by the Australian Government and His Majesty's Government of Nepal. The Project operates in two hill districts of Nepal, Kabhre Palanchok and Sindhu Palchok, to the north-east and east of the Kathmandu Valley. It began operations in its current form in 1978, since when there has been a significant change in its approach to community forestry. In the early stages of the project, technocratic solutions to technocratic problems were sought; the problem was seen as a lack of trees and the solution proposed was forestation. Project activities were directed towards the creation of new forest resources, through the planting of village land, paid for by the NAFP and using local labour. It was assumed that by increasing the number of trees planted there would be an increased supply of firewood and fodder available to all members of society, and in particular to the disadvantaged rural poor. Experience, however, has shown that the benefits of these programmes were limited in extent and did not trickle down to the rural poor. Furthermore, since the early 1980s community forestry in Nepal has undergone a major reorientation; participation has become part of the rhetoric of forestry development and the process by which to achieve a substantial increase in forestation. Involvement of forest users (primarily rural poor men and women) in the sustainable management of their forest resources became one of the major objectives of the NAFP community forestry approach.

Community forestry and the village

NAFP, in common with changes occurring in forestry development in other parts of the world, changed its prime objectives from resource creation and finding technical solutions to technical problems, to that of the local management of existing forest resources. This change required government and project foresters to embrace a whole new set of skills and understandings. This new form of forestry demanded time and the restructuring of decision-making and problem-solving processes within the Project, Department of Forests and the village. The pressure for change from the largely technocratic practices of the first few years of the project came from a number of sources, both external and internal. However, one of the most important factors was the realisation that the new forest resources created were insignificant in area and quantity relative to the existing forests that were being used by villagers to fulfil their daily needs. If forests were to be maintained within the Middle Hills, it was the natural forests that most urgently needed to come under sustainable management systems. The Department of Forests did not have sufficient resources to ensure effective management throughout the Hills, and therefore there was pressure for the villagers to take responsibility for and protect their subsistence resources.

The problem as perceived by the Project was rapid degradation of existing natural forests; the solution proposed was the local management of the forests by the people who used them. This solution implied a move away from the traditional forestry approach which had placed the responsibility for management entirely with the Department of Forests. Forests were no longer a resource to be protected from the people, but a resource to be used and conserved by the people. In the process of change from traditional forestry approaches towards local management of forests, the Project moved from passive participation to an approach which encouraged people's active participation. In the early years of the NAFP the local people were viewed as the "beneficiaries" of the Project activities and the amorphous target at which forestry development was directed. Control over this development was held by the Project and the Department of Forests and the villagers were passive participants in tree-planting schemes. The distinction between passive and active participation has been explained as follows:

> What gives real meaning to popular participation is the collective effort by the people concerned to pool their efforts and whatever other resources they decide to pool together, to attain objectives they set for themselves. In this regard participation is viewed as an active process in which the participants take initiatives and action that is stimulated by their own thinking and deliberation and over which they can exert effective control. The idea of passive participation which only involves the people in actions that have been thought out or designed by others and are controlled by others is unacceptable (Oakley and Marsden, 1984, p. x).

From community forestry to participatory forestry

In 1985 new forms of community forestry were begun in selected panchayats (local village councils) within the NAFP working area. The panchayats were chosen on the basis of already having existing local forest protection systems and thus explicit signs of a collective sympathy and understanding of the need to protect forests. It was felt by Project staff that this was a necessary precondition from which to start local forest management. Thus the initial decisions to begin local forest management were taken by the Project and Department of Forests independently of the villagers.

The process of implementing this new form of community forestry began in one panchayat, Tukucha, which was a group of caste-differentiated settlements with several locally protected forest areas within its boundaries. The first steps in the management process began with an externally taken decision by the Project and the Department of Forests that Tukucha should be the starting-point for the experiment in local forest management. Accordingly, a meeting was called by the District Forest Controller through the Pradhan Pancha (the panchayat leader) to discuss the management of the forests. The meeting brought together panchayat leaders and local men, with a few women sitting on the periphery of the meeting. Decisions were made at this meeting to manage all the forests within the panchayat through a forest committee at the panchayat level. This committee was composed of panchayat members and one woman who was voted on to the committee in her absence. However, the committee was unable to function, as it had no clear understanding of what it was supposed to do; its formation had not arisen out of a perceived need by local people but rather as a response to externally imposed views on what was the most efficient way to manage forests. The Project, therefore, had adopted only part of the participation process in that some local people were partially in control of the decision-making process.

After these initial unsuccessful attempts to devolve control of the forests to local people, the Project decided that a new approach was needed to secure the participation of the forest users in the decision-making process. Again the initiative was taken externally; the panchayat forest committee was called together to decide how to manage the forests, and the members agreed that subcommittees at the ward level should be formed. Meetings started the next day in each ward following an agenda drawn up in Kathmandu and led by Department of Forests and NAFP staff. These meetings produced a set of ward-level committees and priorities for action. Again the meetings were dominated by men and ward leaders while the forest users were not represented, or did not speak out even if they did attend. The information from these meetings was recorded by Department of Forests and Project staff and taken back to Kathmandu to form the basis for future action. Questions were asked at the meetings, for example, about forest product priorities, access rights to the forest, and willingness to pay for firewood and fodder. Initiatives and ideas continued to be generated outside the panchayat, with action in the panchayat arising as a reaction to external intervention.

Internal change within the NAFP, stimulated by experience in the panchayat, led to the next stage in the Project's understanding of the meaning of local participation in forest management. Meetings in the panchayat had provided information on which to act, but had also shown that the method used to elicit participation had ensured that information was obtained from only one sector of the village; male and powerful. Attempts by Project staff to draw women and low castes into the discussions had failed and therefore this group's needs were not articulated. The information gathered clearly did not represent the views of the users of the forest and thus could not form the basis of a management plan. The Project had initiated actions at the wrong level: the committees established after brief meetings at the ward level were unrepresentative of the forest users and had been formed in response to external directives from the NAFP and the Department of Forests.

Project staff returned to Kathmandu for a period of reflection on the action that had been taken in Tukucha. This reflection produced a new set of ideas: forest users must be involved in the planning and implementation of management and in order to reach these people a new approach was needed. The Project decided to focus its efforts in Ward 1 of Tukucha panchayat (there are nine wards within a panchayat) and in this way it was hoped that the staff would be able to reach the forest users.

The initial meetings, called by the NAFP and the Department of Forests staff, to discuss management of the local forest were all held in Pandaygaon (one of the settlements in the ward) and were dominated by local high-caste males.

The location of the meetings in Pandaygaon prevented individuals from other villages attending. The forest used by the villagers of Pandaygaon represented an important local resource; it was a large area of natural woodland which had been protected by the village for the past 25 years, although it was government owned. Villagers from Pandaygaon considered the forest to be their own and stated that access to the forest was the exclusive right of Pandaygaon and one other small neighbouring settlement. The resource use picture presented by the villagers to the NAFP was clear: they said that no other village had rights over the forest and therefore ownership of the forest and control over forest management should be vested in Pandaygaon. These exclusive rights to the forest were later challenged by another village which also claimed rights of access to part of the forest. The Project had obtained information from one group of individuals who were the decision-makers of the village but who were not the forest users. It became clear that in this village the labour expended in collecting forest products was almost exclusively that of women of all castes, but that the decision-makers were exclusively wealthy men.

Although the Project had stimulated change within the panchayat with the formation of forest committees, it had failed to understand the complexity of local control over forest resources which was reflected in the non-representation of women and the poor on the committees. The arrival of government officials and foreign NAFP staff with proposals to formalise management of locally controlled forests led to the elevation of the forest from a local resource of local interest to one of deep political significance. The public forest was used by a number of different groups of people differentiated by class, caste and sex but control over access to the forest remained in the hands of a few individuals. It had become apparent that the Project was excluding the forest users from participation in the management of the forest because of the initial approaches through the formal panchayat structure, a structure controlled by high-caste males. The forest committees had not been set up out of an endogenous desire to manage resources collectively, but from an external intervention which stated that the committee was the desired way to manage forests. These committees were ineffective, unrepresentative and had no control or responsibility. This passive form of participation was not able to produce effective local forest management systems.

Accordingly it became obvious, at this stage, that all the initial actions had been misdirected and that the following implicit assumptions which had guided these actions had been wrongly conceived:

- the "local community" and "local forest users" were synonymous;

- the forest users would come to public meetings about forest management;

- all the people who attended such meetings about forest management would speak freely and honestly at the meeting;

- the meetings would be able to provide the information necessary for the formulation of a management plan;

- the forest committees formed at these meetings would be able to determine and execute their duties and responsibilities (King, Hobley and Gilmour, 1987, p. 3).

Reflection on the above issues began eventually to produce a change within the NAFP, with a move away from the imposition of plans and solutions towards a greater emphasis on seeking the ideas and opinions of the forest users. The initial assumptions of a community united for collective action were questioned; and discussions between individuals on the Project and social scientists suggested a different methodology for action. This methodology focused on ways to involve the people who use the forests for their daily sustenance in the forest management process. The first problem the Project faced was how to identify the forest users, and the second was how to build a rapport with them. Previously, all contacts at the village level had been made with male panchayat leaders and thus the skills needed to communicate with women and low castes had not been developed.

To support this changing understanding of community-level forestry, the NAFP sought advice on methods of building rapport with villagers. A group of social scientists was employed to help both NAFP and Department of Forests staff in the villages. Foresters paired up with social scientists and they spent several days together in Pandaygaon and surrounding villages identifying the different users of the forest. The next important stage of the process was to bring the forest users together in a non-threatening situation where they could voice their needs. Accordingly, the users said that they would be able to discuss their problems in homogeneous groups divided on the basis of sex and caste. Thus, each group was brought together separately to discuss its needs, access to forests, conflicts between individuals over resource use, and any other issues considered relevant to the collective management of the forest.

The outcome of this process of forest user group formation and discussion was the realisation by the NAFP and the Department of Forests that the different groups represented forest users with varying needs and influence. The information provided by these groups was at odds with the information obtained from previous meetings: other villages claimed that they had equal rights of access to the Pandaygaon forest; priorities for different forest products given by the men were disputed by the women; prices for firewood, decided by the wealthy male leaders, were questioned by the poor in the village. It was concluded, therefore, that it was necessary to provide a forum in which these groups could present their views and ensure that they were heard. However, the committee formed at the previous ward-level meeting was not considered to be representative of the forest users; first, it was composed entirely of men and, second, other villages which also used the forest had been excluded from participation on the committee. After discussion this committee was disbanded and a new committee formed from individuals of the different user groups. However, the conflicts were not easily resolved and the ability of women and low castes on the committee to resist pressure from more powerful individuals had yet to be demonstrated; but the committee was able to make some decisions which were supported by the forest users. These decisions included the regulation of leaf collection and firewood cutting, the organisation of labour to cut a fireline in the forest, and the planting of a small area of degraded land. However, a low-caste blacksmith expressed his scepticism about local control over forests, saying that authority for the forest should be held by the Government and not by the local people because he feared that local control by wealthy individuals would prevent him from gaining access to the forest. Whether participation in decision-making by all the forest users has continued after the end of the interventions by the Project is unknown to the author. However, it was unlikely that the women and low castes would be able to maintain their positions on the committee; full participation of such groups was a challenge to the existing power structure and would not be tolerated by the male leaders of the village.

The intervention in this village by the NAFP and Department of Forests staff continued over a period of eight months, at the end of which a management plan was prepared by the villagers. The plan described the way in which the forest was to be managed, the harvesting systems, the distribution of products from the forest and a statement on the right of access to the forest. The implementation of this plan was left to the forest committee which was able to contact the Department of Forests' local staff if technical advice were needed.

Training for participatory forestry

If the local management of forests were to spread throughout Nepal a group of facilitators would be needed to catalyse action in the villages. The outcome of this experiment in participatory forestry was the realisation by the NAFP of the need to retrain field-level foresters. Field-level foresters (rangers) were trained in the traditional forestry format, with the result that their knowledge was restricted to technical forestry and did not encompass the types of skills needed to implement local management schemes. The rangers' relationships with the villagers were generally characterised by mutual mistrust and this situation clearly needed to be reversed. The ranger became the catalyst of change in the village and his or her future work would encompass a range of activities:

–   visits to the village to listen, understand and explain ideas of forestry development to the people;

- building up the confidence of the villagers;

- bringing together the users of the forest and identifying their various interests;

- ensuring that each group had equal representation;

- offering technical advice when sought by the group;

- remaining in regular contact with the forest groups.

This new role was a radical departure from the rangers' current work and would therefore involve training and continuing support to ensure that they were able to build a successful rapport with all levels of village society. This process of education and training, which has become one of the main foci of the present NAFP programme, was based on the experiences gained in Tukucha panchayat from which a new understanding of village forestry emerged: "Village forestry is the control, management and use of forest resources by villagers. It aims to ensure that all villagers have equal access" (Fisher and Malla, 1987a, p. 4).

Rangers were taught the necessary communication and rapport-building skills through a series of workshops and through living in the villages with experienced facilitators. Through these workshops the rangers developed the ability to be self-critical and to become aware of their class and gender biases. They were trained to reject the authoritarian and technical approach in favour of a role which meshed together technical skills and an understanding and respect for local knowledge. Time for these training programmes was limited by the need for rangers to return to work. After the conclusion of their training they were expected to select several villages in their local areas where interest had been expressed in the management of forests. The rangers worked with these villagers, identifying the forest users, listening to problems, stimulating discussion, helping to resolve conflicts and finally bringing together the forest users to manage the forest collectively. At this point a management plan was written by the villagers with the help of the ranger. This was the beginning of the relationship between the ranger and the villagers which would continue as long as the villagers felt it to be necessary. NAFP stressed in their training programmes that the role of the ranger was not to teach the villagers about the forests, but to work with the villagers to help them to help themselves. The ranger must be willing to learn from the local people (Fisher and Malla, 1987a). The emphasis throughout was placed on the forest user and the involvement of that individual, regardless of caste, class or sex in the decisions made about their forest.

In passive community forestry the ranger had a clearly defined technical role, his contacts in the villager were confined to male leaders and the time he needed to spend in individual villages was limited to short stays. The move to active participatory forestry required the ranger to change his role completely. His commitment to the village was expected to be longer term, involving protracted stays in the village; he had to be able to communicate with all the forest users among whom would be women and low castes. He was now expected to be able to resolve conflicts between competing forest users, offer technical advice and facilitate collective action. It will take a long time before a sufficient number of rangers have been trained in these techniques and until then the types of action begun by the NAFP will be limited by the lack of rangers to continue the work.

Critical review of the NAFP participatory methodology

Over the past decade of involvement in community forestry, NAFP has changed its whole approach to the participation of local people. Initially, local people were seen by the Project as passive actors in the process of forestry development which had been planned for them by outsiders. New forests were created through local labour and individuals were trained in nursery techniques, but there was little development of local responsibility for forests. Now responsibility for and control over local forests have been devolved to the users of the forests.

The case study showed the learning process through which both the NAFP and the Department of Forests staff had to progress before they were able to adopt more participatory forms of action. The need for change must first be recognised by the individuals involved and commitment to the new process must be uniform within the Project, the Department of Forests and the village. Time is needed to foster such a change to ensure that it is sustained beyond the end of the work of the external agents.

In the initial stages of work in Tukucha panchayat, the participation of local people was directed and imposed. Ideas and actions were determined by the NAFP and the Department of Forests and fed to the people through meetings called by the Project. It was suggested at these meetings that local forests should be managed and that committees were a "democratic" means through which to implement management. The sense of urgency felt by the foresters to prevent further forest degradation was apparent in their attempts to institute local management which left no time to discuss issues informally with all the people concerned. The Project wanted representation of all social groups on the committees and pushed for the inclusion of low castes and women. However, in a country where personal relations with patrons determines access to resources and power, a committee composed of low castes and women, and so with no access to higher levels of bureaucracy, could not function. The foresters had failed to understand the degree of social change that was needed before there could be equal participation of both women and the poor.

The rural élite in Nepal, who were politically powerful and wealthy, had developed certain necessary skills and experiences which ensured that they had direct access to government officials and immediate control over projects in their villages. As Gow and Vansant (1983, p. 435) state: "Even when groups are formed specifically to serve the interests or defend the rights of the most disadvantaged, effective leadership is most likely to emerge from those individuals who are relatively more advantaged and closely allied with the local power structure." This will act as an immediate barrier to the inclusion of the lower castes in decision-making. These groups will not be allowed to function without the acceptance of the local élite. The sustained vitality of forest committees and their continued representation of all forest users was dependent on local power structures. Ultimately, it was these structures which determined the success or failure of participatory forms of forest management.

The NAFP, however, was not concerned with participation as a form of liberation; conflict between the rural élite and the forest groups was minimised and only those actions which had the consent of the powerful were pursued. The participation of local people was seen as the means to retain forest cover for local use. However, if the forest users continued to act together for the benefit of all, and if they could retain equal control over the forest resource and the decision-making process, the development begun by the Project might be sustainable. This would only possible, however, if power and authority for the forests was not concentrated in the hands of the few but spread between representatives of all the groups who used and needed the forest for their daily sustenance.

Bibliography

The material for this case study is drawn from fieldwork carried out for a Ph.D. from the Department of Forestry, Australian National University (ANU). The views expressed in the case study are those of the author and do not necessarily reflect those of either the Project or the Department of Forestry, ANU. Other texts consulted include:

FAO. 1980. *Forestry for local community development*, FAO Forestry Paper 7. Rome.

Fisher, R.J., and Malla, Y.B. 1987a. *Forestry work in villages: A guide for field workers*, Technical Note 3/87. Kathmandu, Nepal-Australia Forestry Project.

---. 1987b. *A strategy for a community development approach to management plans*, Draft paper. Kathmandu, Nepal-Australia Forestry Project.

Gilmour, D.A., King G.C., and Fisher, R.J. 1987. *Action research into socio-economic aspects of forest management*. Paper presented at IUFRO Symposium.

Gow, D.J. and van Sant, J. 1983. "Beyond the rhetoric of rural development participation: How can it be done?", in *World Development*, Vol. 11, No. 5, pp. 427-446.

Griffin, D.M. 1988. *Innocents abroad in the forests of Nepal: An account of Australian aid to Nepalese forestry*. Canberra, Anutech.

King, G.C., Hobley, M., and Gilmour, D.A. 1987. *Management of forests for local use in the hills of Nepal. 2. Towards the development of participatory forest management*. NAFP Project discussion paper.

Malla, Y.B., Fisher, R.J., and Gilmour, D.A. 1988. *Extension for community management of forest resources*, Paper presented at Planning Forestry Extension Programmes. FAO Bangkok Field Document No. 8 GCP/RAS/111/NET.

Oakley, P., and Marsden, D. 1984. *Approaches to participation in rural development.* Geneva, ILO.

Paudyal, B.R., King, G.C., and Malla, Y.B. 1987. "The development of improved local forest management in Kabhre Palanchok District", in *Banko Janakari* (Kathmandu), 1(4), pp. 16-19.

Nijera Kori: Bangladesh*

Charlotte Harland

Nijera Kori began in 1974, as a project for poor rural women. In 1979, following the addition of 23 new workers from another NGO, Nijera Kori diversified its activities to include men. Now Nijera Kori works with just over 60,000 people, 40 per cent of whom are women, spread over different rural areas throughout Bangladesh. Nijera Kori is founded on the belief that development based on the needs and interests of the poor will not take place unless the landless, including women, have the confidence and opportunity to play a full role in economic projects and development activities. Conventional approaches are seen to exclude the poorest, even if the intention is to spread benefits equally. Nijera Kori believes poverty to be caused by increasing indebtedness amongst the most deprived people in rural areas, rather than only by natural causes such as the flooding and erosion which are often identified as the causes of poverty in Bangladesh.

Nijera Kori has therefore developed its own approach to rural development, which is aimed specifically at the poorest.

In this respect, it is important to distinguish between Nijera Kori, the intermediate supporting agency, and the base organisations of the landless which are serviced by Nijera Kori but which have no representation in the agency itself. The base organisations are the essential dynamic of work with the landless in Bangladesh, and Nijera Kori is typical of the kind of intermediate agency that supports this work. The whole thrust of Nijera Kori's work is to establish the momentum of this dynamic, to build up the organisations of the landless and to develop their strength, understanding and ability to take action. Nijera Kori, therefore, is not a participatory project but an intermediate agency which seeks to build up the basis for the involvement of previously excluded landless groups in the development process.

*The written material upon which the Nijera Kori study is based has come from the project files of War on Want, United Kingdom.

Objectives

The aim of Nijera Kori is to create organisations of the most exploited groups in rural Bangladesh, and to build their confidence and strength in the process of taking control over their lives and environment. In order to achieve this, people's awareness of the powerlessness which maintains their situation in society must be raised. Nijera Kori's understanding of the "most exploited" is defined as those who "do not have a significant amount of resources in terms of ownership and / or control, and as a consequence depend on selling their labour, or some petty trade, fishing and the like".

The basic approach of Nijera Kori is, through a process of conscientisation, to develop local organisations, which become the dynamic of development. Both short-term, action-oriented goals, and longer-term objectives are pursued, in recognition of the people's immediate material needs as well as the causes of their exploitation. This dual approach requires a careful balance in terms of initial direction on the part of Nijera Kori, so as to prevent the short-term, economic-oriented goals from becoming dominant. Thus Nijera Kori adopts a methodology which begins, and continues with, a process of awareness raising and conscientisation. The level of involvement in collective economic activities follows that of awareness and begins on a low key. Other collective activities are undertaken, including agricultural cultivation, social action and campaigns, building primary schools, primary health-care and so on. Nijera Kori, therefore, concentrates upon conscientisation and organisation development in its work with the landless, and support for these groups when they undertake activities of a more economic nature. It does not give material help to the landless groups but tries to develop their strength and abilities to undertake activities for economic betterment.

Elements and instruments of participation

Nijera Kori helps to establish local groups based on the members' livelihood activities; for example, there are groups of agricultural wage labourers, marginal farmers, fishers, and women working for their household. Men and women have separate groups. After the initial stage of awareness creation and discussions have occurred, and members have begun planning their activities, the sectoral groups are merged. This leaves a pair of organisations – male and female – in each village. Nijera Kori aims for at least 90 per cent of each identified sectoral group to be involved, thus enabling a strong and united organisation of the landless to emerge.

The purpose of Nijera Kori's work is that the group as a whole should take responsibility for all decisions, and that power should not rest with one or a minority of members. However, it is evident that in many places, one person has emerged as the chief functionary of the group. This person may also take a major decision-making role, thus reducing the dynamism of the group as a whole. Questions of accountability, suitability, sensitivity and representativeness have arisen in relation to this emergence of leadership which has not been trained or prepared specifically for that role by Nijera Kori. The issue of whether to pay the group leaders has also arisen, and it was decided that Nijera Kori would not do so. This was because of the belief that the central Nijera Kori organisation should gradually diminish in importance as the groups mature, and this could not happen if Nijera Kori were paying salaries. In any case, many of the group leaders said that they did not want or expect payment. However, Nijera Kori has not declared that local organisations should or should not pay their leaders, but left this issue for them to decide themselves.

Organisations of the landless normally hold weekly meetings, at which the process of dialogue and conscientisation continues and the membership plans its activities. Activities vary from group to group ; some may be involved in income-generating activities (through a collective or revolving loan), others in collective work and still others in social action and campaigning. Focus is often on identifying and securing government resources to which group members are entitled, but which often never reach the poorest. Emphasis is laid on working collectively, building economic assets to further the organisation, and a continuing process of conscientisation.

Training: Nijera Kori runs training programmes for the members of village organisations. These programmes are at different levels, and individuals attend successively higher levels. Not all members of an organisation attend ; in the first instance, one or two members of a new group will go. By 1986, for example, 3,529 people had been on a basic training course, and a lesser number on more advanced courses. Training sessions are run on a divisional level, putting trainees from many different villages together. They last for three days, and trainees are compensated for loss of income. On the first day, trainees introduce themselves, and talk about their lives, their families and their work. Group members then synthesise all their experiences into a picture of the position of the poorest in the context of a village. Discussion then turns to the alternatives which local groups have open to them, and ways in which the poorest can collectively work to overcome their powerlessness. More advanced training sessions follow the same format, but at an increasingly macro level of analysis, putting the position of the village in its national and international context. The trained group members become a resource for their organisations, using the experience and the insight they gain for the collective awareness-raising process and to enhance the capacity of the group.

Further technical training sessions are given according to the particular collective activities of an organisation. These could concern the handling of loans, the management of collective enterprises, primary health care or other such matters. Training is given for practical reasons, and is intended to maximise the success of group activities. Training oriented towards the acquisition of this type of knowledge and skills is considered to be a tool, rather than a critical component, in achieving the goals of the group.

Links: Throughout Nijera Kori's methodology, there is an emphasis on establishing links between a number of local-level organisations. From the initial basic training onwards, dialogue between members of different organisations is encouraged. Joint workshops and conventions at all levels are used to facilitate a sharing of experience, to stimulate an interactive learning process and to develop a sense of solidarity between organisations of the poor. It has been noted that women's participation is much stronger in conventions, and that being away from their home responsibilities and environment appears to increase their assertiveness. Finally, there are links at a staff level with other radical NGOs, both in Bangladesh and India.

The change agent

Change agents in Nijera Kori are known as "organisers". However, their role is not made entirely clear by this term since their role is specifically *not* to think, plan and implement activities on behalf of the organisations of the landless. Rather, their role is as the initiator of a participatory process, in which the people control their own activities, and as a partner in this process. The organiser starts the group through the process of dialogue, training and education, with individuals, small groups and large groups. Through dialogue people gradually see the possible benefits, both long and short term, of the collective organisation, and from there the group is established. Nijera Kori aims to achieve a feeling of mutual responsibility between the organisers and group members, rather than to stress the organisers' primary responsibility to the central Nijera Kori body.

The organisers live in the village and receive very low salaries. Their accommodation is of average standard compared with the target population. Recruiting organisers from the area in which they will work has helped to improve the chances of the organiser adapting well to the village. Nijera Kori tries to use as few organisers as possible, in order to reduce dependence on them. One of the organiser's aims is to expand the process of organisation further into adjoining villages, which helps to reduce their intensive involvement in any particular place beyond the time necessary to complete the process of organisation.

Methodological issues of Nijera Kori

In the past few years a number of issues have been identified as potentially significant in Nijera Kori. These issues mostly relate to the fact that

Nijera Kori is now a large movement, and to maintain a participatory process in a movement with 60,000 members can be very difficult. The first methodological issue, therefore, is the need to consider the balance between expanding the numbers of people and groups involved in Nijera Kori against the preservation of some sort of homogeneity within the movement. As the movement develops, gradually moving away from established groups and into new areas, it could be argued that homogeneity does not matter other than within local organisations. Indeed, it may be valuable for Nijera Kori to become the mechanism for a broad alliance of organisations of the landless throughout Bangladesh. On the other hand, if increasing membership is over-emphasised in Nijera Kori, attention to who joins the new groups may be lost in a drive for expansion. It could further be argued that a primary focus on a numerical increase might detract from the quality of Nijera Kori's work.

Nijera Kori has leaders of different kinds, and in a large organisation it is important to ensure that the leadership does not become an élite, or become static. These are questions which have been raised at the village level, and which perhaps should be looked at in the context of the local organisations. As we have seen, Nijera Kori does not impose any leadership structure on the local organisations, but none the less leaders usually emerge. It may be necessary for Nijera Kori to recognise this, and help the group members work through their ideas and expectations of leadership, and come to some collective decisions about the leadership structure they want. This might result in local leaders less likely to form an élite, and the emergence of an agreed structure which could help prevent leadership stagnation. The local organisations of the landless are also involved in a range of activities, including both short-term, income-generating projects, and longer-term social action and change. A problem which has occurred in some organisations has been that the short-term objectives have dominated to the extent that the longer-term aims, which Nijera Kori identify as essential for sustainable development, are lost. Losing sight of these long-term objectives is probably a sign of insufficient or incomplete conscientisation and awareness-raising processes within the local organisations.

Finally, Nijera Kori was originally a project for rural women. Since groups for men were started, they have become dominant. Less than half of the local organisations' members are women, and it is important that this does not fall further. If Nijera Kori focuses on quick expansion as a priority, this could happen. Similarly, if the issue of broadening local leadership is not resolved, women could be marginalised as the men are more dominant in numbers. However, this appears unlikely. Nijera Kori has been to the fore in Bangladesh in promoting women's rights without antagonistically confronting male partners; while men might be numerically dominant in the organisations, it would be wrong to suggest that women have become marginalised from the movement which Nijera Kori has helped to create.

Nijera Kori is a classical example of an agency which sees participation very much in terms of human rights. Participation is essentially a struggle for human, economic, social, cultural and gender rights, for example, and not merely involvement in economic betterment activities. Hence the whole methodology of Nijera Kori is based upon building and developing the conditions under which disadvantaged and marginalised groups can assert these rights. The emphasis, therefore, is on conscientisation and the building of solidarity and strength through organisation. Such a strategy is not based upon isolated and individual initiatives, but builds links and seeks to develop the dynamic of a movement. Methodologically Nijera Kori's approach is both time-consuming and ideologically demanding, and its activities fit better within an open-ended movement rather than a specifically designed development project.

PIDER: People's participation in Mexico

*Adriana Herrera Garibay**

Since 1940 Mexico's basic strategy for development has been one of import substitution and industrialisation (ISI). In support of the ISI strategy, agriculture in irrigated areas and large private properties was modernised in order to increase export earnings and the production of raw materials. As part of the favourable policies that were implemented, access to capital, inputs and new technology were facilitated in these areas. In contrast, most of *ejidal* (communal land tenant) and smallholders' sectors were confined mainly to rainfed areas, with little access to the means of production, difficulties in getting credit and extension services, and lack of access to mechanisation programmes and public investment.[1] In 1970 the small farmers in most of this rainfed agricultural land were cultivating food crops (mainly beans and maize).

By the end of the 1960s it was apparent that the ISI strategy was exhausted, and one of the causes was a production crisis in the agricultural sector. This crisis was the result of three factors: first, a drop in food crop production due to the difficult technical and economic circumstances in which the *ejidal* and smallholders' sectors were producing; second, an increase in the annual rate of population; and third, the decline of production of cash crops due to price changes in the external markets. By 1970 political and social discontent against the Government, a manifestation of the results of the crisis, had been expressed by different sectors of the population.

Within this context, PIDER *(Programa Integral para el Desarrollo Rural)*, the first integrated rural development programme in Mexico, was established in 1973. PIDER was part of the measures implemented by the Government in order to solve the economic crisis and improve the social and

---

*Staff member, FAO Headquarters, Rome.

[1]Mexican land reform measures have created three agrarian sectors: the private sector with the original private landowners, who were allowed to maintain control over 100 hectares of irrigated land or 200 hectares of non-irrigated land; the *ejidal* sector with small plots of state land, which *ejidatarios* use and cultivate without being able to sell, rent, inherit or mortgage; and the small private landowners sector with plots of less than 5 hectares.

economic conditions of the population. It was conceived as a means to increase agricultural production in the *ejidal* and smallholders' traditional sectors, to assist the development of the rural areas through public investment in infrastructure and services, and to overcome rural discontent by encouraging a participatory approach in the planning, implementation and evaluation of the projects.

Origins of PIDER

Since 1973 PIDER has passed through three main periods. The first period, PIDER I, was initiated in May 1975 after the approval of a World Bank loan for US$110 million to assist activities in 30 microregions.[2] This loan financed 49 per cent of the cost, while the balance was provided by the Mexican Government; this included an estimated 3 per cent participation by the beneficiaries. After the first two years of the programme, a new World Bank credit of US$120 million was made for PIDER II, extending the Programme's work to 20 additional microregions. In 1981 the World Bank approved a third loan of US$175 million for PIDER III, which consisted of various rural development investments planned for 17 microregions (Cernea, 1983a).

Since the first period PIDER has had three essential objectives:

■ The generation and retention in rural areas of economic surpluses that have a potential to increase production.

■ The creation of rural employment both by financing productive investments and by channelling the newly generated incomes into productive investments.

■ Guaranteed access to minimum levels of social welfare for the rural poor.

PIDER was essentially a co-ordinating programme and not a self-sufficient or self-contained development agency. It was located within the Ministry of Programming and Budgeting (*Secretaría de Programación y Presupuesto*: SPP) and it did not execute investments itself, but operated as a programme that involved several technical agencies in a co-ordinated administrative-financial mechanism for channelling investment funds into selected projects (see figure 2). As a result PIDER had only limited specialised staff within the SPP at the federal and state levels. Instead, it relied on the support of other SPP departments, full-time and part-time staff of other agencies and state (county) governments in financing, planning and executing development activities. In the planning, implementation and evaluation of investment projects, PIDER was technically supported by the line agencies' staff. Sometimes staff worked full time on PIDER projects, but in most cases they were in charge of technical support for both PIDER and other projects in the microregion.

---

[2] Microregion is a PIDER term denoting a well-defined area which includes a group of communities no smaller than 500 inhabitants and no larger than 5,000.

Figure 2. The PIDER Directorate, Mexico

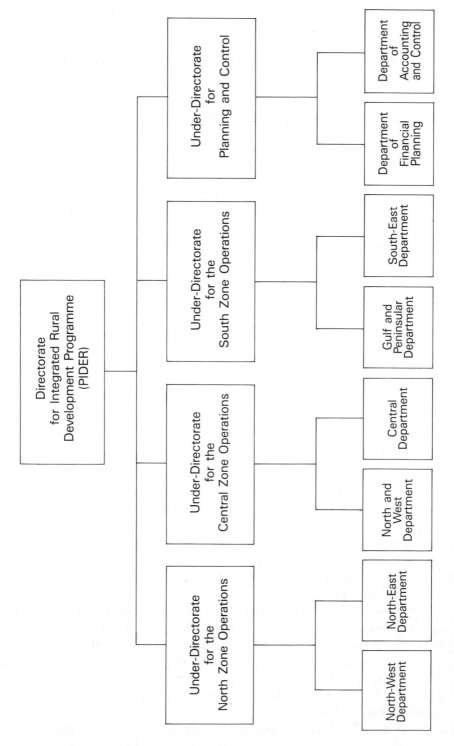

Source: M. M. Cernea, 1983a, Annex III, p. 106.

PIDER's overall development strategy was characterised by five main operational principles:

(1) The first, and possibly the most important, considered productive investments as a priority; thus 70 per cent of the programme budget was assigned to productive investments, 20 per cent to social services investments and 10 per cent to infrastructural investments.

(2) The programme was implemented within a regional structure, based on a microregion subdivision.

(3) All the investments were multi-sectoral. Thus PIDER investment projects were related to agriculture, small industries, education, health and commerce. The function of the programme within this multi-sectoral framework was to co-ordinate the investments through government line agencies and to supervise the projects financed by PIDER funds.

(4) The PIDER programme was decentralised. Most of the planning was done at the local and state levels and the implementation of the projects was not the responsibility of PIDER directly, but of 27 government line agencies.

(5) The participation of both project staff and beneficiaries in planning and implementation was essential for the efficiency and viability of the community-based projects.

Participation as a strategy

From the beginning PIDER stressed the importance of participation by beneficiaries. In 1974 it concluded that the traditional investment and programming system which it was using had serious deficiencies, particularly with regard to the incorporation of beneficiaries' views into the planning of investment projects. This incorporation was regarded as fundamental to the success of the projects. By bringing beneficiary participation into the planning level, PIDER would be in a better position to ensure that the investment projects would be successful in achieving PIDER's goals.

In view of the above, PIDER channelled important research work through CIDER (Centre for Research on Rural Development) and PAPCO (Programme for the Support of the Participation of the Rural Community) in order to build up a participatory methodology aimed at introducing beneficiaries' perspectives into the project planning process. By "beneficiaries' perspectives" PIDER meant the peasants' evaluation of a proposed project, taking into account their past experiences, their resources and their current needs (Cernea, 1983a). It is important to emphasise that the main research efforts were directed at participation in the investment planning phase, this being the main responsibility of PIDER. The implementation and evaluation phases were the line agencies' responsibility.

Methodology of participation

In its operations PIDER worked on the basis of a particular understanding of participation, which was defined as "getting members of rural communities, covered by PIDER, to participate actively and responsibly in analysing their problems, identifying solutions based on their knowledge and available natural, human and capital resources, and taking decisions on accomplishing their development" (SPP, 1982).

The crucial understanding of participation in PIDER methodology was to seek the peasants' opinions regarding a proposed item of investment and to bring PIDER and agencies' staff and the peasants together for joint discussions. This methodology also emphasised that the target population should be those peasant groups which were most lacking in access to resources and development possibilities. PIDER's participatory methodology was structured in four important phases of interaction with the peasants:

- the Information-Motivation Phase;

- the Participatory Programming Phase;

- the Implementation Phase;

- the Monitoring Phase.

Of the above four phases, only the first two were completely developed in PIDER's participatory methodology; the third was only partially developed, while the fourth was never developed at all.

The Information-Motivation Phase

This phase was principally concerned with the members of the rural communities and the agencies' personnel working on PIDER projects. The main objective of this phase, with reference to the rural communities, was to inform and motivate them to play an active and responsible part in their own development. With respect to the agencies' staff, the aim was to make them aware of their important function as a link between public capital resources and the rural communities, as well as playing a significant role in the process of achieving the participation of rural communities in the different phases involved in the methodology.

The Information-Motivation Phase was the direct responsibility of PIDER personnel who visited the rural communities, contacted the local authorities, and through them organised meetings with the people. At these meetings, community members were informed about PIDER and its objectives, and people's rights and obligations if they participated in PIDER projects. As a result of these visits, it was expected that community members would increase their bargaining position vis-à-vis the agencies taking part in the project, and that a more favourable community attitude towards PIDER would be created.

The Participatory Programming Phase

This was the principal phase of PIDER's participatory methodology and involved three stages: field community assessment, preliminary programming and final programming.

Field assessment

This was the most comprehensive stage of the programming phase and involved a range of activities. These included the collection of data on population, infrastructure and resources in the microregion; the assessment of past programmes; the selection of communities eligible for the programme; the study and diagnosis of the selected localities; meetings with local groups; selection of the investment proposals; and the preparation of an assessment report of the proposed strategy. Most of the activities in this phase were undertaken by PIDER and agencies' personnel.

The activities in which the communities participated were mainly study and diagnosis. The first of these activities involved PIDER and agencies' field staff making a familiarisation trip through the village where they took the opportunity to inform local people about the community study. At a later stage, a survey of local needs and priorities was undertaken using selected informants including local authorities and community leaders. The results of the diagnosis were one of the main sources used in selecting the issues to be discussed in meetings with the rural communities. These results constituted the background information for discussions in the meetings.

A second activity involved meetings with the local community groups. These meetings represented the cornerstone of the participatory methodology of PIDER. It was here that PIDER was able to bring about joint discussions between PIDER and agencies' staff and the rural communities, and where the communities' views could be presented. These meetings were conducted in two different ways: either PIDER and agencies' personnel selected issues and discussed them with particular groups separately, or a meeting was held in a large group in which all information of community interest was discussed.

In either case, the discussions at the meetings followed a three-step sequence. First, PIDER and agencies' personnel spoke about the issues identified by the survey and sought the community's view; second, they explained how PIDER could help tackle these issues; and third, the community then presented its understanding of the issues. In particular, the community would comment on the content and location of specific projects suggested by PIDER and suggest the kinds of contributions the community could make to implement the project. Finally, investment proposals would emerge which would then be analysed and priority ranked by PIDER and agencies' staff. When this field community assessment was concluded, PIDER and the agencies would initiate the last two stages of the programming phase.

Preliminary programming

This stage was the responsibility of the agencies. Its objective was to prepare an integrated investment programme at the microregion level.

Final programming

Following discussions between PIDER and the agencies, and their approval of the investment programme and plans, the communities would be asked to attend a meeting where they were informed of what the agencies and PIDER had decided in terms of investment proposals.

The Implementation Phase

This phase was only partially developed in PIDER's participatory methodology. Nevertheless, this phase was seen as both an expression of the community's commitment to a project and also as a way of mobilising local resources. In this sense, participation in the Implementation Phase was considered essentially as community contributions of physical or financial resources, e.g. cash, local available materials and labour. This participation was formalised by the signature of a Community Acceptance Act which was signed by PIDER and the representatives of the community. The Act included a formal agreement on the contributions that the beneficiaries were to make.

The Monitoring Phase

This phase was never really developed in PIDER's participatory methodology. Nevertheless, it was argued that participation was important in the monitoring activities since continuous field-checking of work performed by the local contractors was more efficient when it was carried out by the communities in collaboration with PIDER and the agencies' staff. Although the principle was established, however, there was little direct community monitoring of PIDER projects.

Achievements and outcomes of PIDER's participatory methodology

In the first instance it must be said that to date there is no firm evidence on the impact of PIDER's participatory methodology in rural Mexico. Up until 1985 SPP/PIDER had still not undertaken any substantial research into the extent of the adoption and impact of the PIDER participatory approach. A study on this was aborted in 1982 and in 1983 a planned full-scale evaluation was never implemented. However, a general review of PIDER's work during its first ten years suggests some tentative conclusions:

(1) The formulation, testing and implementation of the PIDER participatory methodology was an important outcome of the programme. It was the first in-depth Latin American experience of building up a participation methodology for a nation-wide integrated rural development programme.

(2) Through the implementation of the methodology, some awareness of the importance of people's participation was developed at the planning and operational levels of government agencies working in rural areas of Mexico. A field review in the state of Chihuahua in 1982 showed how PIDER technicians operated at the microregion level in an effort to involve themselves in the participatory planning process at the community level.

(3) Another important outcome was the decentralisation process initiated under PIDER III. Because of the overcentralised administration of programming, budgeting and co-ordination of the PIDER investment projects, it was decided in 1980 to implement institutional changes. The federal and state administration roles were re-examined and increased authority was assigned to the state governments. The extent and results of the implementation of this decentralisation process throughout the country remained, however, a subject of controversy. Nevertheless, the formulation of decentralisation principles and operational guide-lines, as well as the process of implementation, could be considered as a positive outcome, taking into consideration the highly centralised approach adopted by PIDER I in 1973.

(4) At the same time, it has been suggested that PIDER was unsuccessful in several key areas, particularly beneficiary participation and organisation, and the provision of technical assistance and credit. Regarding

beneficiary participation, several indicators can be used to assess the level of non-achievement:

■   The lack of co-ordination between PIDER and agencies' staff was a problem often found in PIDER microregions. In the opinion of PIDER's local staff, many of their day-to-day problems were related to the lack of authority and influence over the agencies which were in charge of executing its projects. According to the agencies' staff, however, PIDER personnel wanted complete control of the operations. The result of this conflict was a lack of co-ordination and an overlapping of functions, mainly at the implementation stage. This left little scope for attention to people's participation in the implementation phase.

■   The low average of beneficiaries' financial participation could be seen as another manifestation of non-achievement. According to PIDER statistics for 1977-81, beneficiaries contributed 5.6 per cent of the costs of local productive projects, while their contribution to production support projects was only 3.8 per cent. In both cases, the percentage of contribution was much lower than the 10 per cent expected.

■   The beneficiaries' lack of a sense of ownership and interest in the maintenance and operation of the completed productive projects, which apparently was frequently the case, was the result of several factors. First, the beneficiaries did not receive enough training to take over and operate the new assets; second, the projects sometimes used machinery which was very costly or difficult to repair once it was broken; and third, in most of the cases the projects were not in response to the real needs of the majority of the beneficiaries. It seemed that the beneficiaries merely accepted what the Government provided for them without having a real sense of needing or wanting it.

Critical issues relating to the methodology of PIDER

Structural problems

(1) There was a considerable difference between how people's participation in decision-making was defined by PIDER and how it was implemented in the different phases of the methodology. PIDER's understanding of participation was active and responsible people's involvement in the analysis of problems, identification of solutions and the decision-making processes of the projects. This methodology allowed the rural communities to become involved in the meetings where they analysed problems and suggested solutions, but there was no place for communities to participate in decision-making. Decisions were made outside the community and, in fact, when PIDER

and the agencies' staff called for the final meeting in the programming phase, decisions upon which investment projects would be implemented had already been taken without the participation of the people.

(2) PIDER's understanding of participation did not encourage the organisation of rural communities into groups. In PIDER's methodology, the objective was to elicit the community's opinion regarding a proposed item of investment through joint discussions. The methodology was developed on the basis of these joint discussions, but did not encourage any further participation or organisation of the community. The methodology, therefore, did not encourage the organisation of the rural communities into groups as a basis for a longer-term participation in the implementation and follow-up of the projects.

(3) It was difficult for the communities to have a sense of ownership of a project. PIDER's participatory methodology made no reference to community control of a project.[3] PIDER methodology referred to a community's obligations in terms of physical or financial resources as an expression of its commitment to a project, but it did not refer to community control of the activities of a project; this control was exercised by PIDER and agencies' staff. This fact, combined with the lack of opportunities for communities to participate in the decision-making processes, made it difficult for them to feel that the project was their own, and because of this, it discouraged the communities from committing themselves to any longer-term involvement in development activities.

Operational problems

(1) There was a considerable reluctance on the part of PIDER's bureaucratic apparatus to work with a participatory approach. Evidence suggests that a participatory approach in integrated rural development programmes is usually constrained by the reluctance of the bureaucratic apparatus to work with it, because of the kinds of changes that the new approach would involve. The time-consuming nature of participatory activities, the lack of appropriately trained staff, the need for different administrative procedures and poor cost-benefit results, are some of the arguments often made by bureaucracy against the participatory approach. In the experience of PIDER projects, this reluctant attitude was multiplied by the number of government agencies participating in their implementation.

Though PIDER prepared manuals and encouraged measures such as decentralisation and training for government agencies' staff to sensitise the

---

[3]By the control of the project, we mean the organisation, checking, verification and regulation of the activities, as well as the general development of the project according to the project's goals.

bureaucracy and to promote the practice of a participatory approach, the achievements in this respect have been indifferent. In some microregions, such as the ones in the state of Chihuahua, PIDER and agencies' personnel confirmed that investment projects worked better when project staff were fully involved in rural areas and worked in close contact with the beneficiaries of the projects. However, this was not the case in many of the other microregions where planning staff would often never visit the field and where, although extension staff did, they often operated without regard to a participatory approach.

(2) Another operational problem that affected the practice of the participatory methodology concerned the limitations of the line agencies' technical staff. Agency staff, especially the extension agents, were constrained in their practice of the participatory approach by a number of factors: the structure of their institutional work responsibilities, the lack of good institutional infrastructure and support, and the way they had been trained. The way that extension agents' responsibilities had been structured also represented an obstacle to a participatory approach in their field work. The line agencies' extension agents were usually responsible for giving technical support, not just to PIDER projects but to other projects in the region, which meant that they had to visit a large number of communities each week. On top of this, they had to do office work. With all these responsibilities, the extension agents were usually not willing to spend more time and energy on their visits to the communities than what was strictly required. In general, they approached the rural communities through local authorities or leaders, and discussed with them what was to be done. The use of a participatory approach demanded that more time be spent in the communities and closer contact be established, but generally extension agents could not afford the time to do this.

Another limitation was the lack of good institutional support for the extension agents. More generally there was a lack of field transport, inflexible working hours, little technical support and training, low salaries and few promotion prospects. All these circumstances did not permit or encourage field agencies' staff to put much energy and effort into the implementation of a participatory approach.

External factors which limited participation in PIDER

In addition to the structural and operational problems of PIDER's participatory methodology, it is important to consider how the economic and political environment also affected the participatory methodology. In this respect, it could be argued that the confrontation between the Mexican Government's objectives and the objectives of the peasant economy, which were expressed during the programming phase of PIDER's methodology, severely limited the potential for participation. PIDER's participatory methodology aimed at introducing peasants' views into the local planning process. This implied that projects, in their planning, implementation and evaluation stages, could be influenced by the objectives of the peasant economy. Although there are a variety of approaches to define the objectives of the peasant economy, there is agreement on the basic fundamentals of this economy: the household is the basic economic unit, and land and labour the main means of production. The aim of the peasant economy is to be able to produce enough to cover the physical, economic and social reproduction needs of each member of the household (Worsley, 1984; Wolf, 1966; Shanin, 1971). Such reproduction is achieved firstly through the production of consumption needs, and secondly through production for the market in order to generate sufficient cash to buy what they cannot produce but need for the completion of their reproduction process. The logic that rules the peasant economy is production for subsistence, not for accumulation (Worsley, 1984).

In contrast, the goals of the Mexican Government towards the agrarian sector, which were reflected in the objectives of PIDER, were both to increase agricultural production in order to satisfy domestic and international market demand and to integrate the rural poor into the market economy in order to achieve development. The logic that ruled the Government's goals was a logic of accumulation and development. In both cases, production was a basic aim, but the peasants' production was focused on subsistence needs, and for the Government it was focused towards market needs. Accordingly, when the PIDER and agencies' staff attended meetings with rural communities during the programming phase, they had to bear in mind existing national development plans and regional development programmes which defined the funding priorities for project proposals in the area. The communities' views, which were the result of their participation in the joint discussions, had to be analysed and priority ranked according to the Government's development plans and programmes. In this sense the communities' needs and goals would be taken into account only as long as they were similar to the Government's.

In the face of this potential confrontation between the objectives of the Government and of the peasant economy, the solution would appear to be for Government to widen its priority ranking in the regional and national development plans in order to accommodate community priorities. In addition, community participation in decision-making of local and microregion development programmes should be stressed. This does not mean that the confrontation between the two sets of objectives could be avoided, but that it could be mitigated if some common ground could be found. This would appear to be a prerequisite for an effective PIDER participatory methodology.

Bibliography

Materials for this case study are drawn from the author's previous research into PIDER and have included the following:

Cernea, M.M. 1979. *Measuring project impact: Monitoring and evaluation in the PIDER rural development project – Mexico*, World Bank Staff Working Paper No. 332, Washington, DC, World Bank.

———. 1983a. *A social methodology for community participation in local investments: The experience of Mexico's PIDER Programme*, World Bank Staff Working Paper No. 598. Washington, DC, World Bank.

———. 1983b. *Community participation in local investment programming: A social methodology in PIDER – Mexico*. Draft Working Paper. Washington, DC, World Bank.

———. 1987. *The production of a social methodology*, Series Number 430. Washington, DC, World Bank.

Echenique, J. 1979. *Notes on peasant participation in rural development planning*, Paper prepared for the Sociological Workshop on Participation. Washington, DC, World Bank.

Herrera Garibay, A. 1985. *Rhetoric and reality of people's participation in integrated rural development projects with specific reference to Mexico*. Unpublished M.A. dissertation. Norwich, University of East Anglia.

Lacroix, R.L.J. 1985. *Integrated rural development in Latin America*, World Bank Staff Working Paper No. 716. Washington, DC, World Bank.

Secretaría de Programación y Presupuesto (SPP). 1982. *Manual del programa de apoyo a la Participación de la Comunidad Rural*, Mexico, DF.

Shanin, T. (ed.) 1971. *Peasants and peasant societies*. London, Penguin.

Wolf, E. 1966. *Peasants*. Englewood Cliffs, Prentice-Hall.

Worsley, P. 1984. *The three worlds*. London, Culture and World Development.

Flora Tristan and women's participation: Peru*

Introduction

Since the mid-1970s numerous development initiatives have attempted to integrate women into development activities. The United Nations Development Fund for Women (UNIFEM) supports especially those initiatives coming from the poorest communities. Experience in incorporating poor rural and urban women into mainstream development has shown that unless sex-based differences and inequalities are taken into account at all stages of project design, women will not benefit from these efforts. The effective integration of women into development activities offers them an opportunity to participate more fully in the mainstream economy. Women's domestic role, in particular, must not be overlooked; one-third of the women in developing countries are heads of households.

The areas of activity for which UNIFEM provides technical and financial support have several common dimensions. They are innovative; they are often experimental; they provide a direct, immediate benefit to low-income women; and they hold the promise of becoming self-sustaining and of multiplying their effects. UNIFEM-funded projects cover a broad range of activities: from training that makes women's production projects more economically viable, while at the same time providing the opportunity for women to analyse their socio-economic situation, to projects that promote women's access to resources such as land, employment, income, education and health, all of which help to create the conditions to bring about changes in women's position in society.

Project context and description

The project known as "Promotion of Women Workers in the Metropolitan Area," was implemented by the Peruvian Women's Centre, Flora

*This case study was written by staff of the United Nations Development Fund for Women (UNIFEM) based upon existing project files.

Tristan, and supported by UNIFEM. Flora Tristan is a Peruvian NGO which carries out action-oriented research concerning poor urban working women on the basis of which solutions to specific problems are sought. The Flora Tristan Project, which started in 1985, was designed to raise the level of women's awareness so that they could contribute new, creative and co-operative solutions in order to bring about changes in Peruvian society and their position within it. From this perspective, the organisation of women constitutes both an end in itself and a means for the emergence of new forms of participation, conduct and attitudes towards the development of society as a whole. Flora Tristan works directly with women's groups in metropolitan Lima, helping to establish the groups and providing an advisory service once a group is established and functioning.

Peru has 20 million inhabitants, 65 per cent of whom are located in urban areas, mainly along the coast. Over the past 20 years the population has become more concentrated in Lima, owing to a heavy migration of the peasant population from Andean villages in search of a better life in the coastal cities. A great many of these migrants work in the informal and service sectors, and others in industry. In the 1960s the growth rate of the female labour force in Peru increased enormously. This was attributed to the industrialisation process; the establishment of new industrial sectors and the modernisation of old ones; the increased opportunity in education for men and women in the urban sector; changes in cultural values and family structure; and most recently, the negative effects of Peru's economic crisis on family income, which has produced the need for supplementary income.

The Flora Tristan project should be understood within the changing socio-economic context of Peru over the past three decades, which has resulted in the increased participation of women in the labour force, particularly during the 1960s. This increase was concentrated in the service sector or in those sectors requiring what was seen as typical female qualifications (e.g. patience and tact). Hence, women tended to be isolated within the labour market, unable to participate equally at all levels. Neither was women's increased employment accompanied by a social evaluation of women's roles as workers as opposed to their role as caretaker of the family unit. With the subsequent economic crisis that emerged during the early 1980s in Peru, women workers faced additional problems such as the pressure to resign their jobs in favour of men, who are traditionally perceived as the actual bread-winners, coupled with increased pressure at home to make ends meet; this was the result of many men losing their own jobs, thereby reducing the family income.

With the above in mind, the Flora Tristan Women's Centre started to work with electronics workers in 1980, organising workshops every two months for women to reflect on the problems they encountered as working women. In 1982, with the support of UNIFEM, Flora Tristan carried out a participatory research project with those companies in the electronics sector in which the majority of workers were women. The results identified a number of major problems: women's lack of knowledge or understanding of the economic crises and of protective labour legislation; the negative effect of the work on both their physical and mental health; the lack of training and advisory services available to women workers; and the difficulty in harmonising demands at work with those of the family.

The purpose of Flora Tristan, therefore, was to develop a permanent consulting and training programme for organised groups of working women in such industries as textiles, chemicals, canning and electronics. Training was planned at two levels. One involved women trade union leaders who needed better skills to carry out their responsibilities; bi-monthly workshops and monthly classes in public speaking, health, legal and labour issues were organised to help train 15 leaders within a six-month period. The other level entailed a training workshop to sensitise larger groups of working women. These were brought together in *jornadas* – eight-hour intensive sessions – to develop ideas concerning union organisation and its importance in achieving more effective participation in the decision-making process. Six months after the project started, working women were encouraged to participate in trade unions to influence social, family and labour-related decisions in their favour. Moreover, legal, family and mental health consulting services were being planned, as well as an occupational health service with plans to provide gynaecological and pediatrics services within three years.

From the beginning Flora Tristan saw its objectives as follows:

- The formation of a group of 45 women leaders with the ability to express women-specific demands in trade unions.
- The creation of a large movement of working women aware of the need to strengthen their role in society.
- The provision of legal and occupational health-consulting services within female unions.
- The provision of family and mental health-consulting services for female industrial workers.

The consulting and training programmes proposed were followed by the publication of materials (bulletins and articles) assisting working women to get to know their rights and to organise in order to achieve specific demands.

Understanding of participation

Flora Tristan was organised around three main components: training, advisory services and information, and each of these was undertaken with the female industrial workers in a participatory manner. In the field of women and development and gender issues, Flora Tristan proved effective in relating to grass-roots women's organisations in Peru in a way that no other similar institution had been able to do before. Flora Tristan provided the tools to enable these organisations to express their needs and, at the same time, it was able to influence national policy-making through its personal contacts, public recognition and access to the media. The project provided an opportunity for UNIFEM to give direct support to women workers in organising to defend their rights, not only as workers but also as mothers, wives and citizens entitled as a group to be a part of policy-making processes at national and community levels. The nature of this support can best be illustrated by one of the initiatives undertaken by the women during the fifth workshop. It was decided that, in the light of forthcoming Peruvian national elections, it was timely to sign a petition expressing the demands of women workers. Although this was not originally a planned activity within the project, Flora Tristan assisted with the preparation of the petition, which was presented at the National Meeting of Women Workers, attended by hundreds of women. The petition became part of the overall platform of the Central Session of Peruvian Workers. This experience provided an interesting combination of research, training, group motivation, individual counselling, sensitisation and advocacy.

In terms of participation, the general objective of Flora Tristan was to develop a permanent consulting and training programme for organised groups of women workers, allowing them to become aware of their important role in the economic and social development process in their country. In that context, the project was organised around three main components: training, information and advocacy, and provision of services. The immediate objectives in the training component were twofold:

- the training of women leaders from different firms in four branches of industry with the highest percentage of women workers;
- the training of larger groups of workers in these industries, in order to help them with their decision-making process, their articulation of their own needs, and their participation in union affairs.

On the basis of the above training approach, project participants were reached separately on several levels. The first level focused on small groups of union leaders from different branches of industry. The expected outcome at this level was the reinforcement of women's presence in the unions and training them in leadership skills, thus allowing them to compete with men for leadership positions. The second, wider group of participants, the non-leaders, received more widespread training and motivation, in order to begin discussions on the kinds of daily problems faced by women workers. Another objective of Flora Tristan was to influence public opinion generally; more specifically it sought to raise public awareness of several key issues for women workers and to put pressure on policy-makers and legislators.

To disseminate information, Flora Tristan produced educational material on specific subjects concerning women workers, including a videotape and a publication that provided in an organised way the results of the project's training, advocacy and service experiences. The advocacy phase referred to organised legal advice for women regarding such family situations as abandonment, divorce and alimony. While labour problems were usually dealt with by the unions, Flora Tristan's services were set up to provide additional assistance to unions when particular labour problems arose. Finally, the services component of Flora Tristan's work was designed to attend to women's needs in integrated development, including motherhood, attitudes towards breast feeding, health and nutrition, division of labour inside the household, time management, and the improvement of domestic working conditions.

Strategy and methodology

Essentially, Flora Tristan's strategy was to build upon individual women's confidence and to strengthen women's organisations. This was achieved in a variety of ways:

- training of labour leaders through bi-monthly workshops and seminars;
- training of large groups of women through day-long seminars in organisation and reflection;
- consulting services to women's organisations to enable them to:
- examine labour and legal problems, rights and obligations;
- compare different industrial sectors with regard to legal questions, promotion and training opportunities, and wage policy;
- examine working conditions and health risks in each sector;
- examine the differences in standard of living among working women in each sector.

Although the project started with women in four industries where women's participation was particularly high (i.e. metals, chemicals, food and the textile industry), other groups soon became involved, including the electronics industry, the telephone industry and domestic workers. In this work Flora Tristan was innovative for several reasons. First, the women workers were the main participants throughout, presenting themselves not only as workers but also as mothers, providers, decision-makers, women and human beings. The workshops and seminars were a place not only for learning and training, but also for discussions of specific problems that women were facing at the time. They provided an environment conducive to solving these personal problems.

Another interesting feature of Flora Tristan was its integral methodological approach which reflected its concept of participation. The methodology combined research, training, group and mass motivation, political sensitisation, action and advocacy with the actual implementation of services, and direct personalised attention. The aim was to reinforce women's understanding of, and participation in, collective issues in their unions, as well as in their families and communities. Development projects rarely consider the gender-specific situations that may arise, such as sexual harassment, as well as women's political role.

Achievements and outcomes

Overall, Flora Tristan has had a substantial impact and is well known in labour and academic spheres, as well as in related policy-making circles. It has been recognised for its innovative work and has achieved considerable influence in union circles. For example, Flora Tristan undertook specialised motivation and training in leadership courses for 70-100 women, and these women union leaders are now taking an active part in their unions' organisation, in most cases having formal and important responsibilities: several are Organisation Secretaries, and some are General Secretaries. Clearly, one of Flora Tristan's most important political involvements was the formulation of the petition mentioned earlier. Furthermore, the association of such subjects as domestic labour and child education with more traditional union-related matters was unusual in Peru and sometimes misunderstood. An outstanding achievement of Flora Tristan was this introduction to the labour movement of new issues formerly treated as personal matters of concern only to women, including life outside the labour world, domestic and family life. Many women, through the process of motivation and understanding, were able to redefine their roles in the family based upon self-respect and a recognition of the importance of their role in the labour force. Although it is hard to quantify, this aspect is, in the final analysis, one of the most important.

The formulation and negotiation of the petition to the National Meeting of Women Workers, one of the most dramatic actions supported by Flora Tristan, was a model of what can be achieved when women workers are organised and conscious of their own specific needs and characteristics. In addition, it is an example of the catalytic effect that outside intervention, in this case the joint forces of Flora Tristan skills with UNIFEM support, can have to improve the conditions of women workers' lives.

In 1985 Flora Tristan organised the first local meeting of women workers in Lima, as well as a national meeting during which they discussed the petition detailing their demands (e.g. child-care centres, retirement at the age of 50, leave for both men and women for family reasons and penalties for sexual harassment). Two important points were incorporated in a Law on Labour Stability; those providing for a salary bonus of 25 per cent for women workers with more than 25 years within one work centre, and the abolition of piece work. A third point concerning sexual harassment was cited in the Law as a form of hostility, although not treated as the serious offence that the petition had demanded.

The participants in the courses organised by Flora Tristan were very active in both substantive and organisational aspects. Through their activities, participating women became more active agents in the development process of their country. These women can now better relate their work to their health and analyse the effects of the current economic crisis on their personal and labour relations. The training sessions facilitated the development of women leaders capable of analysing problems and proposing solutions, enabling them to plan actions geared toward improving the quality of all women workers' lives. The scope of Flora Tristan was thus widened to include women in other sectors (e.g. domestic workers, workers in the service sectors and university students). Finally, a commission was formed consisting of female senior leaders of different industries. Through this commission, a public political debate on gender-related labour issues was initiated.

The services for the workers set up by the Flora Tristan Centre are ongoing and in growing demand. The identification of the need for psychological assistance proved to be an accurate one, in many cases providing a complement to legal advice. Although the exact impact of this support is hard to evaluate, it clearly became a component of the mobilisation of poor urban women whose influence on the urban scene is becoming evident. In general, Flora Tristan's activities were perceived positively, even if at times within the unions the incorporation of gender issues into overall labour concerns was not easily accepted. Since changes in traditional union attitudes were one of the objectives of Flora Tristan, women workers and participating professionals have become even further convinced of the importance of these activities, and they continue with renewed confidence.

Community involvement
in health development:
Caranavi District, Bolivia

Peter Oakley

Bolivia is a land-locked country of over 1 million square kilometres which lies in the southern cone of the South American subcontinent. The country's population in 1988 was estimated at some 7 million, with over 70 per cent living in the *altiplano* (high plateau) region; in 1988, 49 per cent of the population lived in urban areas. In 1985 over 43 per cent were under 15 years of age, while only 3 per cent were aged 65 or over. The official languages are Spanish, Quechua and Aymara, reflecting the country's ethnic composition and the domination of indigenous ethnic groups. Indeed, the country's strong indigenous base is a powerful source of local community action. Community involvement and action through the traditional *ayllu* structure and communal work practices have established a broad indigenous base which still persists in Bolivia's Andean communities.

Despite the enormous and imaginative efforts that have been made, particularly since 1982, the general health situation of the majority of Bolivians remains precarious. The grave economic crisis of the early 1980s, the collapse of the international market for Bolivia's primary materials such as tin and the political turmoil of the past 20 years have all contributed to the lack of resources available to the health sector; furthermore, where resources were available they were not always most effectively or efficiently applied. The Ministry of Social Security and Public Health's (MPSSP) Three-Year Plan, 1987-89, presented the following overall health profile of the country:

Life expectancy	64 per cent
Overall death rate	48 years
Infant mortality rate	15 per 1,000
Maternal mortality rate	169 per 1,000
Child malnutrition (1-6 years)	48 per 1,000
Population without piped	47 per cent rural
drinking water	57 per cent urban
	64 per cent

Indeed it is estimated that only some 35 per cent of the country's population have any kind of access to health services provided by the MPSSP. Health care delivery and development in Bolivia face enormous obstacles related to the paucity of resources available, the country's formidable geographical obstacles; the chilling statistics attest to the generally very poor health situation and to the precariousness of life for most Bolivian *campesinos* (peasants) and the urban and rural poor.

Health structure and strategies since 1982

A Ministry of Social Welfare and Public Health was first established in Bolivia in 1958, when at the same time the basic regional health structure was established. Essentially, the country was divided into 11 *Health Units*, which largely corresponded to the Departmental administrative divisions of the country, with the exception of Potosi and Beni, which were each divided into two health units. Each health unit was then divided into an adequate number of *Health Districts* (53 in 1987). Finally, the health districts were divided into *Health Areas* (300 in 1987) which became the basic unit of health provision within the country.

The installation of President Siles Zuazo in 1982, and the formation of the *Unidad Democrática Popular* (UDP) coalition, encouraged a more radical approach to health care provision in Bolivia. The central thrust of the UDP was widespread popular mobilisation as a means of building up a political base for the new alliance and of thwarting future attempts at military intervention. This mobilisation was to be based upon programmes of community education, the transfer of new technologies to the rural communities and widespread participation of the Bolivian people in the different aspects of national development. This release of energy and encouragement of grass-roots approaches was taken up by the MPSSP. In July 1983 the Ministry published a document setting out the basis for future health development under the new democratic government. The document was scathing in its criticism both of the appalling health conditions of the majority of the Bolivian people and of the ineffective and disorganised health service still largely dominated by a clinical as opposed to a public health approach to Bolivia's health problems.

The new approach argued the need for a more effective regionalisation of existing health services, with health priorities based upon primary health care, and mother-and-child and environmental health. It pointed out that Bolivia had an enormous richness and tradition of popular organisations (e.g. workers' and peasants' unions, and neighbourhood and community associations) and that these organisations could be involved in future health development. The approach laid great emphasis upon the concept of participation and proposed to structure organisations which would allow for effective people's participation in health development. In the first instance this new health strategy established two basic priorities as a way of giving some immediate direction to future health development:

■ An immediate programme of massive popular mobilisation for vaccination campaigns, e.g. polio. Nation-wide campaigns were launched and used as the means by which people could be brought into health activities.

■ The structuring of people's participation and the setting up of a nation-wide structure within the health service which would facilitate people's participation. The basis of this was the People's Health Committee (PHCT).

The thinking behind this new approach can perhaps best be summed up by this short proclamation which accompanied the publication of the MPSSP's document in 1983: "Health is a social right, and as such it cannot either be bought or received as a present; it can only be achieved by organised, popular mobilisation."

In terms of the implementation of the above approach, there were two main lines of thought:

– to strengthen the existing health structure, with emphasis upon its regionalisation and more effective co-ordination between its different levels and departments;

– to strengthen the means of people's participation.

The central objective was co-management *(cogestión)* of the health service between health professionals and local people via a structure of popular organisation. The idea of *cogestión* became the rallying cry of the new approach, but was not greeted with great enthusiasm in all circles. Similarly, the approach sought to break the essentially "assistencialist" character of the Bolivian health service, to give it more of a public health orientation and to lessen its dependence upon medical professionals. The implementation of this approach was conceptualised and largely put into practice as follows:

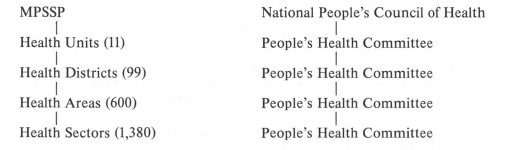

MPSSP	National People's Council of Health
Health Units (11)	People's Health Committee
Health Districts (99)	People's Health Committee
Health Areas (600)	People's Health Committee
Health Sectors (1,380)	People's Health Committee

(Note: Numbers are theoretical estimates based upon plans drawn up in 1983.)

The conceptualisation envisaged two parallel, collaborative and mutually supportive structures which would lead to a far wider people's involvement and mobilisation of local resources in support of health development. It would not be a competitive structure, but both sides would have an agreed role to play. In this respect the relationship was conceptualised as follows:

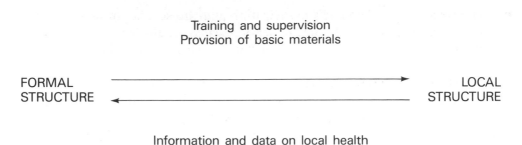

Training and supervision
Provision of basic materials

FORMAL
STRUCTURE

LOCAL
STRUCTURE

Information and data on local health
Referral of serious cases

The Health District of Caranavi

The Health District of Caranavi lies to the north-east of the Department of La Paz about 175 km from the national capital; its lifeline with La Paz is a single dirt road which, while it is passable in most weather conditions, is extremely winding and narrow in places and subject to landslides during the rainy season. Caranavi is in the *yungas*, an area of humid, semi-tropical valleys lying at between 800 and 2,000 m. The Health District does not conform to existing administrative boundaries but is made up of the provinces of Noryungas and Larecaja and part of the Province of Sudyungas. It covers approximately 14,000 sq km and enjoys a semi-tropical climate with temperatures varying between 10°C during the winter season in some of its highest areas and 35°C in the lower areas around 800 m. The Health District has a total estimated population (1988) of about 92,000 inhabitants, of which some 15,000 live in the towns or larger settlements of Caranavi, Guanay, Tipuani and Cangalli, while the rest live scattered in some 780 rural settlements. This scattering of a relatively small population over such an enormous area presents a fundamental logistical problem for the health service and was indeed one of the reasons behind the new health approach.

Caranavi is one of seven Health Districts within the La Paz Health Unit. The Health District is centred upon the hospital and health post in Caranavi where the District Medical Director is based. Apart from the District Health Service, there are several other health-care bodies in the District. Some 20 doctors with different private practices are located principally in the main towns. The Spanish NGO, *Medicina sin Fronteras*, operates from and gives considerable support to the Palos Blancos Health Area; an Italian NGO, *Acre*, provides medical support in the Borg and Caranavi areas; and the government-sponsored *Agro-Yungas* Development Programme provides some assistance for health development in different parts of the District. There are, however, no social security programmes providing health care in the District. The District Health Service, therefore, is the only comprehensive health structure existing in the District and correspondingly plays the major role in health-care provision.

The structure of the District Health Service is shown in figure 3.

The Caranavi Health District is divided into six Health Areas which are subdivided into 26 Health Sectors. There are three hospitals in the District, in Caranavi, Borg and Guanay, but only two ambulances to provide transport for the whole structure. Of the six Health Areas, perhaps Caranavi, Guanay and Palos Blancos have relatively better situations; Caranavi and Guanay are the two main towns in the District, while Palos Blancos has the assistance of *Medicina sin Fronteras*.

The breakdown of the professional staff in the Health District is shown in the following table:

Caranavi	Guanay	Mapiri	Palos Blancos	Borg	Popoy
3 doctors	3 doctors	1 doctor	4 doctors	1 doctor	1 doctor
1 dentist					
1 laboratory technician					
2 nurses	1 nurse		2 nurses	1 nurse	
13 health auxiliaries	3 health auxiliaries	3 health auxiliaries	3 health auxiliaries	4 health auxiliaries	4 health auxiliaries

Notes: *(a)* Of the 13 doctors, two are provided by *Medicina sin Fronteras* from Spain, while nine are attached to Caranavi as part of their post-graduation provincial year. Only two doctors have longer-term appointments in the Health District. *(b)* Four of the six nurses are also completing their provincial year, while two are provided by *Medicina sin Fronteras*.

At all levels of the district health structure, the health services available are basically twofold: immediate health care and treatment on the basis of individual consultation, and the promotion and implementation of MPSSP health programmes such as mother-and-child health, immunisation (e.g. polio), nutritional surveillance, and control of acute respiratory infections, tuberculosis and diarrhoea.

The beginning of the experiment: 1986

Little appears to have been written encapsulating the thinking behind the experiment, but there is a very distinct impression of individual initiative which transmitted verbally a particular philosophy of district health

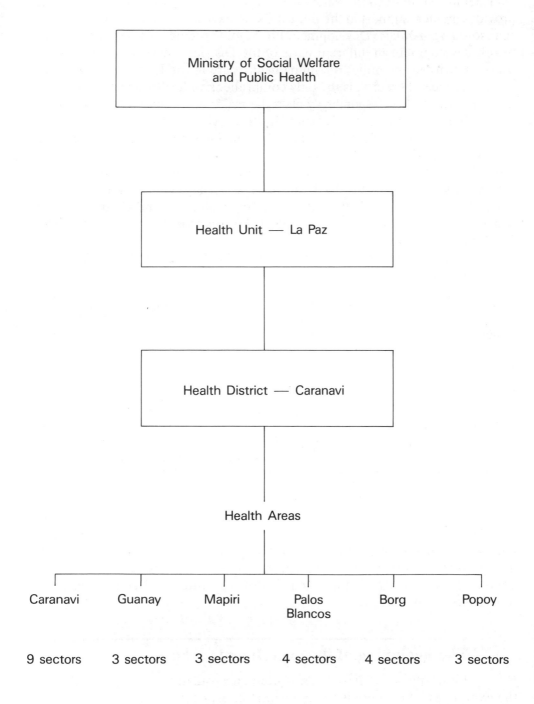

Figure 3. The structure of the District Health Service, Caranavi, Peru

development and then took off. Fortunately, there are still some professional staff working in the district who can act as oral historians of what took place in early 1986. Essentially the Caranavi approach argued that the existing professional staff were simply not enough to extend health care more widely within the district and that the only way this could be achieved would be if the local people became more involved in the health service. From this broad statement, two main lines of thinking emerged:

■ The local communities within the district should play a part in the health services; it was both their right and their duty to assume some responsibility for health-care provision.

■ The systematic development of appropriate local-level health structures and the identification and training of key individuals to assume particular responsibility would be the two basic instruments to stimulate this local involvement.

The approach to community participation, therefore, was seen very much in terms of local-level collaboration with the existing services and of the assumption by local communities of a greater responsibility for their own health care. It did not initially extend the concept of participation into areas of local knowledge or expertise in the health field, nor suggest any greater community involvement in defining health priorities or in health service management. Furthermore, the approach was essentially functional and appeared not to stress the educational aspect of participation other than in purely technical terms. Finally, the approach was very much limited to the health sector and, while recognising the validity of community involvement in other development processes in Caranavi district, it initially limited this involvement to the District Health Service.

The structure of people's participation in the Caranavi Health District

People's Health Committee

The new health development strategy of 1983 suggested a parallel health structure which would advise, collaborate with and support the formal health service. This parallel structure was based upon a People's Health Committee (PHCT) at different levels, with a People's Health Council at the national level. The notion of the PHCT was launched in 1983 with great vigour, and subsequent MPSSP documentation sought to project the PHCT as the fundamental vehicle within the health structure which would encourage people's participation. It was expected that PHCT would be set up nation-wide in city suburbs, mining encampments and in the rural communities as bodies representing local interests in the formal health structure. Each PHCT would have a President, Vice-President, Minutes Secretary and several other members. In the earlier literature on the new health strategy, the PHCTs were seen to have the following functions:

- to strengthen existing communal structures through planned development activities;

- to develop a greater local critical consciousness of health issues;

- to seek to improve the living conditions of local people and to defend their interests;

- to support existing health services so that they function better.

The PHCT was regarded as essentially a people's organisation, which would seek to involve people locally and would tackle local health problems. It was to be a representative and democratic body which would stress the value of communal action and the joining of forces to tackle local health problems.

In reality in Caranavi Health District the PHCT is a more complex structure than the People's Health Centre, and little really is known about how well or in what ways it functions. It would appear that there is no common pattern either to the tasks which PHCTs undertake nor to how they function. PHCTs appear to range from the active to the sporadic and to the dormant and inactive. PHCTs in or nearer the towns or larger settlements are more active, while in many instances little is known about what is happening in some of the more isolated settlements. In this respect, the health auxiliary is a key figure; he or she has to get the PHCT going and the energies and the level of involvement of the health auxiliary have a direct influence upon the PHCTs in any health sector.

People's Health Centre

In the health strategy which was elaborated in 1983, the People's Health Centre (PHC) theoretically was given the pivotal role as the first point of contact between the health system and the rural or urban community. The PHC was to be the physical presence of the health service even in the most isolated rural areas, functioning with the support of legal and traditional authority within the community and administratively responsible to the area health centre. The expected activities of the PHC were understood as follows:

- the prevention of disease by means of environmental education, immunisation campaigns or other relevant actions;

- the implementation of health service programmes;

- the strengthening of traditional medicine by the use of local medicinal plants;

- preventive medicine, with priority towards mothers and children;

- the referral of seriously ill patients for further medical care;

- the control of transmissible diseases.

The above is indeed an impressive list of activities which, even in normal circumstances, it might be difficult for a village-level health organisation to undertake even with adequate resources. The reality in Caranavi Health District is that the PHC is essentially the place from where the People's Health Agent (PHA) can give direct medical attention and undertake some preventive or health education work. While exact numbers are not known, only a small number of the PHCs have separate premises; in most instances they are also the base of the PHAS. Where PHC buildings have been put up, these have often been financed by other development programmes, e.g. *Agriyungas*.

Health auxiliary

The health auxiliary is the basic front-line professional health auxiliary most directly involved in promoting greater people's participation. Most health auxiliaries have completed a nine-month basic health training course and operate from a health post. These health posts are equipped with basic medical instruments and drugs and a great part of the health auxiliary's work is essentially clinical. However, in terms of the structure of participation, the health auxiliary has three important functions:

- the training of People's Health Agents (PHAs) in basic health-care practice and the supplying of drugs and instruments;

- supervision of the PHAs within the health sector, often on the basis of a monthly visit;

- serving as a link or support to PHAs in their work in the settlements.

While the role of the health auxiliary within the Caranavi approach is conceptually as described above, it is impossible to say how relevant or effective this role is. No detailed studies have yet been undertaken on the health auxiliary's role, but there is the clear impression that it is perhaps the key to the whole approach and that at present this role is very much left to personal initiative. The health auxiliary is the link between the formal health service structure and the still embryonic community-based structures; furthermore, health auxiliaries are also more permanent and most have been in their sectors for several years or more. For the moment, however, it would appear that their crucial link role is more clinical than educational, and that they have yet to receive the substantial support and preparation they would need to build upon their educational work. They appear to be overburdened with paperwork – some 12 forms a month to submit to the Health Unit – and this greatly reduces the time available to work more directly upon building up local structures. Furthermore, while health auxiliaries are supposed to be responsible for the training of PHAs and for continually updating this training, little time has been given to their own training. The Caranavi experiment has rightly identified health auxiliaries as key people in the development of community-based health structures, but it has yet to institutionalise an effective system for their training and support.

People's Health Agent

The key to the implementation of the Caranavi health development experiment is the People's Health Agent (PHA). The PHA is a locally based health worker, selected by the community, trained by the District Health Service, equipped with the basic means to function and expected to serve as the community-based link between the Health Service and the people. The PHA is the symbol of participation, the democratisation of the health service and the means by which people on a far wider basis could be brought within the ambit of health care. In terms of selection, it was suggested that a PHA should be literate, preferably young and with initiative, be willing to "serve the community" and reside within it. In the earlier literature on the new health strategy, the basic functions of the PHA were seen as follows:

- to promote the participation of the community in health activities;

- to treat basic illnesses, with priority to mothers and children;

- to seek to prevent diseases by means of health education;

- to implement the District's health plans;

- to maintain a supply of basic drugs and health equipment in the PHCs;

- to undertake a local census;

- to complete a monthly report on births and deaths.

This is indeed a formidable list of activities which, if effectively implemented, might well extend the health service base and create more active take-up of health services. The reality, however, is somewhat different. While detailed knowledge of PHA activities is not available, it would appear that, where they are functioning, PHAs are essentially undertaking three tasks: basic medical treatment, management of vaccination campaigns, and a monthly report on birth, dates and monthly pattern of illnesses and treatment. Some of the more active PHAs do get involved in educational work, by giving talks at local union meetings or by holding classes within their village. There is little evidence, however, of any systematic transfer of medical knowledge or the democratisation of this knowledge, for which the PHA was supposed to be the key mechanism. Similarly, and apart from the particularly energetic activities of a small number of very keen PHAs, there is little indication that the PHA has either attempted or been able to promote any form of noticeable people's participation.

The current situation is that the presence and performance of PHAs in the Health Areas are subject to considerable variation and fluctuation. In each of the Health Areas a hard core of original PHAs probably still exists, and these tend to be the more active ones. In Borg, for example, of 60-70 PHAs in 1987, only 32 were believed to be working in 1989; in Palos Blancos there are believed to be over 100 original PHAs, but only ten have appeared for training; and in Popoy, of eight original PHAs, only one is currently functioning. Essentially, however, not even the Health District capital knows the real picture. Undoubtedly a widespread network of PHAs was set up quickly in 1986-87, but nobody has any substantial information as to what extent and how well it is still functioning. In discussions concerning problems associated with the performance of the PHAs, the following were mentioned:

-   a continual lack of basic drugs, without which the PHA is unable to function or maintain credibility in the community;

-   irregular or sporadic contact between Health Service staff and the PHA, which often results in an PHA simply ceasing to function;

-   PHAs are often not linked to traditional medical care within the community and thus lack support;

-   some PHAs are closely linked to political structures within the community and selected on that basis;

-   PHAs are usually literate and Spanish speaking, while in the settlements illiteracy is high and most people speak Aymara or Quechua;

-   PHAs are trained as the last link in a vertical health service structure; inevitably they transmit this vertical authority to the villages in the way they deal with local people.

Comment and assessment

(1) Undoubtedly the considerable activity in the Caranavi Health District between 1986 and 1987 introduced both a distinctive approach to

district health development and established a structure to put this approach into practice. Given the general paucity of resources for district health development in Bolivia, the Caranavi experiment would never have got off the ground without support from the Pan-American Health Organisation (OPS). This OPS support was crucial, but unfortunately it has not been sustained. Caranavi shows, however, that with an initial external impetus and concentration of resources, experiments in health development can take hold and can quite quickly have a structural impact. Today the District Health Service is the only "development" service which potentially reaches even the most isolated settlements, and clearly it has helped both to break their isolation and to integrate them into development activities.

(2) Caranavi similarly demonstrates the clear link between district-level structures, which are seeking to promote people's involvement, and health service decentralisation and local autonomy. People's involvement must be built from the base upwards; it is not enough merely to proclaim it at the national level. In order to do this effectively at the district level, there must be some degree of local autonomy, control at the district level over health resources and a district health service budget. Currently Caranavi has none of these facilities. Perhaps the central problem here is the fact that the Caranavi experiment did not originate in the La Paz Health Unit; it was largely a private initiative and had no real institutional base in the Bolivian Health Service. Whatever the explanation, however, the experiment does suggest that the building of local-level structures and the development of a health service in which people have a major role can best occur when district health services have some degree of local autonomy and a district-based health budget. It is impossible for the Health Unit to develop and build upon local initiatives; this can only be done at the district level.

(3) It is difficult to be sure what the notion of "participation" has meant in the context of the Caranavi health experiment. The Health District and the experiment were born out of an ideological reappraisal of health and health development in Bolivia; but the actual practice has been far less radical. The notion of "participation" which has emerged in Caranavi has largely been dictated by the resources available. While philosophically there is a broader commitment to the "democratisation of health knowledge", the "awakening of people's consciousness" about health problems and the "control" of health activities by local people, the reality is more pragmatic. Participation has come to mean extension and collaboration; that is, the extending of access to basic health services and the involvement of local people in providing basic health data and information, and implementing health programmes such as vaccination campaigns. There have simply not been the resources, the trained staff nor the necessary longer-term perspective to develop the more radical

aspects of the experiment. With hindsight the Caranavi experiment has been something of a "leap in the dark"; it sought an immediate and widespread impact and has never had the opportunity to plan and conduct an experiment over a longer period of time, which might have given it the chance to build a more secure base.

(4) Finally, if we consider it as an experiment, we can learn several things about people's participation and district health services from Caranavi. By examining the three-year period and looking at the way in which participation developed, we may identify four stages:

(a) initial contact: broadening the coverage of the health service;

(b) active local involvement in specific health activities, e.g. vaccination campaigns;

(c) generating a more general interest in health development issues;

(d) strengthening of the educational component of participation and development of more direct involvement in health service organisation and management.

The practice, of course, is not as clear-cut as the above, but certainly there is evidence of these different stages in several Health Areas. At this moment most Health Areas in Caranavi have progressed to stages *(a)* and *(b)*, although with varying degrees of sustainability. There would appear to be some initiatives around stage *(c)* in one or two sectors, largely build around the training of PHAs. Stages *(a)* and *(b)* are the least difficult to achieve; stages *(c)* and *(d)* demand more substantial support and appropriately trained staff.

Bibliography

Cuellar, Julio M. 1986. *Bolivia: Salud y conciencia nacional*. La Paz, UNICEF.

Granados, R.; Valencia, A.; Sotelo, J.M. 1988. *Sistemas de salud a nivel de distrito: Las Experencias de Caranavi y Sorato*. La Paz, OPS.

MPSSP. 1983. *Bases para la política de salud del gobierno democrático y popular*. La Paz.

———. 1986. *Estadísticas de salud 1970-1984*. La Paz.

———. 1987a. *Plan Trienal de Salud 1987-89*. La Paz.

———. 1987b. *Los sistemas locales de salud en la República de Bolivia*. La Paz.

OPS. 1986. *Las condiciones de salud en las Americas: Bolivia* Washington, DC.

———. 1988. *Estrategias de participación social en los sistemas locales de salud: Estudios de factabilidad*. La Paz.

4

Participation as a strategy

Everybody speaks of people's participation. A bureaucrat going into a rural area in his brand new imported jeep, and having a few words with the village people, comes back to his office and speaks jubilantly of "people's participation in planning". That is just poppy-cock (A.T. Ariyatne).

The more important level of understanding of participation in this study is to examine how it is beginning to emerge in practice in development projects. There is, of course, little specific literature on this aspect of participation and few examples of any systematic inquiry into the functioning of participation at the project level. Oakley and Winder (1981), Galjart (1981), Rahman (1985), Paul (1987) and Castillo (1983) have all, to some extent, considered this issue and examined different aspects of the operationalisation of participation. Rahman's and Paul's works in particular, on participation in NGO and World Bank projects respectively, are useful in their analysis of the key elements of participatory projects. Otherwise the only substantial source of information is project documentation. Both international and non-governmental organisations keep files, or some such equivalent, on the projects they support, and these files are at this moment the most substantial source of information on the practice of participation. The case studies which we have seen in Chapter 3 have all been written essentially on the basis of material in project files and confirm the assertion that much of our knowledge of participation in practice is still buried in these bureaucratic files.

An examination of both the conventional and the project-based literature confirms the noticeable gap between writings on the theory and concept of participation and evidence of its practice. There are, of course, a number of well-documented supposedly participatory projects: SFDP (Nepal), Grameen Bank (Bangladesh) and Six-S (Burkina Faso), for example, but these are relatively few. Generally, there is a need to trawl quite extensively to uncover the participatory element in projects. Projects have a distinctive shape of their own in terms of content: context, project objectives, approach, expected achievement and financial basis. All too often the weight of project information concentrates on quantifiable achievements and financial and budgetary issues. In terms of the development projects reviewed in this study, we can distinguish between two broad types of participation:

- Participation as an *element* in the overall project objectives: projects which are essentially technical (agriculture, water and forestry) include participation as an element in their approach. Overwhelmingly the project is a technical intervention but it seeks to develop the technical objectives in a participatory way.

- Participation as the *fundamental dynamic* of the project. In such projects, and whatever the specific objectives, the whole approach is participatory. An emphasis on less technical activities is apparent in these projects and there is often a much stronger educational element.

As a very broad generalisation we could argue that, where participation is an element, these projects tend to be big, in terms of resources and geographical coverage, and supported by government or larger international aid donors; where participation is a fundamental dynamic, they tend to be small and supported by NGOs. Similarly, in the former type of project the element of participation is at times difficult to identify or, at least, any substantial analysis or assessment of it is rarely undertaken. On the other hand, where participation is a fundamental dynamic, the participation is more apparent and its outcome often evaluated. This broad generalisation is presented, however, not to suggest that all projects fall into one or the other category, but as a first level of analysis with which to examine participatory projects in more detail. Since participation is not a science, there is little in the way of models or proven strategies that we can argue as the way to put participation universally into practice.

Notwithstanding the above, it is important to move our understanding of participation one stage further. While there are no universal models, there is a broad strategy of participation which is beginning to emerge in practice. On the one hand, in projects where participation is seen as essentially an element, there is little in the way of a discernible strategy; much of the approach is ad hoc and an attempt to reform existing approaches in such a way that they become more participatory. It is difficult to argue that such projects have developed a coherent strategy of participation. On the other hand, however, it is now possible to trace and identify the basis of a strategy in projects where participation is seen as the fundamental dynamic and where fairly radical changes of approach have been put into practice. It is, of course, difficult to draw the line and we could not argue that a particular project was exclusively either one or the other; but highlighting such alternatives throws their differences into clearer perspective and gives us the chance to identify more clearly an emerging and effective strategy of participation.

This chapter, therefore, will develop the main elements of this emerging strategy. It takes participation as the fundamental dynamic of a development project and suggests what are the key elements in the implementation of this strategy. Eventually all statements on participation come down to their ideological origins, and this study argues that authentic people's participation in development projects is only authentic where the participation is central to the project's activities and where the analysis employed by the project sees participation as essential to the empowering of local people. The strategy which is illustrated in this chapter is not drawn from one single text, but is a compilation based upon an extensive review of project practice. It is not presented as a universal model, but as an understanding of current practice and as an attempt to give this practice some shape. The strategy presented is essentially a framework which can be used to understand better the key elements in the practice of participation.

Important principles of participatory practice

The principles of any form of development practice are inextricably linked to the development analysis which the practice employs. The majority of development projects see change as inevitably linked to the introduction into rural areas of new technologies and ideas; the principles which guide this approach, therefore, will be directly related to this form of intervention and will stress such things as the appropriate packaging of the technology, the nature and approach of the delivery system, the most efficient use of resources, the quantitative evaluation of results and the need to "understand the rural community". Whether these elements can be elevated to the status of principles is a debateable point. What they have done, however, is to cause emerging alternative strategies to stress the importance of "principles" as basic guides to practice and to argue that a major failing of technology-oriented practice has been the absence of any set of principles to guide this practice. In the first instance, in both the literature and project documentation we can identify three major principles of a strategy of participation.

The primacy of people

Drawing from development as essentially a humanising process, participatory development must be consciously based on people, their needs, their analysis of issues and their decisions (box 8). It also implies an implicit faith that people, whatever the condition of their poverty and oppression, can progressively transform their environment with the help of, but not dominated by, external agents. In essence, participatory development demands that rural people move from being objects to becoming subjects of development projects:

> Conventional modes of rural development, explicitly or implicitly, treat people as objects of change and the relation between the development agent and the people often takes the form of a subject acting upon an object; (rural) people have been told what to do. The outcome is a delivery approach – that is, an attempt to bring development to people through deliveries of knowledge and resources from outside (Sethi, 1987, p. 52).

Box 8. Principles of participatory development

■ Programme activities must be based upon a "bottom-up" approach. Only through this sort of approach can the programme attain any meaningful and lasting success. The community's awareness of the necessity and effectiveness of their active participation in their own development will ensure that progress shall continue even after the formalised project ends.

The programme's next purpose is to nurture the enthusiasm and capabilities of the target group in order that they may attain self-sufficiency. The group members will be encouraged to identify and utilise whatever resources, however meagre, are available to them. Outside inputs shall be limited to the role of stimulants, only assisting the groups in more effectively utilising their own assets. In no way shall the beneficiaries become dependent upon the programme itself for financial or bureaucratic survival (OXFAM, Indonesia Project 161).

- People generally act on the basis of self-interest; consciousness-raising along everyday issues e.g. water, land eviction, gets early success.

- Move from simple, concrete short-term personal issues to more complex, abstract, long-term and system issues.

- The establishment gives people the opportunity to become angry and militant.

- Tactics against the powerful should be within the experience of the powerless, and outside the experience of the powerful.

- Throughout the organising process, people make their own decisions (Castillo, 1983, p. 487).

The underlying assumption is that rural people are able to initiate development but that the very nature of development interventions to date has denied a practical opportunity for them to do so. While few would disagree with these sentiments, the implications for project practice are profound. Chambers' (1983) suggestion of "putting the last first" aptly sums up what is required and he rightly points to the major transformations that would be required on the part of "development professionals" to pursue a participatory approach. Tilakaratna (1987), in his impressive work on the role of the development worker in participatory rural development, argues that these workers can become the major stumbling-blocks to authentic people-led development because of their tendency to impose their "own biases, values, visions and attitudes on the poor". This important principle of a people-led development is now enshrined in the literature, but there has yet to be the substantial turn-about in project design and implementation to suggest that, in certain types of development projects, the principle is yet affecting the practice to any great degree.[1]

---

[1] Midgeley et al. (1986), Ghai (1988) and MacDonald (1989) are all recent studies which include an analysis of a range of sectoral projects. They would all tend to confirm this statement.

People's knowledge

A major corollary to the people-led nature of participatory development is the principle that people's knowledge is as appropriate a basis for development action as that knowledge brought in by professionals. This assertion has given rise to a reorientation of some development practice and the incorporation of local knowledge into development projects. For too long, it is argued, external forces have not only controlled the means of material production, but also the means of knowledge production and, in particular, the power to determine what is valid or useful knowledge. While in certain fields such as health care, artisan production and irrigation control, local knowledge has to a limited extent been recognised, until recently development projects have rarely sought deliberately to incorporate people's knowledge into project design and planning. But now this process, in theory at least, is beginning to change. Several important works, including Fals–Borda's (1987) study of the relationship between knowledge and people's power, have examined the dimensions of people's knowledge as an input into development.[2] The principle, however, is still somewhat in its infancy and few substantial development initiatives have incorporated people's knowledge as a major component. Intellectually there are arguments to establish the scientific basis of people's knowledge just as professionals bring scientific knowledge to rural areas; there are even arguments that rural people should be "intellectually self-reliant" from outside experts. Certainly participatory development argues for the recognition of the creative tension between two knowledge streams, namely rural people's essentially experiential knowledge and the formal knowledge introduced from outside.

This principle of people's knowledge is struggling to influence project practice. It is widely acknowledged in the literature, which perhaps gives a false impression of its acceptance in practice. Decades of scientifically conducted research and higher-level professional training will need to be radically altered if the principle is to become firmly embedded in development practice. The change in mentality and attitude will be quite phenomenal; furthermore, there is a danger of the whole exercise becoming over-dogmatic with the result that the supposed science of the people becomes a science for the people, conceived by external intellectuals and handed down in a traditional manner. The principle is fundamental to participatory development but its implementation demands at least an extremely thoughtful and sensitive approach.[3]

---

[2] See note 14, Chapter 1. In the agricultural field the recent collection of papers by Chambers, Pacey and Thrupp (1989) is the most thorough analysis to date of the concept of farmers' knowledge in agricultural development programmes.

[3] An excellent study of this interface between external "intellectuals" and local people is H. Sethi: *Refocussing praxis (New Delhi, UNU-UNDP Interaction Programme, 1987)*. See also World Council of Churches: *People's participation and people's movements*, Vols. 1-3 (Geneva, 1981).

People include women

A third fundamental principle of participatory development emphasises women's position as an equal partner in the mass of rural people. This principle is, to a large extent, a reaction to a dominant feature of other development strategies which for so long have been largely directed at men as the supposed main rural producers. It is important, however, to understand the basis of this principle. It does not imply merely a re-orientation of delivery services so that resources previously only available to men are now made available to women, both as household heads and legitimate agricultural producers. For the past decade or so this male domination has been recognised, and more and more development projects are now directed exclusively at women in an attempt to develop their skills, build up their assets or lighten their heavy domestic burden. In another vein, projects that are aimed at women's education in the broadest sense and seek to build up women's abilities to resist the forces that exploit them are also increasing; in this respect Bhasin's (1985) study on the process of empowerment among rural women in Asia is a seminal text. An ILO study on the struggle for self-reliance among a group of women in the Philippines cogently summarises the principle in practice:

> It should be realised also that the struggle for total human development and authentic social change, which seeks the liberation of the oppressed from the oppressor's clutches, and the women from the structural and male exploitation, must be waged by both men and women of the oppressed class. It would be valuable from this point of view if the husbands are involved in the struggle of the [women] ... so that their consciousness also develops in parallel with the women's consciousness (ILO, 1982, p. 25).

Participatory development must not seek deliberately to divide women from men but, where possible, should see them as equal constituents of the rural people. Such a principle is, of course, culturally specific and it cannot be dogmatic. It is critical, however, if it is to break the male domination of development practice. In this respect the work of UNIFEM has been important in ensuring that women have a role to play in development. UNIFEM's approach has been to support women's projects with the tools and mechanisms to enable women, both practically and strategically, to improve the basis of their livelihoods. Women are seen as partners and equal constituents of the rural people and their greater involvement in development constitutes a major challenge to existing perceptions of the development process.

Other principles

The above constitute the three major principles of participatory development which appear to be emerging and which distinguish it from previous strategies of planned change. We can also identify other principles which, while they do not carry the universal weight of the above three, appear in differing degrees to be beginning to influence this practice. These other principles do not constitute a model nor are they listed in any systematic way; and they are certainly not presented as any kind of check-list of project performance. They include:

Long term as opposed to short term:	The importance of projecting a project over the long term and not merely structuring it in order to achieve an immediate quantifiable impact.
Autonomy as opposed to control:	Seeking to invest, as far as possible, direct responsibility for the project with the people and not keeping absolute control in the hands of outside professionals.
Structural as opposed to physical understanding:	Ensuring that the analysis of the context in which the project is located details not merely the physical problems but also the structural issues affecting people's participation.
Spontaneity as opposed to fixed objectives:	Allowing for some element of unplanned, qualitative changes to occur within the project rather than limit all actions within predetermined objectives.
Local actions as opposed to local responses:	Encouraging rural people to determine and to take action within the parameters of the project and not merely to respond passively to project initiatives taken by others.

There is certainly no suggestion that the above principles constitute any kind of magical formula or absolute truths for the implementation of participatory projects. Indeed it could be argued that, as principles, they are relevant to the practice of development in general. Together, however, they do constitute a substantial reorientation of the practice of development projects. It could further be argued, and the evidence is widespread, that a major failing of development projects is that many of them embark on a course of activities with the geographical area defined, the technological package in hand and the professional staff at the ready, but with little, if any, basis for their practice. Refreshingly, some participatory projects seem to be establishing this basis before taking the first step.

Participatory projects

Box 9. Two extremes of project practice

- It is no caricature to say that a conventional development project is conceived and designed from outside by national and international experts together with the paraphernalia of feasibility studies, appraisal reports, specification of inputs and outputs and sophisticated cost-benefit analysis. The people for whom this is supposed to be done exist only in the abstract as numbers where output and productivity are to be enhanced and where needs are to be satisfied. Their participation in the preparatory phase, if they are lucky, may at best consist of some hastily organised meetings with the "experts" and bureaucrats where they are briefed about the objectives and activities of the planned projects. In the implementation phase they are expected to carry out their pre-assigned roles (Ghai, 1988, p. 14).

- Some participatory projects are showing the highest standards of promoting the people's self-reliant development. In such [projects] external intervention is of a catalytic nature, stimulating and sensitively assisting people's collective action, taking care not to create a dependence of the people on the external [agent], raising people's awareness and capabilities, and eventually withdrawing, leaving behind self-reliant, forward-moving people's processes (ILO, 1987, p. 1).

The statements in box 9 represent the two extremes of project practice, with the greatest number of development projects probably lying somewhere along the continuum. The assumption of the statements, however, is that "participatory" projects are different from "conventional" projects. The project is a notoriously complex instrument of development which acts as the framework within which development activities occur. Given the present-day central position of projects in development practice, there is a voluminous literature which looks at such issues as, for example, project design, implementation, management and evaluation.[4] As instruments of development, participatory or non-participatory projects are not greatly different in the broad dimension of their activities; the differences lie in such things as interpretation, style of

---

[4] As the basic instrument of rural development intervention, the concept of the project has been much examined in the literature. See, for example, U. Lele: *The design of rural development* (Washington, DC, Johns Hopkins University Press, 1975); D. Rondinelli: *Development projects as policy experiments* (London, Methuen, 1983); *FAO: Guidelines for designing development projects to benefit the rural poor* (Rome, 1984); A. MacDonald: *Nowhere to go but down: Peasant farming and the international development game* (London, Unwin and Hyman, 1989). Each of these studies examines in detail the different aspects of project practice – assessment, formulation, setting of objectives, implementation and evaluation – and attests to the major difficulties involved in attempts to alter radically the almost juggernaut qualities of these projects and create opportunities for greater people's involvement.

intervention, nature of activities and methods of implementation. Verhagen (1985) examined these differences in considerable detail and presented an analytical framework which identified some 15 different characteristics of conventional as opposed to participatory projects, e.g. nature of co-operation, target group, generation and use of capital resources, method of articulation and role of change agent. Participatory projects are what Rogers (1988) calls an alternative to "input-based development". While Gezelius and Millwood (1988) raise doubts about the project as a rational way of promoting participation, for the moment we have to accept it as the most widely used instrument. If we accept Ghai's statement as characterising the majority of development projects then, on the basis of current practice, we need to identify the critical aspects which distinguish participatory projects from Ghai's conventional project. In the first instance we can begin to understand this by examining how several authors have explained the general structure of participatory projects in terms of their principal, identifiable stages or components:

Decision-making benefits	Project beginnings	Exploratory/ national	Information sharing
	Economic activities	Preparatory/ regional	Consultation
Implementation	Project organisation	Exploratory/ village level	Decision-making
Evaluation (Cohen and Uphoff, 1977)	Sociological knowledge	Preparatory/ group level	Initiating activities (Paul, 1987)
	Replication (Galjart,1981)	Management	
		Monitoring (Delion, 1986)	

The above are not presented in any way as universal characteristics of participatory projects. They are, however, evidence that practitioners are beginning to think out and structure participatory projects with the purpose of ensuring that the element of participation is strong and not merely a perfunctory exercise. Galjart and Paul's works make for interesting comparisons; Galjart's is based on a review of largely NGO-supported projects which seek to strengthen people's abilities to manage their own development, while Paul's work is based on World Bank supported projects which see participation more in terms of involvement in externally conceived projects via contributions and accrued benefits. The above structures are not presented here for detailed examination but more to indicate the kinds of important stages of participatory projects which are beginning to emerge from the practice. While these stages will, of course, be influenced by the nature of the participation in the project concerned, the examples above do suggest that participation cannot merely be proclaimed within a project but requires some form of systematic implementation.

The practice of participatory projects is now sufficiently established for us to recognise a number of critical aspects which influence the projects' outcome in terms of participation. We have already seen in Chapter 1 the kinds of more general issue which can influence the implementation of participation; here our concern is with a number of aspects which appear to be critical in terms of a project's ability to develop people's participation:

(1) In terms of objectives, participatory projects lay greater emphasis upon participation as an explicit objective of project activities (box 10 gives examples of such objectives). A statement of objectives is a fundamental component of most development projects and the basic means whereby a project's outcome can be evaluated. It must be recognised, however, that currently most rural development projects do not include participation as an overt objective; influenced by the present debate, however, many projects are now seeking to incorporate participation or to function more sensitively in response to rural people's wishes and needs. The exceptions to this statement can be divided into two groups: *(a)* projects which see participation in terms of rural people contributing or benefiting from the project and which state their objectives in these terms; and *(b)* projects which first and foremost seek to develop rural people's skills and abilities to participate and state their objectives in those terms. The difference is essentially whether the objectives are expressed in *quantitative* or *qualitative* terms. Non-participatory projects state their objectives almost wholly in quantitative terms and seek to achieve those objectives through varying degrees of people's participation; participatory projects have more qualitative objectives directly linked to the participatory process.

(2) In conventional project practice, situation analysis is generally considered to be one of the more important first stages of the project cycle and substantial human and physical surveys and inventories are often a project's first step. Increasingly also a multi-dimensional study is undertaken and analysed before projects are designed and structured. Participatory projects similarly seek to examine the local context in which they will intervene, but this examination often has different priorities and is undertaken in a different way. Participatory projects lay great stress upon the initial contact and the nature of the interaction with rural people and see these as the crucial first steps which will determine the nature of the participation that develops. Establishing contact and a rapport with the rural people takes precedence over the flooding of an area with teams of enumerators or other research personnel. Similarly, any study undertaken will not be limited to detailing the physical characteristics of an area or community, supported by a much more limited socio-economic and political analysis; Buijs (1982) suggests a range of different local contexts in which the potential for people's participation will clearly be different. Rural

people are not normally constrained from participating in development simply through apathy or inertia; hence the importance of studying the forces which prevent their participation. In this respect Cernea's (1985) study of the sociological dimension of development projects illustrates clearly how a lack of understanding of these dimensions frustrated projects' efforts to involve rural people. Of particular importance is the need to understand possible reactions on the part of élite groups which may now wish to see project participation on a broader basis (Paul, 1987). Equally important is the way in which any research into rural areas is conducted and, in this respect, the concept of participatory research has emerged as a radically different approach to researching in rural areas.

Verhagen's work (1987) underlines the central role that the local people have to play in this initial situation analysis and indeed argues that, without the people's involvement, the analysis may be invalid.[5]

(3) Development projects normally proceed through a pre-established sequence of stages around which different objectives and inputs are correspondingly organised. The experience of participatory projects suggests that this sequence needs to be re-examined. Projects with economic or other material objectives invariably place these objectives in the forefront and trust that people's participation will ensue; other projects, however, see participation as an objective in itself and, in the sequence of project activities, give initial and equal emphasis to the activities designed to strengthen the basis of this participation. In a review of rural public works' projects in Nepal, Pradhan (1979) recognised the importance of this sequence of activities and showed how a lack of attention to developing the basis for people's participation caused these projects to fail to involve the local people. Rahman's (1988) review of a number of participatory projects in Africa similarly confirmed the importance of starting a project by building up people's confidence and abilities as the basis for their participation. Few development projects, however, organise the sequence of project activities in order first to build up the basis of people's participation; most still seek to involve them during the course of the predetermined sequence of activities which usually gives priority to making as immediate an economic or physical impact as possible.

[5] Since the early 1980s the concept of participatory research has emerged as a major challenge to the more empirically based social science research methodologies. Participatory research is very much a product of the concern with participation in general and, particularly in the NGO field, it has begun to have some influence. It would be wrong, however, to suggest that it has radically altered dominant social science research paradigms, although it has obliged them to pay lip-service to a more participatory approach. See W. Fernandes and R. Tandon: *Participatory research and evaluation* (New Delhi, Indian Social Institute, 1981); A. Rahman: *The theory and practice of participatory research* (Geneva, ILO, 1982); W.F. Whyte: *Participatory approaches to agricultural research and development* (Ithaca, New York, Cornell University, 1981); B. Hall: *Participatory research: An approach for change* (Toronto, International Council for Adult Education, 1979). This emerging school of participatory research has taken shape in the past five years and has been given impetus by a series of regional networks which periodically bring practitioners together in seminars and workshops.

Box 10.   Objectives of participatory projects

■ Help women to develop their awareness of the conditions that dominate their lives and of their subordinate role; and thus promoting their organisation and participation in the process of social change (War on Want, Peru 5).

■ The main objective of the project is to help the rural masses to educate themselves, so that they will be able to assess critically their situation, organise themselves as a powerful group and creatively work to change society towards building up a new world. It is a programme of adult education in order to dispel wrong attitudes, create new ones and awaken people to revolutionise social structures so that they can be the masters of their own destiny (CAFOD, Sri Lanka 59).

■ The programme of women's meetings is being organised to fulfil its main objective of helping women who are suppressed to raise their voices. We are starting our programme with women's literacy and will work towards awareness building and consciousness raising among the villagers through their organisations (OXFAM, India/UDP 081).

(i)   Fight local conformist feelings and help develop a more participatory outlook.

(ii) Develop local knowledge and encourage local peasants to use their knowledge as the basis for understanding the issues which confront them.

(iii) Develop leadership within the people.

(iv) Encourage the peasants to take over the organisation themselves (Christian Aid, Brazil 13a).

(i)   To promote adequate forms of self-help groupings and organisation of subsistence farmers, which they regard as their own, for the satisfaction of their specific economic and social needs.

(ii) To identify, plan and implement income-generating activities for and with such groupings with a view to increasing economically viable group action.

(iii) To increase the effectiveness of the service delivery system and to stimulate improved access for the rural excluded to existing programmes and services (FAO/PPP).

---

(4)   An important issue which emerges in the practice of participation is the issue of time. Development projects invariably have fixed targets within predetermined budgetary time-scales and are driven to achieve these targets in time; many also, for a variety of reasons, seek to make an immediate impact and deliberately hasten project activities. Participatory practice, however, overwhelmingly reveals that to achieve meaningful and durable participation takes time. But, as Paul (1987) observes, time has a cost and the building of participation is a complex and costly exercise which many projects are not prepared to consider.

Whatever the interpretation of participation, and unless it refers simply to project participants as beneficiaries, project participation takes time. In the more limited instances, time will be needed to allow rural people to understand the technological component of a project or to assume whatever administrative responsibility is assigned to them (e.g. water users' committee or forestry management group). Where, however, participation is interpreted more fundamentally, the time required can often stretch into years. One such project with the rural poor in Sri Lanka reported:

> Four years of work with the action-reflection method has brought good results in terms of people's participation. The people of our villages have changed considerably; they have caused basic changes in the life of their villages, they continue to be agents of change and they are more and more becoming an awakened people. Five years of people's education work has also shown us the fact that only an awakened people can cause real social change (CAFOD, Sri Lanka Project No. 59).

In a similar vein, the tireless work of a female animator in Brazil showed how time and patience are needed to break down the decades of mistrust and oppression before poor fisherwomen could be ready to seek to get involved. The animator's work began in 1975 and she spent an initial period of a year merely observing the work of the fisherwomen from a distance. Her approach to the fisherwomen was gradual and she preferred to let them take the initiative. After several contacts during which the fisherwomen invited her to their homes and also to join them in fishing, the animator suggested that the fisherwomen might like to meet one evening to talk over some issues. Sixteen fisherwomen attended the first meeting. By 1981 this number had grown to 50, and two other fisherwomen's groups had been formed in neighbouring villages. The fisherwomen registered legally with the government-controlled fishing colony and in late 1981 several stood for election to the colony's board (Oakley, 1981).

The cases quoted above are examples of projects which first and foremost sought to establish the basis for people's participation. Such practice is not general and, while their particular approaches to time may not be universally applicable, these projects do underline the qualitative nature of participation and the fact that time must be allowed in the project cycle for the basis of participation to be laid.

(5) A final issue concerns the size of the project. Here size is measured in terms of magnitude of inputs, numbers of people involved, complexity of project organisation and level of technical sophistication. Buijs (1982) sees these project dimensions as having a crucial impact on people's participation. On the one hand, enormous projects with complex structures and technologies will be beyond the competence of the vast majority of rural people; in such projects outside professionals will inevitably dominate and people's participation be reduced to managed contributions or passively accepted benefits.

On the other hand, an evident characteristic of those projects which lay emphasis upon consciously developing people's participation is that they are smaller in all senses of the word. The vast majority of them are outside the formal sector, often comprise no more than a small team of professionals, function within a reduced geographical areas and operate on the basis of limited resources. Size is critical at the initial stage of building up the participation; such projects often link up and regionalise later when the structures of people's participation have been well established. Furthermore, in terms of project size we must clearly distinguish between the size of the external agency and the size of the project organisation. Many of the external agencies which support processes of participation, e.g. BRAC (Bangladesh), AWARE (India) and FASE (Brazil), are themselves substantial bodies; what is important is the size of the project organisations which they support. Interestingly, in his study on self-help organisations in Brazil, Indonesia and Thailand, Verhagen (1987) concluded that "... small is beautiful, but not too small".

The belief is still strong that there is a direct relationship between active people's participation and project success. The evaluation of EEC-funded projects by Crombrugghe et al. (1985), for example, concluded that people's involvement in project planning and implementation were critical to the chances of project success. While this belief is widespread, there are some who argue that encapsulating participation within the rigid targets, budgets and administrative procedures of a project greatly reduces its opportunities to develop. Leconte (1986), for example, sees projects as unrealistic scenarios for promoting participation since, by their very nature, they are externally oriented and confined by certain parameters, no matter how sensitive or qualitatively oriented these might be. Certainly it could be argued that the range of scenarios examined in the project documentation do not all constitute projects in the more accepted sense of the term and that indeed participation can emerge and develop in less highly structured environments.

Participation as a process

In many rural development projects participation is seen essentially as either another input or a distinguishing characteristic of project operations. In those instances where participation is largely to do with mobilising people's contributions to project activities, then appropriate mechanisms or even conditions will be established to help incorporate these contributions. In other projects participation will be basically to do with people's access to the benefits that will accrue to their involvement in the project and in these cases, similarly, project design will take account of the need to give rural people access to these benefits. Both these forms of project participation are widespread and, with the accumulated experiences, have led to a whole range of project administrative mechanisms for facilitating the participation. The common characteristic of both of the above forms is that they see participation as a clearly recognisable project *component*, and this is taken into account in project design and preparation stages. The impact on the conventional project approach has been limited and the common ingredients of development projects – external agency, change agent, clientele and economic impact – have not been challenged. It is not untrue to say that the vast majority of rural development projects have been largely unaffected by the participation "debate", other than in terms of participation as contribution or benefit, and that where they have been affected the participation is seen largely as yet another manageable project input.

A radically different view is to see participation at the project level essentially as a *process*. Participation as a process is not a totally random or an unstructured series of activities but is more linked to project issues such as objectives and time, as we saw above. Process suggests the notion of a series of activities or outcomes over a period of time and, as such, all projects can be seen as processes in that they usually seek to structure these activities towards a series of predetermined objectives. The importance of participation as a process, however, lies in the recognition of participation as an integral outcome, if not the central objective, of a development project. Participation as a process is contrary to the notion of participation as a manageable input and sees the whole project outcome as directly related to strengthening the basis for and the abilities of rural people to continue to play a part. Fuglesang and Chandler's (1986) study of participation as a process in the context of the development of the Grameen Bank in Bangladesh describes the evolution of the process over time and in a range of project activities: economic development, social development, joint enterprises and women's participation. Earlier Buijs (1982) discussed the participation process and suggested a number of key stages (see below). Projects which seek to develop the basis for rural people to sustain an active involvement in development emphasise the processes implicit in this and seek to develop them in project activities.

Encouragingly the nature and content of this process is now beginning to emerge in project practice. Where participation is a basic objective of a project, there is evidence that these projects, usually as part of project evaluation, are beginning to explain how the process of participation evolves. Characteristically, none of these projects suggests that participation can merely be announced or assumed in project activities; rather, they suggest that it is a constructive process and demands its own series of activities designed to help it develop. Characteristically, also, such projects see the process of participation as consisting of a number of stages which follow a particular sequence; participation develops as each stage is consolidated and the process unfolds. The following are a number of examples of the stages of the process of participation at the project level:

Promotion and mobilisation
phase
First action phase
Construction phase
Consolidation phase
(Buijs, 1982)

Awareness of issues
Developing community leadership
Sharing decision-making
Learning together
Analysing options
Planning together
Evaluation
(Kenya: Christian Aid)

Context analysis
Entry point/priorities
Establishing outsiders
Creation of consciousness
Pattern of organisation
Comprehensive development
(India: Bhasin and Vimala, 1980)

Contact with people
Structuring of organisation
Identification of issues
Group meetings
Articulation
(Brazil: OXFAM)

The purpose here is not to examine the above in detail but to use them to illustrate how some projects have explained the stages or phases of the process of participation. While each of the above is unique to a specific context, we can recognise a common thread that appears to run through each one : that is the move from some initial contact with the people, through a period of activities designed to develop and structure participation to a stage where it is assumed that the basis for continuing participation has been achieved. Each of the examples suggest, therefore, the kind of activities which will have to be undertaken if a project wishes to develop participation. The examples are a direct response to those who see participation as an extra ingredient which can merely be added to an existing cake. Each of the examples reinforces the view that there is a distinctive process which projects will need to pursue if they wish to build up rural people's abilities for sustained participation.

Key elements in the practice of participation

The practice of participation in development projects is now substantial enough to enable us to identify what appear to be its key elements. Apart from project documentation, the literature to date has been largely dominated by analyses of the concept of participation or prescriptions of how it should be incorporated into project design. Several authors, however, have begun to examine this practice and to suggest a number of its key elements: Galjart, 1981; Rahman, 1984; Tilakaratna, 1987; Ghai, 1988. Similarly, in different sectors – agriculture, health and water, for example – a range of publications, often accompanied by detailed instructions or guide-lines, has emerged. Project documentation, and particularly project evaluation, are also now beginning to be structured in such a way as to identify these key elements.

These key elements essentially reflect the understanding of the practice of participation presented earlier. They have been identified in and extracted from projects in which this study believes there is an authentic process of participation. The elements are a construct of what appear to be the key elements in projects which seek to develop a sustainable basis for people's participation. They are not drawn from any one source, nor have they been proved in research. Certainly they will be alien to a great number of development projects which manifest few, if any, of these elements. This study, however, argues that on the basis of current practice, there is now evidence that a number of key elements must be present within a development project if it is to promote the sustained participation of local people; these elements will be easily recognisable and understood, but will differ radically in their interpretation and characteristics from more conventional project practice.

External agencies

While some purists might argue that participation should be a wholly internal process and should be allowed to emerge solely on the basis of internal abilities and direction, the practice reveals the inevitable presence of some kind of external agency in projects which seek to promote participation. Furthermore, this external agency inevitably takes the initiative. Although in some contexts, particularly the Indian subcontinent and parts of Latin America, the spread of participatory development has resulted in rural people approaching agencies for their support, more commonly an external agency takes the first step in initiating the process. The term "external agency" is extremely broad and covers a wide range of formal, informal and ad hoc bodies which have mobilised resources in order to intervene in a particular area. In terms of participatory development, the term also applies to projects in a general sense; any project which seeks to promote participation can be regarded as an "external agency". The process of participation begins, therefore, with initiatives taken by an external agency and its future nature and direction are largely influenced by the style and approach of that agency.

The current debate regarding external agencies revolves around whether government or non-governmental organisations (NGOs) are "better" agencies to promote participation or whether equally they can play a useful role. While there are other more substantial debates regarding such issues as the relationships between governments and NGOs, the partnership between North and South NGOs and the role of NGOs in development, our concern here is specifically with the issue of the external agency in the process of participation.[6] Although Midgeley et al. (1986) argue very strongly that government agencies, since they have access to central decision-making and to a greater volume of resources, have a more important role to play than NGOs, there is a strong feeling that, for a variety of reasons, NGOs may be the more suitable external agencies for promoting participation. The arguments put forward in both cases are summarised below.

Government development agencies

This umbrella term covers the whole range of government departments, ministries or specially established development agencies. The projects which such agencies manage tend to be big and linked more directly to central government development plans and practices. Overwhelmingly in such projects participation is seen as an input or characteristic which the project seeks to include in its overall programming. Such projects, therefore, try to incorporate participation into predetermined plans but do not see it as any kind of independent process. Government agency projects are closely linked to the state bureaucratic apparatus, are dependent upon this apparatus for their efficiency of operations and usually operate within strictly defined goals and procedures. Questions arise about the sensitivity and commitment of such projects to participation and whether government agencies can possibly, given the closeness of their ties with the prevailing political structure, seek to promote genuine participation.[7]

Non-governmental organisations

Where an NGO is the external agency, projects invariably are smaller, function as independently as they can within the limitations of the context in which they operate, are usually more flexible in the use of resources and are more able to be innovative in response to local conditions. Characteristically also, a great number of NGO projects see participation as a distinctive process

---

[6] Over the past two decades NGOs have emerged as legitimate and authentic agencies promoting development. The term covers a very broad church both in terms of the nature of the NGO and the development activities it promotes. A number of recent studies encapsulate the many dimensions of the current debates concerning NGOs and development; see, for example, A. Gordon Drabek (ed.): "Development alternatives: The challenge for NGOs", in *World Development*, Vol. 15, Autumn 1987, Special issue; M. Cernea: *Non-government organisations and local development* (Washington, DC, World Bank, 1988); H. Gezelius and D. Millwood: *NGOs in development and participation in practice: An initial inquiry* (Stockholm, University of Stockholm, 1988).

[7] See Midgeley et al. (1986) and Ghai (1988) for discussions on the role of government in promoting projects of people's participation.

and seek to support and develop this process without the constraints of time and targets. Participation in such projects is more linked to wider, structural issues and not limited to contributions or project management. Finally, it is argued that NGOs are often staffed with people openly committed to the radical changes that participation implies and less constrained by the professional nature of their work. Box 11 gives an example of how an NGO operates in Bangladesh.

Box 11.   An NGO in Bangladesh

Working here since 1980, this NGO has organised some 140 base organisations of the landless in about 100 villages in this district. Seventy-one to 72 of these are organisations of women. The membership varied from about 15 to nearly 100. The NGO has a three-member staff living in the house of one of these three who comes from a family in one of the villages of the district. They are doing *(a)* organising work, *(b)* assisting in pressure group work of the organisations mostly against corruption of official agencies and the union council, and *(c)* para-medic work, concentrated at this time on attending to cases of diarrhoea and other intestinal diseases and fever, and distributing saline and anti-dysentery and anti-fever tablets which the NGO obtained from a foreign agency (Rahman, 1987, p. 2).

The above are, of course, caricatures of actors in an extremely complex process and it is impossible to be dogmatic about the issues raised by any comparison between the above two types of external agency. The issue is emotive and there are passionate views on both sides. Many NGOs are still bound by essentially traditional views of development practice, and many governments are genuinely seeking to promote more widespread participation in the benefits of development. There is no universal truth in this situation. One thing that can be said, however, is that the NGO influence in development is widespread and that NGOs have been particularly active in supporting participatory projects. While Padron's study (1982) has argued that NGOs are more effective external agencies in promoting participation, Gezelius and Millwood's (1988) work suggests that it is difficult to state categorically that NGO-supported participatory projects are more effective than government-supported ones. What is not disputed, however, is that potentially NGOs are better equipped to deal with the demands of a process of participation. Uphoff (1987), for example, suggests that NGOs have a number of advantages over government agencies in working with a process of "participation" in certain situations:

– where NGOs are administratively and financially stronger than a weak government;

- where government is either not interested or unable to work in a particular area;
- where government lacks the technical or other skills required to support the process;
- where government wishes to support participatory development but lacks the knowledge or capacity to be effective;
- where government is unable to co-ordinate the activities necessary to support participatory projects;
- where government is obliged to work within the pattern of traditional values and relations and is less able to work with groups outside this pattern;
- where government is favourably disposed towards NGO initiatives in promoting participatory development.

In terms of the extent of the practice of participation, it would appear that NGOs are more dominantly involved, although this can be misleading since the distinction between government and non-governmental agency is sometimes difficult to determine. What we can say, however, is that NGOs clearly have a number of "advantages" over government agencies and that in many countries this has led to a situation where the NGOs are the major influence in participatory development. This conclusion is borne out also by Cernea's study (1988) on NGOs and particularly their role in promoting grass-roots development.

Whatever the nature of the external agency, the practice suggests that there are two critical issues which affect the agency's performance; the basic *objective* of the agency's support for participation and the actual *role* that the agency will have in the process. In the first case, the basic objective will be linked to the agency's understanding of the meaning of participation; either the agency helps to develop participation essentially as a supportive mechanism to existing development plans, or it develops participation as more of a process of empowering rural people. The difference in objectives is a fundamental distinguishing feature between the two broad types of external agency. In terms of role, the practice suggests that the external agency's role can vary between directing, supporting or facilitating the process of participation. While it is clearly difficult to argue that each of these roles is mutually exclusive, they do imply both quite distinctive approaches and outcomes. The point to stress here is that the external agency does have a recognisable role in the process of participation and that its influence cannot be seen as merely benign and passive. The very nature of the role that the external agency, consciously or unconsciously, assumes will have a major impact on the evolution of the participatory project and its eventual outcome.[8]

---

[8] An interesting example of an external agency and its influence in determining the nature of people's participation in development projects is the BMZ Unit of the Government of the Federal Republic of Germany. See, for example, F. Von Thun and G. Ullrich: *Fighting rural poverty through self-help* (Bonn, German Foundation for International Development (DSE), 1985).

The project agent

As we have seen from the previous section, a process of participatory development rarely evolves as a spontaneous phenomenon; on the contrary, rural people need to be stimulated, encouraged and assisted to embark on such processes. In all of this the project agent is the key person. While the practice does not agree on what to call this individual – animator, change agent, activist, facilitator, catalyst, group organiser or simply development worker – there is common agreement that he or she plays a key role in the process. For the purpose of this study and reflecting both the more common term used in the practice and the inherent nature of the job, we shall use the term project agent. Furthermore, the term project agent is used in respect of those agents who essentially work for an external agency and support local groups or organisations. We are not here referring to another level of agent – leaders within these groups or organisations – who equally support the process of participation. Paul's (1987) review of World Bank experiences with participatory projects concluded that the project worker was a key instrument in such projects and identified the success of these projects with staff appropriately trained in participatory techniques; Sethi (1987) came to a similar conclusion based on a review of participatory projects in India.

Success in promoting participation appears to be directly linked to the approach and style of work of these project agents (box 12). Often their training in terms of participation is rudimentary and they do not possess any particular technical skills; emphasis is more commonly placed on non-technical skills and particular personal qualities which suit them for participatory development. In all the projects reviewed a project agent was directly involved in project activities and responsible for promoting the participatory aspects of these projects. Who are these project workers working closely with the process of

---

Box 12.   The role of the project agent

■ An outsider who comes with ready-made solutions is worse than useless. He must first understand from us what our questions are and help us articulate the questions better, and then help us find solutions. Outsiders also have to change. He alone is a friend who helps us think about our problems on our own (Tilakaratna, 1987, p. xii).

■ The prejudices that development workers have of communities are well known: they believe that communities are ignorant, do not know what their problems are and that they do not know solutions to these problems. As for themselves, development workers believe that they know everything, including the problems of the people and that they have ready-made prescriptions which should be accepted by the people (OXFAM: Tanzania 249).

---

participation? In the first instance we have to recognise that many development projects do not have project agents who work directly and exclusively on developing the participatory aspects of the project. Many projects entrust these critical aspects to other professional staff who are supposed to develop their work in a manner which promotes people's participation. In such projects there is no discrete role as such for a project agent, with the result that the participatory element is little developed. In other projects, and particularly smaller projects supported by NGOs, project staff work exclusively in promoting participation and their activities have given rise to a whole new understanding of the project worker. An important point to underline is that the practice confirms that participation will not evolve at project level unless a number of project staff work exclusively and explicitly on its development. The implication is that projects need to include staff who will do this specific work.

In terms of project agents who will work with the participatory process, we can examine the practice and begin to suggest a number of broad distinctions between agents on different projects:

Government or NGO:	Project agents who work within the formal structures of government services and whose style and limitations of operation are dictated by the demands of those services; and agents who work in the informal sector, in smaller, less hierarchical structures and whose approach to their work is correspondingly different.
Professional or non-professional:	Project agents who have received professional training, usually at higher-education level, and who function as agents within the framework of an established professional group; and agents, many of whom have much less formal education and whose role is not circumscribed by any professional restrictions.
External or internal:	Project agents who do not live in, identify with or belong to the context within which they operate, but are able to maintain distance between their role as agents and their private lives; and agents who live at village or community level and see a close identification with the people's lives as intrinsic to their work.

The term project agent, therefore, covers an extremely broad range of people and there have been few studies which can offer us a more detailed profile of who they are. The FAO *Manual on the Small Farmers' Development Programme* is probably the most detailed account of the agent (called "group organiser") within a more formally structured participatory project; similarly, Van Heck's study of group promoters on field projects of the FAO's People's Participation Project contains useful information on the tasks and selection of these promoters.[9] Tilakaratna's study (1985) of the social background of external animators working in Sri Lanka found a high level of formal education and a range of experiences before the animators began their work. He further added:

> There are many common features in their family and class backgrounds. All have been born and bred in villages and belonged to lower middle-class families having some property ownership and engaged in either agricultural or petty trading activity. In all cases, the parents had played an active role in ensuring a formal education for them in the expectation that salaried jobs with security, social status and regular income would follow (Tilakaratna, 1985, p. 37).

For many project agents working with a process of participation there is an intense struggle between the demands of a close identification with the work involved in participatory projects and alternative styles of life which education and professional training can bring. Rahman (1987a) observed that in Bangladesh the drop-out rate among NGO animators was high and the conflict between commitment to the cause of the people and the pressures of belonging to another class was apparent. For some the work of promoting participation is undertaken within the relative security of a professional service; for many, however, it is unstructured, insecure, poorly paid and highly demanding of time and energy.

A major aspect of the agent's work is the role that he or she will undertake in promoting participation. In this respect we can leave aside that role where agents are merely seeking to organise people's contributions to projects or to function in a way that is more sensitive to rural people's views. If a project wishes genuinely to promote people's participation, then it must recognise that the agent's role must be a distinctive and substantial aspect of project activities. In this respect the agent's role is essentially both to create the conditions whereby people can begin to get involved in development and also to relate to and have some influence on the activities before they begin. This is the key aspect of the agent's role; if it is undertaken in any other way the agent will end up basically trying to accommodate rural people within existing projects.

---

[9] Two detailed attempts to spell out the function and role of change agents in a supposedly participatory form of development have been FAO studies; see FAO: *Small farmers' development manual*, Vols. 1 and 2 (Bangkok, 1979); B. Van Heck: *Training of group promoters in field projects of the People's Participation Programme* (Rome, FAO, 1983); also R. Charlick: *Animation rural revisited* (Ithaca, New York, Cornell University, 1984) for an examination of the animator in developing local participation in West Africa.

This role has led the project agent to be variously described as an educator, catalyst, facilitator, broker, intermediary or activist, and this broad range of terms does reflect the diffuseness of the agent's role and the difficulties of encapsulating it within commonly understood parameters. A review of participatory projects suggests the following as the major dimensions of the project agent's role:[10]

Animation: A process of assisting rural people to develop their own intellectual capacities, that is, to stimulate their critical awareness; this critical awareness enables rural people to examine and explain issues in their own words and, as a result, to realise what they can do to bring about change.

Structuring: The development of internal cohesion and solidarity among rural people, and of some form of structure or organisation which can help bring the people together and serve as the forum for their continued involvement.

Facilitation: A service role which assists rural people to undertake specific actions designed to strengthen their participation; these actions can include the acquiring of particular technical skills, gaining access to available resources or translating their own ideas into feasible projects.

Intermediary: To serve, in the initial stages, as a go-between in relation to other external services or forces; to help establish contacts with existing services and introduce rural people to the procedures and mechanisms for dealing with these services.

Linking: To help develop links between rural people in similar contexts and facing similar problems; this linking at district and regional level creates a wider base of support for participation.

Withdrawal: A progressive redundancy, whereby the agent consciously withdraws from a direct role with the people and increasingly encourages them to undertake and manage the projects in which they are involved.

The above is a synthesis of a considerable amount of project and other documentation and reflects the major dimensions of the agent's role in participation which have currently emerged from the practice. Essentially, agents seek to work with rural people and not for them, which is a major reversal of conventional practice. Similarly, they seek to support as opposed to direct rural people and their activities; and critically they seek to make themselves dispensable and encourage rural people fully to assume active responsibility.

[10] Huizer (1983), Fugelsang and Chandler (1986), Tilakaratna (1987), Rahman (1987), Sethi (1987), Werner (1988a); and also a number of project files.

The above dimensions have major implications for everyday project practice since they fly in the face of decades of project agents' style of intervention. Where participation is no more than a greater degree of sensitivity or allowance for some limited discussion with rural people, then the project agent's role can make a few minor adjustments; but where participation is more closely linked to people's active involvement, then the above suggests a very different range of activities that project agents will have to undertake. Box 13 provides an example of the role of a project agent.

Box 13.   A project agent in the Philippines

Diwa is a 25-year-old community organiser. She has had previous experiences with a number of peasant groups in the country so that she came with some experience of working with people's organisations and movements. When she took the option to integrate herself in the community, she did this because she did not want "merely to use the residents as a training ground". Her stay at the resettlement area motivated her to continue to assist the resettled people because, like the peasant groups she had previously worked with, she saw them as "similarly oppressed". Vis-à-vis the vanguard group, Diwa perceived her role as "only to assist" the women to organise the community and to stimulate or hasten the development of the vanguard group's consciousness and resolve to confront their problems. In the course of her two-year stay, Diwa came to be viewed by the vanguard group as a "reliable partner and friend". They provided Diwa with free board and lodging and, through their economic projects, some support in her movements. However, as this was not enough, Diwa requested the Farmers' Assistance Board for additional support. Diwa then became the conduit through which the FAB and the vanguard group interacted with each other. The FAB on its part did not impose any package development model on the women. The programmes and projects in which the FAB was able to participate with the vanguard group evolved in a dialogical manner. The vanguard group conceptualises and implements their programmes, the FAB contributes the technical skills needed, and some resource to implement these projects (ILO, 1982, p. 22).

To undertake the above roles, it is argued that professional or other appropriate qualifications are not enough, but that certain qualities or characteristics are vital to the agent in participatory development. In a more general sense, references have been made to the need for such qualities as commitment, flexibility and readiness to learn from others, emotional maturity, compassion and sympathy and ability to inspire trust and confidence, which agents will need to possess for their work. Tilakaratna's work (1987) is the only detailed study we have of the agent in participatory development; his study of animators in Asia caused him to conclude that there were seven social or behavioural skills that it was important for an animator to possess:

- a scientific method of social analysis and study;

- the ability for continuous learning;

- two-way (horizontal) communications;

- facilitation;

- ability to adjust to the life and work styles of rural people;

- ability to cope with tension and conflict situations;

- ability to make himself or herself redundant to the participatory process.

The only common theme running through the project documentation studied is the assertion that the professional qualifications alone of project staff are not necessarily sufficient to promote participation in projects. And yet it could be argued that most development projects recruit staff almost entirely on this basis. The suggestions of Tilakaratna and others on the other major skills and aptitudes required for project staff to work with a process of participation raise substantial issues of project staff selection and training.

Participatory development undoubtedly demands a new type of project agent and the changes in practice will be profound. The larger government and international agency development projects are still overwhelmingly staffed by professionals whose relationship with rural people is one essentially of teacher and pupil; it is in the NGO-supported projects that a new generation of project agents is emerging. These agents are "breaking the traditional relationship of submission" that characterises the relationship between project workers and intended beneficiaries (Fals-Borda, 1988, p. 28); they are beginning to operate as "the invisible operators" (Rogers, 1988, p. 8); and they are helping to redefine the relationship between development agency and rural people. To date, however, this new kind of agent is more a feature of NGO projects than of the more substantial government projects. While these agents are assisting in the spread of their form of participatory development, particularly in the Asian sub-continent and Latin America, the challenge remains to introduce this kind of agent into existing government services and more extensively into conventional project practice. The signs are that this is occurring only to a limited extent, and there is still a long way to go before we will have large numbers of agents promoting authentic participation on a wider basis.

Project groups

Participatory development has caused a major reassessment concerning the client or target audience of project activities. While many conventional development projects still refer to "farmers", "small farmers", "rural families", "rural youth" or "rural communities" as their indiscriminate and aggregate

targets, a dominant characteristic of participatory development is its identification of discrete groups of rural people as the basic social unit for project
implementation. The Small Farmer Development Programmes, which have
sprung up in several Asian countries since 1974, organised small farmers into
groups as the basic unit for development; a resulting manual has detailed the
processes involved in establishing and working with these groups. In Latin
America, and particularly in projects in which the Catholic Church has had an
influence, the formation of base groups has been a basic method of operation.[11]
Similarly, studies by Verhagen (1985), Fuglesang and Chandler (1986), Buijs
(1982), Baldus and Ullrich (1982) all report the use of groups in participatory
projects. Conventional development projects have a package of objectives and
inputs which are directed at the rural population and those who meet the
required characteristics or resource level become the project target group;
participatory development involves a deliberate act of group identification and
formation before the project begins.

There would appear to be two basically different approaches to working
with groups in participatory development. Both of them have a series of
arguments for the use of groups and also a different approach to group
development. We can summarise these differences as follows:

Groups as social action: in which groups serve to forge social and economic
links between people and can help develop the
cohesion and solidarity which are the basis for the
groups' taking action. Groups help overcome the
impotence of individuality and also to break the
isolation that many rural people experience. In this
type of group it is important that the approach
should be a slow building up of trust and confidence,
the developing of the groups' structure and the
emergence of group members able to take responsibility for future direction.[12]

---

[11] The use of *grupos de base* (grass-roots level groups) has been a fundamental strategy of
NGO and church-supported development work in Latin America for the past 20 years. An early
study of the work of these groups based upon OXFAM-supported projects was P. Oakley and D.
Winder: "The concept and practice of rural social development: Current trends in Latin America
and India", in *Manchester Papers on Development* (Manchester, University of Manchester), No. 1,
May 1981, "Studies in rural development", pp. 1-71. See also T. Bruneau: "Brazil: The Catholic
Church and Basic Christian Communities", in D. Levine (ed.): *Religion and political conflict in
Latin America* (Chapel Hill, North Carolina, University of North Carolina Press, 1986). Bruneau
commented: "The formation of the Basic Christian Communities implies substantial change for
the Church itself as the laity assume broader roles and responsibility in many cases coming to
define the change in a decentralised and participatory format that bears little resemblance to the
hierarchical and highly structured institution it is commonly assumed to be."

[12] See, for example, S. Mainwaring: *Grassroots popular movements: Identity and
democratisation in Brazil*, Working Paper No. 84 (Notre Dame, Indiana, University of Notre
Dame, 1986).

Groups as receiving mechanisms:

in which groups serve essentially as vehicles or mechanisms for receiving inputs and technologies which the project wishes to diffuse. In these cases groups are often formed in order to increase the coverage of a particular service or to try to make more resources available to these services via group contributions. In this type of group the approach is often limited to incentives to rural people to form groups by the command of a local official. Group formation can be extremely speedy and it is not uncommon for a project to form 50-60 groups in one month.[13]

There is also a strong hint of self-help or self-reliance in such groups. These two terms are notoriously difficult to define and, while some see them as implying the abdication of government from its responsibilities to the rural poor, they do also imply groups with the abilities and skills to negotiate their own development.[14] Similarly, the deliberate formation of groups is a tactic to frustrate élite domination of development resources and as such it implicitly recognises the social and economic differentiation in rural areas. While there is, therefore, considerable similarity in the rationale for groups in project practice, we can note a distinct difference of approach which is essentially linked to the interpretation of participation. At its crudest, we could say that projects that see participation more in terms of contributions and benefits will use groups as receiving mechanisms; those that see participation as more of a qualitative process of rural people assuming more direct responsibilities will use the groups for social action. In this latter respect, Unia's (1988) study of OXFAM-supported project groups in India suggested that Social Action Groups (SAGs) shared a number of common characteristics:

- a shared analysis of the causes of poverty and underdevelopment, and a shared belief in the necessity for social change through a process of empowerment of the poor;

---

[13] In the classical examples of groups as receiving mechanisms, a common feature is that the groups are formed very quickly; and equally quickly they fall apart if the external support is not sustained. Groups established by such bodies as the Small Farmer Development Programme (Nepal), the Coffee Federation (Colombia) and the People's Participation Programme (Ghana and Sierra Leone) are all well-documented examples of groups as receiving mechanisms. See also, for example, United Nations Economic and Social Council for Asia and the Pacific (UNESCAP): *Poverty, productivity and participation* (Bangkok, 1985).

[14] J. Galtang et al. (eds.): *Self-reliance: A strategy for development* (Geneva, Institute for Development Studies, 1980); Galtang's study is still the most authoritative on a concept which is widely used but immensely difficult to define. See also R. Baldus and G. Ullrich (eds.): *Promotion of self-help organisations of the rural poor in Africa* (Bonn, FAO/DSE, 1982); and K. Verhagen: *Self-help promotion* (Netherlands, Royal Tropical Institute, 1987).

- a shared methodology of theory-practice-action-reflection;

- emphasis upon creating awareness and building people's organisations;

- a core group of between five and 20 people;

- a range of activities which include non-formal education, street theatre, leadership training and para-legal training;

- activities centred around putting forward demands for such things as drinking water, loans, tenancy rights and access to land (Unia, 1988, pp. 6-7)

The above comprehensive range of characteristics is certainly confirmed by other agencies' project documentation. Unia (1988) emphasises that while SAGs in India share the above characteristics, there is a wide variation in terms of the blend of characteristics and basic perspective. In terms of the latter, he distinguishes between three broad SAG approaches: the *issue-based approach*, where emphasis is laid upon one specific activity; the *struggle-based approach*, where the central issue revolves around the struggle to gain access to or defend a particular interest or asset; and the *organisation approach*, where the emphasis is placed upon building an organisation to serve as the base for future participation.

Whatever the perspective or approach, the use of groups in participatory development raises a number of important issues. Undoubtedly some projects merely proclaim the existence of their groups and, within months of a project beginning to operate, a whole network of groups has been formally established. This is far too hasty a procedure and runs the risk of falling foul of one or more key issues which the practice suggests influence the eventual outcome of group development:

(1) The *membership of the group*: Emphasis is laid upon the social and economic homogeneity of group members, in order to ensure a common basis of problems and issues and also to avoid potentially divisive internal contradictions; Levi and Litwin (1986) call this "ideological homogeneity". Whatever the term chosen, there is overwhelming evidence that thought must be given at the outset to the composition of the group and it should not be a process of free and uncontrolled access.

(2) The *internal structuring of the group* is critical if it is to begin to develop a particular identity and establish a basis for independent action. This structuring can take on a variety of forms and is a process which takes time. Initially the group may be no more than a loose and informal gathering; as it evolves it takes on a more formal structure. The important issue is that the structure should not be imposed from outside but allowed to develop in response to the group's interests.

(3) The *group's relationship with the external agent* is the critical axis upon which the group's development depends. Too often agents or other project staff set up and continue to direct the activities of project groups; in such cases the groups rarely develop the abilities needed to participate actively, and they merely enjoy the benefits available for the project's duration. From the beginning it is essential that the approach of the agent is to minimise the group's dependence upon his or her contributions.[15]

Work with the groups in participatory development is, of course, a more complex issue than just deciding to establish groups and assigning resources for this purpose. The case for developing groups as the basis from which previously excluded people could participate in development is strong and the practice suggests that groups which have been patiently supported and allowed to develop their own skills and abilities have succeeded in gaining access to development activities. Some pitfalls, however, do litter the way. Group development often comes up against traditional authority and other political groups within rural areas with the result that rural people are reluctant to move outside their traditional obedience and accept the responsibilities that participation implies. In such situations it would seem critical to painstakingly develop the process of participation before making material resources available in order to ensure equitable access to these resources. A highly controversial issue of group development concerns the use of incentives in the act of initial group formation. Such incentives are usually material and can involve immediate access to such things as credit, inputs or some other capital resources. The issue is whether the incentive destroys the potential for future authentic participation. In this respect the conclusion of an ILO study is apposite: "The potentially patronising effect of credit supply programmes creating small functional groups could seriously undermine the sustainability of these groups ..." (ILO, 1984, p. 6).

Incentives in one form or another have become a common feature of many participatory projects and, while they are attractive and can cause an immediate economic impact, their longer-term role in helping to develop participation is debatable. Furthermore, we should not assume that, once formed, project groups continue effortlessly to exist; regrettably the experiences of group developments which fail are numerous. A major cause of such failures relates to a sudden discontinuance of inputs or project agent's support; when this happens, many groups simply fold. Few studies exist which have monitored groups in this respect and group failures are variously attributed to internal tensions, poor leadership or a conflict of individual interests. Remarkably, group failure is often regarded with apparent disinterest

---

[15] Galjart and Buijs (1982), Levi and Litwin (1986), Verhagen (1985) and Oakley and Marsden (1984); see also ILO: *Group-based saving and credit for the rural poor* (Geneva, 1984).

by project staff who presumably, once the inputs begin to roll again, will be able to either resuscitate or form new groups.[16]

It is difficult to avoid the conclusion that groups in participatory development must be more than mere vehicles or instruments of project implementation. The use of the group approach in many development projects is, however, still limited to this function. Where the project is explicitly concerned only to increase production or some other material objective, then this particular use of groups is limited and uncomplicated; there has yet to be a major breakthrough in development projects in the use of groups for alternative objectives. On the other hand, where a project uses the group approach as an instrument to increase rural people's abilities to participate, then the processes involved are more complex and the implications for project practice more profound. Hilsum's (1983) comments on the changing purpose of women's groups in health development in the Dominican Republic aptly describes the direction of this process: "The groups are orientating themselves increasingly towards becoming a movement to demand the rights of each person which the Government should fulfill, and to impress upon the authorities that they must provide at least basic services to communities" (Hilsum, 1983, p. 129).

The organisation

Organisation is a critical dimension of the practice of participation. In its simplest terms, there is the very common argument that an organisation is vital as a mechanism by which rural people can relate or gain access to existing development services. This argument has held sway for several decades and already there is an enormous literature on different forms of rural organisations, their nature, objectives, functions and rules and procedures: this literature covers organisations such as co-operatives, rural unions, farmers' associations, credit and saving associations, and so on. For example, Esman and Uphoff's (1984) substantial study of local organisations as intermediaries in rural development takes the perspective of organisations as external constructs which have been introduced into rural areas in order to promote and sustain development. Implicit in these kinds of organisation is the assumption that they serve as a bridge, a vehicle or a receiving mechanism whereby rural people can participate in development. Our concern here is not to synthesise this vast

[16] MUCARD (Muslim Christian Agency for Rural Development) works to promote group development and vividly described the kinds of problems this work confronts: "... in the beginning the groups are on an upward curve when the members are full of enthusiasm, everything seems to be going well, policies are implemented, members are participating and there are regular meetings and training seminars. The top of the curve represents the peak of achievement when everyone is enthusiastic and membership is growing. Then the problems start to surface as credit increases, attendance at meetings lessens and seminars stop. The group starts on a downward slope. At this point it is important to stop and evaluate what is happening and where the problems are; if the group doesn't it will continue on its downward path until it either breaks up or is forced into a complete reorganisation" (Christian Aid, Philippines, 117).

literature nor to review its traditional arguments. The link between organisations and participation is widely acknowledged and agreed; in the past decade, however, there has been a reappraisal of the nature and approach of organisations if they are effectively to strengthen this process of participation. This reappraisal is linked to the emergence of participation as an alternative strategy and has had profound implications for the more traditional and highly structured approach to the promotion of organisations for rural development. In practice the link between groups and organisations is not always clear; in many instances the terms appear interchangeable. More commonly, however, organisation is seen as a stage in the evolution of a group; as groups develop so they begin to take on a more permanent form and, if they are to sustain this development, a more solid organisational basis is required. In other instances where a group with common interests forms itself relatively quickly, e.g. the landless or small-scale fishermen or women, the development of an appropriate organisation becomes a critical first step. Organisation in participatory development turns upside down the conventional approach and sees organisation as intrinsic to the process of participation and not merely as a means to facilitate project implementation. This about-turn in practice can be best illustrated by the following comparison:

Conventional rural organisation	Organisation for participation
Externally designed and directed	Based upon indigenous patterns of organisation
Functions as receiving mechanism or a means for people's contributions to projects	Organic growth of organisation
Emphasis upon strong leadership and central decisions	Spontaneous evolution
Motivated by immediate economic benefit	Members' self-management
Government supporting	Emphasis upon action linked to tackling exploitative situations
Emphasis upon management procedures and professionalisation	Redefining leadership and decision-making in order to avoid repression
Formal and legal structures	Threatening to existing structures
Large membership and representative	Small membership and participatory

The above two outlines are, of course, caricatures of two extremes and it would be hard to argue that all rural organisations are at either one extreme or the other. There are, for example, large participatory organisations and also people's organisations which seek a formal and legal structure but not with any threatening intention. The purpose of such a divisive continuum, however, is to emphasise the radically different approach to rural organisations that participatory development might imply, and to suggest what these radical changes might be. The essentially non-participatory nature of conventional organisations can be clearly seen and organisations which function on such a basis hardly succeed as vehicles for the mass of rural people to participate. The features of organisations for participation are in direct response to the inadequacies of conventional organisations. The key features of such organisations are the building, where possible, upon existing patterns of local organisation; the importance of time and allowing organisational structures to evolve; the redefining of the notion of leadership and the need for professional, external management; and the emphasis upon action to tackle issues and not the passive response to externally identified problems. Organisations for participation, therefore, arc not designed and implanted but are themselves a process which occurs over time (Constantino-David, 1983; Castillo, 1983; Rahman, 1984). Box 14 illustrates some of the aspects of building up a local organisation.

Box 14. Building up a local organisation

A cluster of disadvantaged women find it even more difficult to participate in organisations due to the difficult local gender, caste and class oppression. The Working Women's Forum (WWF) organisation therefore adopted the following strategies to ensure participation. The WWF process is a reversal in hierarchy and learning. Existing forms of co-operation, e.g. credit groups, were identified and patterned into new collectivities. Local knowledge, nuances, terminology and understanding were part of the process of local organisation. Creating a familiar atmosphere with an informal group of people and with a common issue facilitated participation. Group leaders who belong to the same socio-economic background were a major incentive for women to join the organisation. Leadership was accountable and a means of assistance (Nandini Azad, 1986, pp. 142-143).

The experience of different forms of rural organisation as a basic vehicle for people's participation was the central issue of an international symposium sponsored by the FAO and the German Foundation for International Development (DSE) in 1987. This symposium brought together policy-makers and practitioners from a range of Third World countries and based its discussions on the experiences of 13 case studies of organisations of the rural poor. The symposium identified the following as the key elements which characterise the development and growth of these organisations:

Process: Work with establishing organisations of the rural poor is a lengthy, time-consuming process. Essentially, the organisations should not be imposed but must be allowed to evolve. Similarly, an internal structure appropriate to the organisation must be allowed to emerge and not be hastened on.

External support: Such support, both from within and outside the country concerned, is critical to the eventual emergence of an authentic organisation. The external support can take on a variety of forms and roles but essentially it must support the process of organisation and not dominate it.

Problem of limited resource base: Inevitably the rural poor have limited economic resources. The initial resource base of organisations of the rural poor is, therefore, often quite low and this is a serious obstacle in terms of trying to get something done.

Education and training: The process of organisational development is essentially an educational process in which the rural poor learn about how to manage the organisation. In this respect, specific training is often required.

Inclusion of women: Organisation of the rural poor should encompass both men and women and should not seek to divide the sexes. In many countries women have a vital role in agricultural development and must not be excluded from such organisations. Indeed women can make positive contributions to the successful development of such organisations.

Linking up: Organisations of the rural poor grow stronger as they link up with similar organisations within the district or region. This linking-up promotes solidarity and gives the rural poor the chance to share experiences and knowledge. It also enables them to develop a broader base for action.

Taking action: Similarly, organisations of the rural poor grow stronger and gain in experience and confidence as they undertake actions decided by themselves. Eventually the internal development of the organisation must lead to external action, and this action is important in giving the organisation a direction.

Continual dynamic: The development of organisations of the rural poor is a continual dynamic and not a one-off activity within the time-limits of a particular programme. It is a continuous process which gains in strength as it develops and as it extends its contacts and actions into the area where it is located.[17]

Each organisation, of course, will be the product of a particular socio-economic context, the nature of the supporting agency and the level of resources available and will reflect the above lessons in its own particular way. The above is a very broad framework for understanding the development of participatory organisations but, in contrast to the manuals on the establishment of formal organisations in rural areas, the key elements represent a substantial shift in the practice. The emphasis upon such issues as education, linking-up and organisation as a continual dynamic capture the essence of participatory organisations. The role of the external agency in supporting such organisations is critical and will determine whether they achieve independence or are forever dependent upon external funds. A crucial issue also is whether such organisations eventually seek legal recognition within the existing statutory framework; there is evidence that government often seeks to impose this condition and that this is seen as an attempt at co-option.[18] Ultimately, however, participatory organisations do have to relate to the existing statutory framework and formal registration can help legitimise access to available services.

The educational process

As we have seen, effective people's participation in development cannot simply be proclaimed; it has to be developed. The task involved in asking rural people, many of whom for years have been excluded or treated as mere

---

[17] P. Oakley (ed.): *The challenge of rural poverty: How to meet it* (Bonn, FAO/DSE, 1988). The international symposium brought together representatives of international agencies, governments and NGOs around the central theme of organisations of the rural poor.

[18] This common threat of the co-option of people's organisations by government was well illustrated by a project in Peru which sought to promote women's organisations: "One of the greatest challenges at present is to maintain the independence and autonomy of the community organisations in the face of efforts to co-opt them as a base of support for the Government. Therefore great emphasis has been placed on awareness-raising and educational components of the programme" (CAFOD, Peru 118).

instruments of development projects, to seize the initiative and to participate actively in development activities is formidable. In this respect we must not be deceived when rural people flock to gain access to a development project; when there is the possibility of support from whatever source, people will seek to benefit. This is the way development has worked for years, but the dynamic too often depressingly fails as resources dry up or the immediate political objective has been achieved. In order to avoid this scenario, it is argued that participation must be seen in part as an educational process and that the demands of this process must be considered in project design. Having said this, however, it is important to distinguish between two distinct interpretations of this educational process:

- *Education as information:* Where the educational element in a participatory project consists essentially of informing people about a project and preparing them to contribute to its implementation. In this approach people are educated for a predetermined project and, although they may be consulted or given a limited voice, the education is concerned to prepare them to participate within already defined parameters.

- *Education as awareness:* Where the educational element in a participatory project is more concerned to break people's mental isolation, to reverse the deeply embedded feelings of inability and inferiority and to prepare people to explain things as they see them, to speak out, to analyse, to plan and to carry through a course of planned action. This form of education liberates people from the moulds of deference and impotence and provides the basis for their active involvement in development.

Education as information is the classical extension approach to working with rural people. Whilst in many instances this "education" manages to combine consultation with people and sensitivity to their views, with some involvement in project management, it is usually limited to project objectives and confined to the project's physical environment. Education as awareness, on the other hand, is the basic dynamic of the group and organisational development that we have seen above. In the process of participation, it is seen as the first step which ensures the basis for sustained participation. It is predicated on the argument that uneducated, resource-poor people can understand, analyse and interpret the issues which affect their development.

In development projects it would appear that there is a stronger case for education as awareness as a basic precondition for developing and sustaining participation. This case appears to be increasingly recognised and, although there is still a dominant tendency in development projects to see education for participation in largely information terms, the need for some alternative to this is now widely acknowledged. In project documentation, this educational process is referred to variously as social awareness, conscientisation, human development, people's education or popular education. Each of these terms demands its own analysis and in content they range from the highly structured, almost intellectual processes of conscientisation to the more general principles of non-formal education. The origin of education as awareness is clearly to be found in the work of Paulo Freire and the internationalisation of his practice is indisputable. Essentially, Freire argued that poor rural people, marginalised, oppressed and made dependent by an external dominance which rigidly supported the status quo, could reverse this situation by breaking the mythological barriers which enforced their marginalisation. Through an educational process in which they acted as subjects of their own development and not objects of another person's development, poor rural people could emerge and actively intervene in the forces which influenced their development.[19] It is not untrue to say that Freire's concept of an educational process of awareness has launched a thousand efforts to translate the process into a variety of contexts. The statements in box 15 are examples of this diffusion.

An analysis of the statements on education as awareness reveals a number of critical dimensions of this process. The process begins with people structuring and explaining the dynamics of their own reality; that is the social, economic and political context in which they gain a livelihood. This structuring of reality helps to develop people's critical faculty, in which they move from passively accepting the content of their reality to critically examining it and analysing its contradictions. As people's critical faculty develops, the need for reflection emerges and possible courses of action are examined. Finally, there is the taking of action by people who become fundamental elements in that action and not merely passive onlookers. The above process is a radical departure from the more conventional "education as information" approach of development projects; yet it is indispensable if an enduring basis for participation is to be constructed.

Education as awareness is linked closely in the practice with the notion of empowering. In the vocabulary which has sprung up around participation, empowering is the latest and perhaps most dynamic term to emerge. The whole purpose of awareness creation is seen as empowering rural people; that is, equipping them with the analytical and action-oriented skills necessary for them to become actively involved. Delion (1986) sees this empowering as having three major dimensions:

---

[19]The two basic texts of Paulo Freire which together describe both a philosophy and methodology of development are *Cultural action for freedom* (London, Penguin, 1970) and *Education: The practice of freedom* (London, Writers and Readers Publishing Co-operative, 1974). See also W. Smith: *The meaning of conscientização: The goal of Paulo Freire's pedagogy* (Amherst, University of Massachusetts, 1976); also *New Internationalist*, No. 16, 1974. For a critique of Freire's ideas and methodology see P. Berger: *Pyramids of sacrifice: Political ethics and social change* (New York, Basic Books, 1974).

Box 15.   Education as awareness

■ The purpose of this new education is to help people look at their own situation and begin to take responsibility for shaping their lives. Through group discussion, participants think about different aspects and problems of their lives and are encouraged to look for solutions to these problems. For example, the participants not only talk about water, but look for ways to solve this problem.

■ The most exciting aspect of this method is that the participants come to realise that they are important, that they can take responsibility for their own lives and that they can improve their own future.

■ More and more we are discovering that no one knows the reality better than the people themselves. Therefore, we continue to insist that the local people have the right and duty to design, make decisions and implement community activities that concern their own lives. This demands, however, a tremendous effort in raising the people's awareness and in empowering them to take action (CAFOD, Kenya 293).

■ The central element of a participatory process was identified as conscientisation which is seen as a process of liberating the creative initiatives of the people through a systematic process of investigation, reflection and analysis undertaken by the people themselves. People begin to understand the social reality through a process of self-inquiry and analysis, and through such understanding, perceive self-possibilities for changing that reality. People's intellectual faculties open up and their critical thought processes are liberated. In the words of a Sri Lankan peasant: "The rust in our brains is now removed." The awareness that is created has a transforming potential for, simultaneously with the understanding of the reality, the people also begin to perceive possibilities for changing that reality. Critical awareness forms the basis for organised action (Tilakaratna, Sri Lanka, 1987).

■ The process of popular education is an integral part of the activities of the project group. For example, often a discussion which began as a collective reflection on a particular page of the Bible, leads to an immediate debate to try to agree the group's participation in some activity; perhaps to show solidarity with a strike which is going on at that moment, or mobilising themselves to present demands to the Government for certain improvements or the organisation of a short drama to be presented in the community. This process of education is a continuous one of thinking, reflecting, analysing, criticising, redefining, but all done by the people themselves (Christian Aid, Brazil 53.) [20]

---

[20] The Brazil example is taken from a well-documented conscientisation project based in Sobral in the north-east of the country. The project is essentially a regional movement which has been most imaginative in its use of its team of project agents, its educational process and the instruments it employs, e.g. radio, pamphlets.

- power through greater confidence in their ability to take action success-fully;
- power in terms of the increasing relations they establish with other organisations, thus broadening their basis of operation;
- power as a result of their increasing access to the economic resources, e.g. credit and inputs, which will help their development.

Mazumdar's (1986) study of female rural workers in India placed the emphasis in the process of empowering upon employment generation and organisation which she argued were indispensable for the process to succeed. While, in terms of rural development, previous development strategies have greatly increased the power of those who are already in control of the major rural institutions and have access to the greater share of available resources, empowering the rural poor is a different process that has to be structured over a period of time. Lubett's (1987) study confirms this and shows how the success of the process is closely related to the support of external agencies. Similarly, Bhasin's (1985) study of empowering among a group of women from the Asian subcontinent showed the process as essentially an educational one in which the external agent has a key role. Finally, Werner's (1988) study in the field of health development shows how the concept of empowering has begun to extend its influence on development practice.

As a result of the practice some aspects of education as awareness, however, have come under scrutiny. Berger's (1974) seminal critique of conscientisation has influenced many who doubt the motives of outsiders and question whether rural people can ever become the subjects of a process which is "influenced" by outsiders. Fuglesang and Chandler (1986), in their major study of the Grameen Bank in Bangladesh, argue that conscientisation needs to be reassessed and they are particularly critical of those who have used it as an "intellectual construction superimposed on the problem of poverty" (p. 25). Indeed they go further and argue:

> It is not a precondition that people must be conscientised and develop skills before they can enter into a participatory process. The strength people need starts to grow from their stomach. Access to and control of a resource is the first step. All other development follows in the process. Contrary to a cherished development assumption, adult literacy (conscientisation) is not an absolute premise for change (p. 192).

While there are few who would disagree that "access to and control of resources is the first step" towards filling stomachs, it must be recognised that Fuglesang and Chandler are writing in the context of an internationally supported and well-resourced rural credit programme and that only a fraction of the rural poor have access to such programmes. Many would agree that people can begin to grow when they gain access to resources such as credit; similarly, many would see the Grameen Bank as unrepresentative of the lives of the majority and would argue that it is only as a result of a process of awareness that most rural people can even contemplate access to such institutions. Other critics point to the small scale of awareness-creation projects and are not confident that they can provide the mass basis for participation. Awareness creation takes time and this, as we have seen, is at a premium in development projects. Although there are those who rightly point to some of the intellectual obtrusiveness of conscientisation and question its relevance, there are few who challenge the view that some form of education as awareness is an important first building-block of a process of participation.

The economic base

A debatable issue in projects which seek to promote participation is the emphasis which should be given to developing the economic base of the project as a kind of springboard for the broader process of participation. Earlier participatory projects, and particularly those supported by NGOs, placed less emphasis on the economic as opposed to the educational base of these projects. As government and the big international development agencies, however, have brought their considerable resources to bear upon participation, so the issue of the economic base has received greater priority. Even though there is now a widespread recognition of the importance of the economic base in participatory projects, there is still a clear divergence of opinion on the exact purpose of this base:

- projects in which the whole participatory process is defined in terms of participation in the economic benefits of the project; in such projects there are no assumptions made about the interpretation of participation other than participation in the benefits of the project; participation, therefore, is to do with bringing previously excluded groups into contact with economic resources and assets;

- projects in which the economic base becomes a mechanism for helping to develop the broader participation process; the project's economic base is established not only to generate economic benefits, but as a focus around which other aspects of the participatory process can develop.

Proponents of the former type of project might protest that it is no different than the latter type of project. While, however, both types of project actively seek to develop the economic base of project participants, the former is essentially entrepreneurial and leaves existing forces to determine the eventual impact of the project; the latter more consciously seeks to link the availability of economic resources to the broader struggle for inclusion.

What is not in dispute, however, is the fact that the vast majority of rural people in the Third World have limited economic resources and have little opportunity to add to these resources; indeed many are threatened with the loss of the few resources they have. Rural areas are harshly differentiated between those who have and those who do not have access to productive assets, e.g. land, water and credit, and this differentiation is reinforced by the political and social privileges which accompany the ownership of such assets. The chronic poverty that the vast majority of rural people in the Third World suffer has been amply described and documented, and all explanations are grounded in the absolute lack of resources from which to begin to climb out of this poverty. In Bangladesh the Grameen Bank was established in response to lack of resources available to the rural poor:

> The economy of poverty is at the losing end of the rope despite its labour and skills. Its resource base is too narrow. Poverty is poverty because it cannot on its own overcome the inherent and chronic gap between production and consumption. Much less can it start and sustain the process of accumulation that is a premise for progress. The poor have no land or a very limited access to land. They have no access to credit or an access to credit which is highly exploitative. They are underpaid for their work and this cycle of degradation is compounded by the inadequacy of food intake which depletes their only remaining resources, their labour (Fuglesang and Chandler, 1986, pp. 27-28).

The case in general terms for developing the economic resource base of the rural poor is clearly proven and, particularly since the early 1980s, an increasing number of development projects have seen this as the important first stage of participation. More specifically, there are a number of arguments for seeing the development of the economic base as a critical element in the process of participation. First, the economic base acts as an incentive or evidence of a tangible benefit which can result from active involvement; it is argued that rural people will be more willing to become involved if they feel that some tangible benefit will eventually be forthcoming. Second, there is the link between the educational process within participation and the need for concrete action; economic activities can provide this scenario and achieve the twin objectives of developing both the resource base and confidence and solidarity among project participants. Third, there is evidence of an increasing move away from projects which concentrate solely on awareness-creation activities; such projects often lose direction, provoke frustration and lack the strong focus that an economic activity can provide. Economic activities have indeed begun to emerge as a key and tangible dimension of the promotion of participation.[21]

[21] For example, Rahman (1985) commented upon the fatigue and frustration that can often follow a long drawn-out political campaign which leads to nothing. He added: "This led to a rethinking among the NGO staff, and many started de-emphasising conscientisation work and concentrating on deliveries to raise incomes and employment of the rural poor." Action India (OXFAM, New Delhi 67) reported the same kind of issue: "To sustain any level of group activity, it is essential to organise on the basis of an economic activity but this economic activity is not the ultimate goal."

In practice we can distinguish broadly between two different approaches to the establishing of this economic base in participatory projects:

(1) Externally determined economic base

In terms of resources made available, the more dominant approach involves the designing and structuring externally of substantial programmes and projects which seek deliberately to make resources available to previously excluded rural people. Such programmes are often nation-wide and explicit in their objective to direct resources to those rural people with few economic resources. Such programmes as the SFDP (Nepal), the Grameen Bank (Bangladesh), the PPP (several African countries) and PIDER (Mexico) are well-documented examples of attempts to improve the economic base of the rural poor. They are often presented as examples of the radical reform of delivery systems and of a commitment to bring the benefits of development to those people whom other programmes had previously neglected or ignored. The main armoury of such programmes usually consists of credit or other productive inputs which are made available on favourable terms to rural people who were previously totally beyond the reach of such resources. These resources are mobilised externally, are directed at a clearly defined target group and seek to make an immediate impact. The effect is like a massive injection which is supposed to trigger a chain-reaction and result in previously excluded people building up their resource base from which to participate more actively in development. Although this type of programme does equally stress the importance of developing the organisational base for future participation and seeks to build group solidarity and commitment, there is a strong element of individual economic benefit and programme evaluation inevitably emphasises economic as opposed to other non-material results.

(2) Internally determined economic base

In contrast, there is an extremely wide range of development projects, often small and supported largely by NGOs, in which economic activities are decided internally either wholly by the project group or in discussion with the supporting agency. Such projects are usually based on such activities as crop and livestock production, irrigation water supply or group savings and credit. They are rarely plugged into existing services and are largely supported by external funding. Characteristically these projects often seek to undertake economic activities in a way which increases the resources of the group as a whole and not of a number of individuals; similarly, such projects are used to strengthen skills and knowledge relating to project management and implementation which will enable people to assume greater responsibilities in the future. Importantly also, these economic projects are used to develop the people's understanding of the economic system in which they operate so as to prepare them as and when they negotiate with the system in some future economic activity. These projects are important in themselves for the additional resources they might generate; but they are equally important in the way they mobilise rural people around a common activity and strengthen links and commitment.

Box 16.   Two types of economic base

■ The economic programmes for women were accompanied by educational activities, mainly in the form of night schools which provided a forum where women could discuss their problems, but also where they could acquire the necessary knowledge and training for their socio-economic uplift such as literacy and knowledge about food, health and child care. These programmes were based on the double strategy, namely that of combining the effort to raise women's economic status with that to raise their social, political and cultural status in society and to enable them to fight against their oppression through their own organisation. Although this double strategy seemed to be the only possible one in the given situation, it was not free of contradictions in its implementation. These contradictions are part and parcel of all economic programmes aiming at income generation based on the individual family or the individual woman. By granting loans to individual women for one of their schemes, for example for a buffalo, the general aim of the education programme, namely to strengthen women's solidarity and unity and to increase their bargaining power, was partly jeopardised. Some women were selected as beneficiaries of these schemes and others not, therefore divisions among the women were bound to arise (Bhasin, 1985, p. 84).

■ The experience of working on communal vegetable gardens has shown that such projects can be a way of tackling the lack of nutritious foods, of supporting the family budget and of confronting the constant increases in food prices. But for the participants it is above all a way of creating a consciousness that they can move forward with their own resources by means of their organisation and that, at the same time, they can give an example to the rest of the community (CAFOD, Chile 147).

Box 16 contrasts these two types of economic base in participatory projects. While there is general acceptance that the development of the economic base of the rural poor is of critical importance, there is less unanimity in terms of its role in the process of participation. Some of the larger input-oriented programmes tend to press on regardless and seem prepared to be judged solely by the economic statistics which emerge, assuming that these statistics imply increasingly widespread economic participation. Others find the mix of economic activity and the promotion of participation more problematic and are concerned with the possible outcome of the sudden availability of unbridled economic resources. These concerns tend to focus around a number of critical issues:

- The relevance of developing the economic base in all contexts and the need to relate the strategy to the demands of the particular situation; in work with the Harijans in India, for example, it was felt that the immediate needs were more political and social than strictly related to economic activities.[22]

- The need to ensure that economic activities do not detract from the equally important issue of developing the organisational base for participation; experience in the Philippines, for example, led to the basic principle that "organising should never begin with an economic project; rather economic projects should evolve from the people's own efforts during the process of organising".[23]

- Economic activities often provoke reaction from established economic forces, e.g. middlemen and moneylenders, and can often be squashed by them before they get under way; in examples in India, several project groups preferred to begin with health and education projects, which would be less likely to provoke opposition, and this gave the project group a chance to build up its strength and experience.

- Economic activities based upon individually available resource packages can be divisive and lead to tension and conflict among project beneficiaries; such activities are difficult to distribute on a totally equal basis and, as a result, can often help destroy whatever group solidarity and commitment they were supposed to create.

The relationship between economic power and the ability to participate in the benefits of development is undisputed. What is disputed, however, is how to go about this in the context of a rural development project. Simply to throw resources at the rural poor is not enough. Making these resources available is vital, but it is the manner in which they are applied and used which is more critical in terms of the overall process of participation. In this respect Bhasin's (1985) comments on the issue would appear to summarise much of the present debate:

> The poor are not going to be interested in consciousness-raising for its own sake. All consciousness-raising must lead to an improvement in their material conditions and vice versa. In fact this dichotomy between organisational work and programmes for economic development is false and misleading. The economic position of the poor can be improved by removing scarcity and exploitation and if these two tasks go on simultaneously, it is of course ideal (p. 5).

---

[22] S. Martine: "Harijans can act: An experiment in liberating education", in W. Fernandez (ed.): *People's participation in development* (New Delhi, Indian Social Institute, 1981).
[23] E. Belamide: "Building self-help groups", in *Ideas and Action* (Rome, FAO), No. 171, 1986/6, pp. 13-18.

Concluding comments

The purpose of this chapter has been to sketch the key elements which current practice suggests are fundamental to the promotion of people's participation through development projects. This is a very broad task and hence the brush used has been broad. The purpose has not been to sketch a universally applicable model, but more to provoke some thought and further analysis of conventional project practice. Participation demands a radically different approach on the lines of the elements presented. Certainly a review of current practice must conclude that participation is beginning to emerge as an identifiable, coherent and plausible strategy. But it is a struggle, and it would be wrong to suggest that practice has been turned upside-down and that a whole new genre of development projects has been born. At this moment the practice is extremely uneven. Larger, government-supported projects still see participation largely in terms of cost-sharing, project effectiveness and efficiency and maintain a narrow and short-term view of its role. NGOs, on the other hand, are usually less rigid, see participation more in terms of building people's capacities and skills and are often prepared to be innovative and experimental. Neither approach is mutually exclusive and it would be wrong to emphatically characterise both government and NGO projects in this way. But a division in the practice is beginning to emerge despite an often greater similarity in the language employed.

What is emerging clearly, however, is that participation within development projects must be seen as a distinctive process and not merely as some kind of manipulable mechanism for achieving project objectives. Whether the project is concerned with physical development or with more qualitative objectives, participation must be seen as a distinctive activity. Similarly, the process is not instant, nor can it be encapsulated in a single declaration or decision. Participation as a process evolves through a series of stages and through a combination of different elements. Ghai (1988), for example, sees this process as the key characteristic of participatory projects: "... they build gradually from what is known and familiar to progressively more complex and larger-scale activities; the capabilities of the participants grow in harmony to ensure that they are an effective control" (pp. 35-36).

Pradhan (1980) similarly concluded that projects which seek to promote participation must begin simply and then move towards more complex issues. Complex, area-wide development projects which are designed and directed by professional staff and call for people's participation are totally misconceived and, apart from those people able to share in project benefits, are meaningless in terms of developing the basis for sustained participation.

Perhaps the most unequivocal lesson to emerge from this chapter is that participation as a strategy has dramatic implications for the practice of development projects. While we may differ on the detail of style and content, few would disagree that there are certain universal characteristics of "conventional" development projects. Such projects are essentially anti-participatory: in approach, they are the complete antithesis of a participatory project and often promote participation indiscriminately with little consideration for project context, social traditions, "beneficiary" characteristics or project objectives. How to turn such projects around is the major challenge. The emerging practice to date has suggested which key elements in development projects will need to be re-examined; the more difficult task is to incorporate these elements more broadly into project practice.

5

Emerging methodologies of participation

All action should start from what the peasants are, what they know, what they can do, what they live and what they want (Six-S Association, West Africa).

Participation is not a smooth, easy or painless development process (ORAP — Zimbabwe).

There are now sufficient examples of participation in practice in development projects for us to begin to discern elements of methodology prevalent in this practice. The more substantial studies on participation inevitably paint with a broad brush and outline the kinds of strategies which we saw in Chapter 4. Project files, however, reveal further detail of this practice and give us glimpses of the actual methodological tools used to promote participation. Given that project files are notoriously cumbersome and largely oriented towards justifying expenditure, these glimpses are usually descriptive and uncritical and appear to go mostly unnoticed by the staff concerned. Few projects have conducted substantial reviews of their methodology, yet many whet the appetite with the expectation of methodological innovations which still await detailed study. In the more general literature, for example, such projects as as the Small Farmers' Development Programme (Nepal), Grameen Bank (Bangladesh), the Organisation of Rural Association for Progress (Zimbabwe), the Six-S Associations (West Africa) and PIDER (Mexico) have been the objectives of major studies and have methodologically influenced practice within their continental areas. Yet it could be argued that several of these projects have far outgrown the parameters of the "everyday" project seeking to promote participation and that their usefulness as studies is debatable. These large, relatively resource-rich projects cannot be held up as everyday examples of development projects seeking to promote participation. Their influence has mushroomed in the absence of detailed knowledge of less substantial projects. It is within the practice of these latter projects that the essence of an authentic methodology of participation is being formulated.

Research into project files reveals that methodologically participation is still largely in a period of experimentation. Commitment and social support are widespread; proven methodological tools are much rarer. In terms of the different continental areas, the evidence suggests that in very general terms participation is more "developed" methodologically in Asia and Latin America than in Africa. In particular, it is the Indian subcontinent which has the richest vein of innovative approaches; in Latin America methodology is often overwhelmed by detailed contextual analysis with more emphasis upon the correct ideological perspective and analysis than upon the mundane detail of project activities. Methodology is important to the practice of participation since, as a process, it cannot be expected to emerge, like a plant, within a fixed period of time. Just as an agronomist, in conducting a series of crop trials, will plan out and methodologically arrange his or her work over a period of time, so it could be argued that project staff responsible for promoting participation should similarly plan out and methodologically structure their work. Participation is not an objective which can be achieved by the periodic manoeuvring of project staff and resources; it must, in conjunction with local people, be carefully thought out and its development equally carefully nurtured.

Issues in the methodology of participation

Project files are full of suggestions and ideas of how best a methodology of participation might be implemented. These, however, are scattered randomly across agencies and projects and few have systematically attempted to analyse the practice and present a coherent methodological statement. The World Council of Churches (1981), Crowley (1987) and Unia (1988) have, in the context of different agencies and different projects, reflected overall on the methodology involved and have suggested a number of guiding principles. More generally, however, such principles have to be unearthed by the careful reading of project files.

Certainly the impression is created that a methodology of participation demands particular thought and is not merely abandoned to the vagaries of project practice. If we pull together, therefore, a diffuse body of ideas and thoughts, the following are the four main principles of the methodology of participation which can be culled from the project files reviewed:

- Emphasise the process of participation as opposed to immediate quantitative outcomes. Projects which promote participation must be flexible and willing to experiment and must not allow the demands of immediate, quantifiable impact to undermine or overwhelm the process of participation.

- Ensure a balance between awareness creation and economic activities since both aspects of project practice are important and indeed mutually supporting. Neither awareness with no tangible objective nor short-term tangible gain with no substantial base for longer-term participation are satisfactory recipes. Projects which over-emphasise economic activities on the assumption that these will naturally provide the base for future participation run the risk of a collapse of the process when project inputs are no longer available.

■ Build where possible upon a local base to ensure a secure and locally available foundation for future activities, as well as minimising the inevitable external dependency. This local base includes not only local people generally, but traditional leaders and local institutions, e.g. schools or clinics.

■ Maintain regular contact between the people and project staff since participation is a labour-intensive process and develops better where there is continuity. External support is fundamental to the process but it must be both reliable and regular. A process of participation can only take a hold if, in the early stages, there is this regular contact; otherwise it becomes limited to periodic responses or contributions.

The above principles, of course, overlap and are not mutually exclusive. Collectively they represent a solid point of departure for a project which seeks to promote participation. It could be argued that when projects fail to promote participation (or indeed when development projects generally fail to achieve their objectives) this failure can be traced back to the lack of a sound basis for the project's practice. Certainly there is little evidence in the files reviewed that many projects have given much thought to the above kinds of methodological principles before the project began, and a lot of evidence that failure to promote participation can be traced back to this omission.

On a more general level, there are also a number of key issues which, the practice suggests, also have an effect on the methodology of participation. Again these issues are to be found scattered throughout this practice and it appears that nobody as yet has attempted to pull them together. These issues essentially characterise the methodology of participation and begin to give it some form and shape. Methodologies of qualitative processes are often not readily apparent and need a number of key reference points before they become visible. Indeed it would appear that all too often there is little visible form to the methodology of participation and more an expectation that somehow it will happen. A number of key features which appear to give this methodology some shape and purpose include:

(1) *The systematic nature of the methodology of participation:* The methodology should not be ad hoc, reactive nor subject to impromptu manoeuvrings but should, where possible, be pursued systematically. Some projects are indeed structured to facilitate the process and pursue a course of action deliberately designed to promote it. Verhagen (1987) and Annis (1987), for example, stress the importance of a planned approach to promoting participation; the Tanzanian case study similarly shows the

importance of systematically trying to promote people's participation. Participation which is pursued in an inconsistent and entirely ad hoc manner will inevitably disappear in the maelstrom of project activities.

(2) *The pace and rhythm of the project are important :* Rahman (1989) argues that the process of participation must unfold in rhythm with the pace of the life of the people involved. If people are to participate meaningfully, then they must do so at a pace which is consistent with their livelihoods. Too often projects proceed at a pace consistent with the demands of an immediate visible impact and the people either get left behind or plunge into the accompanying frenetic activities in the hope of some eventual benefit. Participation demands a different approach:

> We are well aware that the formation of groups among marginalised people is extremely slow; it is important to go forward with patience and hope that the people will discover what they need. This does not mean that we have to adopt a passive attitude, but more that it is important to determine the moment in which to hold a training course, put a proposal forward, allow something to develop, but always in the rhythm of the people (CEBEMO, Colombia 8866).

(3) *The first contact and step :* The nature of the first contact with the people and the first step undertaken may well determine the outcome of the process of participation. The very style, approach and purpose of the first contact will set the tone not only for the ensuing relationship between the external agency and the people but also for the expected participation. All too often in project practice this first contact is hasty and cursory, and the first step is undertaken with undue speed. Approaches, for example, which nudge the people into forming groups or organisations quickly and on command and which are then followed up by promises of inputs result in a shallow base for participation which is washed away once project impetus wanes. Thought must be given to this first contact and how it should be conducted in order to avoid these misfortunes. A classical example of the importance of this first contact is exemplified in the work of an animator among fisherwomen in North-East Brazil:

> She spent the first nine months merely living in Bomtempo observing the women and being observed by them. One afternoon one of the fisherwomen stopped to speak to her after a day's fishing. This was repeated on successive days. The animator was then invited to fish with the women — her baptism in the mud — and that evening sat and chatted with a group of fisherwomen outside one of the houses. In the animator's words, she had broken the barrier and begun to establish the friendship and confidence which she felt would be indispensable for her future work (Oakley, 1981, pp. 237-238).

While it is not suggested that the animator's style is a model to be copied or is appropriate to all projects, and particularly those concerned with cost-benefit analyses of staff time, it does serve to emphasise the point. The animator's work turned out to be extremely successful; the isolation of the fisherwomen was broken, their formal registration in the government-sponsored fishing colony was recognised, the original group spawned a whole network of other fisherwomen's groups, the women became active in the fishing colony and, five years after the process began, one of the women was a candidate for the Presidency of the colony. The animator always insisted that it was the women's process and that her most difficult decision had been how to make initial contact and suggest a first step.

(4) *A team approach to methodology:* A common feature of many projects which promote participation is the presence of a project team which serves as the basic dynamic of the project's development. Unfortunately, however, there is usually little discussion of the team or cadre as a specific element in the methodology or of how the team approach is beneficial to the process. De Silva (1983) and Bhasin (1985) have both presented accounts of the workings of a team in the broad process of awareness creation, and there is a general assumption in the practice that a team approach has distinct advantages. Projects such as the Mobile Orientation and Training Team – MOTT (India), the Pastoral Team in Negombo (Sri Lanka: CEBEMO), the Agricultural Development and Training Society – ADATS (India: Novib) and the FASE Team (Brazil: Christian Aid) are all examples of the use of teams in the process of participation. Such teams are usually multi-disciplinary, with a combination of both technical and social science backgrounds to reflect the twin pillars of the process. They are also usually highly mobile, spend most of their time in the field and can be mutually supportive. Given the complexity of a process of participation and the fact that in its initial stages at least it is labour intensive, a team approach has obvious advantages over the lone and often isolated field worker. Participation is essentially a dynamic which energises project activities and such energy can often best be generated by the collective actions of a team. Equally, a team allows both for the sharing of experiences and for the mobilisation of resources when the occasion arises. Although, therefore, there has been little systematic study of the team as a basic tool of the methodology of participation, the practice suggests that the team approach is widely used and seen as the best way of structuring the support which project agents can give. Box 17 gives an example of the work of a project team.

The above range of principles and key issues have been squeezed out of documentation which is heavy on description but less rewarding on those important characteristics of the methodology of participation. Several of the principles and issues are, of course, relevant to development projects across the board and their absence can account for project failure. With projects which seek to promote participation, however, they are more crucial since the processes involved are more complex and the outcomes less predictable.

> **Box 17. The project team**
>
> When we started work in Negombo, I never thought in terms of a team or of a centre. When the workload increased I got a person to help me and that was the beginning of the team. Gradually over the years as a number of groups emerged, the services of more hands were necessary. Thus we now have four full-timers and three volunteers. The methodology of the team is the action and reflexion method. The assignments for team members do not come from the top or from a director. This is done in the spirit of sharing and every effort is made not to make our centre an institution. As the workload of the team increases, this tendency is there but team members are aware of the danger. We have a weekly evaluation session on a Tuesday at which we discover our successes and our failures (CEBEMO: Sri Lanka).

Certainly, without such basic principles, the methodology will lack form or purpose.

The stages of a methodology of participation

One of the more difficult tasks in a review of project practice is to identify clearly the methodology used in the implementation of participation. Indeed it must be said at the very beginning that in many of the projects reviewed no distinctive methodology was discernible other than the range of activities associated with conventional project planning, e.g. identification of problems, analysis, project planning, implementation and evaluation. In many projects participation has become just another factor to be built into overall planning and, apart from the allocation of time and certain human resources to this activity, it merits little particular attention. It could be argued, however, that participation is more than just another project ingredient, that it is a process which should be central to the project's evolution and that methodologically it merits particular attention. We have already seen that participation does not occur overnight; it evolves over a period of time and in relation to a particular interpretation. Participation can, therefore, be understood as a *process* divided into a series of *stages*; equally the methodology involved would consist of a series of stages towards an ultimate state or objective. Galjart's (1987) review, for example, of the practice of a range of participatory development projects suggested the following distinctive stages in the process:

- Promotion — mobilisation.
- First action.
- Expansion.
- Stabilisation.

At each of the above stages a series of different activities takes place. Each stage is important since each contributes to the implementation of the process of participation. The implementation of participation, Galjart concluded, is a protracted, step-by-step affair which can spread over a period of six to ten years; it is not a one-off event but a series of unfolding stages.

Several writers and projects have sought to take matters one stage further and have examined the methodology of participation also as a series of stages. Oakley and Winder (1981), Castillo (1983), Rahman (1984), Uphoff (1987) and Verhagen (1985), have all contributed to this exercise from different contexts but from similar perspectives. This perspective seeks to understand participation over a period of time and to identify the key methodological elements or stages of this process. Many of the projects reviewed and several of the case studies (Ghana, Lesotho, Mexico), however, take a different perspective which results in a different understanding both of the methodology and of its stages. Indeed if we examine the wide range of both literature and project files reviewed in terms of the stages of a methodology of participation, we could distinguish three distinct approaches. The borderlines between these three approaches have been arbitrarily drawn for the purposes of breaking down an extremely amorphous body of practice, but the exercise is valid in that it highlights how different interpretations of participation lead to different methodologies of implementation. The three approaches to methodology can be summarised as follows:

(1) *Projects which methodologically follow a conventional project planning cycle and seek to make it more participatory:* In these types of projects, which are numerically substantial, a distinctive methodology of participation is difficult to pinpoint, largely because it is basically non-existent. Where it can be said to exist is in terms of attempts to make the project planning cycle more sensitive to people, consultative and less an entirely top-down process. In such projects participation is predominantly defined in terms of participation in benefits. This interpretation does not imply any radical re-thinking of project methodology but more an emphasis upon greater project coverage and the incorporation of more people into the ambit of project activities. A review, for example, of a number of UNIFEM projects suggested the following methodological approach:

- Group together a number of women around a production activity.
- Injection of capital resources, e.g. loans.
- Structuring of group to assume formal status, e.g. co-operative.
- Link up group with existing banks or other sources.
- Participation of women in development.

The above methodology, of course, is not explicit in UNIFEM-supported projects but has been deduced from a review of these projects. It is essentially a conventional project approach directed exclusively at women and sees women's participation in terms of their ability to build an economic base. In this sense the methodology has been highly successful but it appears to be limited to ensuring that the project is women oriented. A considerable number of development projects, therefore, have no distinctive methodology of participation other than minor adaptations to conventional project planning either to direct project activities to a particular group or to mitigate the worse excesses of top-down project implementation.

(2) *Projects which methodologically seek to involve people in externally managed development projects:* A number of the case studies fall into this category, e.g. Ghana, Lesotho, Mexico and the United Republic of Tanzania. In these projects methodology is more explicit although still often difficult to disentangle from conventional project practice. Quite clearly, participation is seen as more than the mere enjoyment of eventual tangible benefits and, from the beginning, the projects consciously think of how to get the people involved. In many instances the mechanism employed is some form of organisation; in others the role of the project agent is extended to include the promotion and development of people's awareness and, correspondingly, their greater involvement. The methodology of participation in these kinds of projects is illustrated by the two examples in box 18.

Box 18.   Stages in type (2) methodology of participation

Training of catalysts (development officers)	Survey of village health needs
Conscientisation and awareness creation	Village-level health education seminars
Group formation	Health training for village leaders
Provision of support for group activities	Building up community understanding of health problems
Assistance for proper functioning of groups	Villagers decide upon action projects
Involvement of groups in planning of project activities	Villagers organise own health education-action programme
Involvement in monitoring and evaluation (United Nations, ESCAP, 1985, pp. 115-117)	(CEBEMO: Sri Lanka)

In the above the thrust of the methodology is to mobilise the people in support of some externally determined policy or line of action and it is not normally seen as a one-off action. The methodology is projected over a period of time, a number of sequential stages are clearly identified and there is an explicit emphasis upon building the people into the project. Activities undertaken are usually physical in nature; where education is mentioned it is usually in terms of knowledge of project policy and activities, and there is little overt move to project the people's involvement outside these parameters. The project proceeds on a predictable course and the ultimate stage of the methodology corresponds with the achieving of project objectives.

(3) *Projects which seek to promote a base for continuing people's participation:* It is in this category of projects that a more distinct and innovative methodology of participation can be seen. These projects seek to develop a base among people and set out to do this over a period of time. As a result the methodology unfolds and responds to the different stages of the process. Of the case studies Nijera Kori and SARILAKAS are clearly in this mould, while it could be argued that the PPP in Ghana was moving in this direction. There is currently a whole new kind of development project, particularly in the non-governmental sector, which is experimenting with this methodology of participation. In many instances the methodology is not explicit and one has to dig deep into project records; but there is no doubting its increasing influence. These projects constitute a very broad church and at times employ a confusing array of terms, but there is also a common perception of the methodology which derives from a common understanding of participation. The illustration in box 19 is a composite of the stages of this methodology taken from over 50 development projects. As it is impossible at any stage in the methodology to find a common term to characterise or describe that stage, a range of the terms used by the projects is included.

Box 19.   Stages in type (3) methodology of participation

Entry — Observation — Initial contact — Exposure to village life — Identification of project group

Problem analysis — Mobilisation for self-analysis — Orientation to village context — Context diagnosis

Development and strengthening of people's structures — Setting up co-ordination mechanisms — Emergence of appropriate organisation

Preparation — Awareness creation — Animation — Leadership training — Identification of internal cadres — Briefing

Progressive advance on key issues — Group action — Making outside contacts — Programme management — Doing something concrete

Linking up — Replication — Building alliances — Articulation — Outside support — Expansion

Stabilisation — Establishing base — Autonomy — Functioning alone

---

It must be stressed that the purpose of the above breakdown is to illustrate as comprehensively as possible the kinds of stages involved in a methodology of participation, and accordingly as a framework it is both undisciplined and sprawling. However, it does confirm the range of terms employed. Furthermore, on closer examination it contains a certain coherence, in that as a methodology it has both a starting-point and a finishing-point and a series of intermediate stages. The framework is evidence that projects are not merely proclaiming participation or building it into existing procedures where they can, but are consciously projecting the participation over time and determining methodologically how best to achieve it. One obvious conclusion from the above is that there is no one methodology, but a framework of key stages which should be adapted according to the context. The above framework does, however, suggest a certain sequence of key stages and also that the different stages are equally important in the overall methodology. Many of the terms and expressions, of course, demand further explanation since as simple terms their meanings are not all entirely explicit, but collectively and even in their jumbled fashion they do suggest the key stages in the methodology of participation. In project files much of this is buried under the greater weight of other documentation and indeed few files consciously seek to understand or highlight the project's methodology. One of the problems is that few of the projects have been studied in great detail; furthermore, this kind of methodology is often more in the heads of the people involved than in written form. The evidence of the above examples, however, suggests that a distinctive methodology has clearly emerged, albeit in unwieldy form, and that in different contexts people are experimenting and seeking to develop a process of participation as a series of stages over a period of time (box 20).

While a general conclusion must be that a great many development projects pay little particular attention to the methodology of participation but prefer either to incorporate it into existing project practice or, at the most, devise a few basic mechanisms to facilitate it, there are encouraging signs that elsewhere considerable thought and effort are going into devising appropriate methodologies to consolidate the process. The distinction to be drawn is between projects which see participation merely as an ingredient and methodologically develop it with one-off mechanisms (e.g. a forestry or irrigation management committee), and those which see the participation as a process and project its methodology over a series of stages. This latter approach is the more authentic and fortunately a body of knowledge is now being built up on its implementation. Indeed, such is the widespread impact of this authentic methodology, particularly among NGOs, that a distinctive trend can now be observed. Whereas ten years ago such projects generally worked backwards in terms of explaining their methodology, and indeed largely devised their methodologies as they went along, now we can note that experience has been gained and projects are embarking upon a carefully thought-out methodology

---

Box 20.   Distinctive methodologies of participation

Survey of possibilities and scope of work

Identify issues for campaign

Workshops on consciousness raising

Identify leadership

Develop educational material

Link up with other organisations

Link up with issues of national importance

(OXFAM: India: DEL67)

Mobilisation for self-analysis

Facilitation of group action

Identification of internal cadres

Forging links among organised groups

Progressive advance

(PIDA: Sri Lanka)

Analysis of the context of the groups involved

Local contacts and visits

Reflection and analysis

Structuring of organisation

Integration with local association

(CAFOD: Brazil 190)

Coming together

Forming a nucleus

Beginning an activity

Consolidation

Self-reliance

Transfer of power

Sovereignty

(CWDS: India)

Build up the organisation of the women's groups

Analysis of socio-economic reality of women's groups

Development of critical consciousness

Formation of new women's leaders

Develop links of solidarity with other sectors

Active involvement in the District Federation of Women's Groups

(CAFOD: Peru 118)

---

from the beginning. This is a major advance and suggests that the networking between these projects, even at an intercontinental level, functions well and experiences in one context have influenced projects in others.

The lesson to be drawn and vigorously re-emphasised is that to implement a process of participation demands a carefully thought-out methodology which projects the process over a period of time (box 21). The examples we have noted fully support this contention. The starting-point is the first contact or entry and the finishing-point is a group of people with the basis and conditions for active participation. Development projects must pursue this process methodically and both structure their interventions and staff their activities accordingly; the alternative is ad hoc adjustments to existing practice.

Box 21. Stages in the methodology of community organisation (CO)

(1) CO usually starts with a pair or group of trained organisers entering a community in response to perceived problems there. They may be invited by local people or engaged by groups interested in enhancing people's ability to share in decision-making and resources.

(2) The organiser starts with groundwork or legwork. This is a process of going around the community on foot and talking to small groups or individuals about problems and issues in the community. This one-to-one series of consciousness-raising dialogues can sometimes take weeks.

(3) When the organiser feels with some of the people that it is time to begin bringing larger groups of people together, his conversations begin to focus on specific issues and suggest specific actions such as the holding of a meeting to discuss light and water issues.

(4) When the meeting actually takes place, part of the organiser's role will be to help the group identify the target person to be confronted. This person takes the role of the "enemy" in this strategising process. It is much easier to get people emotional over a person than an abstract institution.

(5) Once people have decided what action to take, one that probably entails confrontation of some persons in authority, the organiser teaches them how to role play (rehearse) the impending meeting.
The experience of being part of a mass confrontation has the effect of erasing ordinary people's fear of conflict ... Tactically people never request or ask for something; they demand it.

(6) The object of mobilisation is to win victory, that is, to attain the goal demanded. The action has to be something manageable that stands a good chance of success. People insist calmly until they get their way.

(7) The next step calls for people, leaders and organisers to return to their communities and engage in group reflection sessions to analyse their tactics and outcomes.

(8) The group is not formalised by electing leaders or drawing up a constitution and by-laws, although formal organisation is an important part of the CO process. They wait until the group feels strong and united after a series of actions (Castillo, 1983, pp. 488-489).

Instruments of a methodology of participation

Any methodology of development intervention requires appropriate instruments for its implementation. Such instruments are the mechanisms whereby the stages of the methodology can be successfully completed. In the case studies, for example, we can see a range of conventional instruments used to implement the methodology: various forms of communication to advise

---

people of the approach and purpose of a particular project; local committees to represent people's interests; key individuals or informants who are trained and then expected to give a lead; incentives such as credit to encourage people to get involved; public meetings to advise people generally of a particular issue, and so on. Such instruments are conventional in the sense that they are commonly used across the spectrum of development projects and, furthermore, they are closely associated with an approach to participation that seeks to get people to contribute to existing development initiatives rather than to redefine these initiatives and give people a central role in the practice. If, however, we examine some of those projects that seek to develop a sustainable base for continuing participation, we can see a number of novel instruments being employed. References to this innovative practice are scattered and there is no universally applicable set of instruments; but there is a consistency in the broad nature and purpose of the instruments and also in the manner in which they are employed. We present here a synthesis of the range of instruments found in the project files.

Economic or physical activities

Implicit in many of the project files is the overall notion that economic or physical activities undertaken by the project group are important not only because of immediate tangible benefit but, more importantly, because they serve as a means to build up and strengthen the future base for participation. Production projects, therefore, are not just useful for the targets they might achieve but also for the ways in which they help develop group cohesion, solidarity and organisational skills. Much of the recent project support work of UNIFEM, for example, follows the above formula; direct support to economically productive projects which result not only in tangible gain but also in increased women's consciousness and solidarity. As a result such activities are not judged solely in economic terms, but equally on their broader qualitative effect. Criteria such as "efficiency", therefore, are not over-emphasised; "effectiveness" and "relevance" are more important. While it would be wrong to suggest that such economic activities are undertaken in a casual or undisciplined manner, there is a willingness to experiment and to take risks. More clearly, however, there is a tendency to see economic activities are part of a larger overall process and to encourage people widely to begin to undertake such activities in order to promote their involvement in this larger process. A small market garden project in Chile sums up this approach:

> The experience of working in communal vegetable gardens has shown that, although not perfect, this can be a good way to tackle food shortage, to provide additional income for the family budget and to act as a kind of therapy to help overcome family tension. Most of all, however, these projects are a way of developing a consciousness among the participants that they can do something and that through organisation they can achieve some improvements in their lives (CAFOD, Chile 147).

Project group meetings and discussions

A critical instrument in the process of participation is the regular meeting of and discussion between those involved in the process. These two instruments constitute a basic dynamic in the whole process and are indispensable to developing a continuing base for people's participation. However, it is important to emphasise that we are not talking about the more traditional kind of farmers' or village meetings which are a common feature of, for example, community development and agricultural extension work. These are not meetings and discussions merely to communicate existing policy or information about a particular programme, or indeed to tell people how to participate or to adopt some new technological practice. Such meetings and discussions are commonplace but essentially communicate things to people and see them as potential contributors to an already agreed programme; the project staff talk and the people listen, the project staff decide and the people comply, the project staff execute and the people contribute.

Meetings and discussions in a process of authentic participation are very different. The basic purpose of the meetings is to help develop the process of participation, and as such they have a character of their own. The meetings essentially function as a forum to get people involved; to help create awareness of issues and, subsequently, solutions; to serve as a basis for a future, more formal structure and to help build solidarity, cohesion and unity of action. The meetings, therefore, are not merely arenas for debate but, in the context of the Freirian praxis, also vehicles for the taking of action. Box 22 gives a number of examples of descriptions of meetings taken from projects reviewed.

The above kinds of meeting are essentially the interface between group members and project staff but conducted on the basis of an equal partnership. The meetings are also conducted in the language of the people and at a pace and style which is appropriate to their livelihoods. They are often characterised by their open-endedness and, at times, apparent lack of structure; this is deliberate so as to ensure that they never become dominated by the outside agent. Indeed, they are meetings at which the people can air their views and begin to break down centuries of enforced silence. The very nature of these meetings has powerful implications for the normal practice of field staff who in conventional project practice would expect to both direct and control project meetings. Project staff attend such meetings as partners and facilitators and must not undermine the processes involved by assuming a too interventionist role. Meetings are held regularly in order to maintain the dynamic and they become a regular feature of project development; Galjart and Buijs (1982) reported 12 meetings in a four-month period in Sri Lanka and eight in three months in Thailand. Meetings are, however, influenced by the demands of people's livelihoods, with a greater frequency in the agricultural off-season. It would

---

Box 22.   Examples of project group meetings and discussions

These intense discussions among the farmers of the zone are supported by animateurs from the project. In these discussions all contribute to sketching out the broad framework of a simple organisation, which will serve as the foundation for efficient and united groups. Furthermore, the question of the division of responsibilities in the group is discussed and together the group's main problems and aspirations are identified (OXFAM: CHD 41).

The meetings tended to last until midnight as members passionately debated thorny issues. Everyone took part, even the cook who voiced strong opinions not only about the kitchen but the whole range of services in Sapecho. Participants clearly stood on an equal footing. The level of interest and patience people displayed trying to build solutions through consensus was amazing (Healey, 1988, p. 34).

A *Jajam* is the monthly meeting of the Sathins, organised by them at the village level. It is a platform for exchanging and sharing their work experience. For the village women, the *Jajam* is a place where they can openly talk about their problems, think of alternatives and reflect on their present position. It is also a festive event for them, with everyone joining in the singing and dancing which last sometimes until the early hours of the next morning (Mathur, 1984).

A lot of people began to get together and meet, many more than in the time of Lula, and they discussed matters to do with agriculture and the marketing of their crops. João and others went to meet with other peasants to see in what way they could strengthen the movement. The Patron heard about this new regime and didn't like it. Recently he assaulted João with a revolver saying that he didn't like those meetings and that João was putting ideas into the people's heads. Some 30 men and women later went and reported the Patron to the police station (Christian Aid: Brazil 13).

---

appear that the content of the discussions at these meetings can be wide-ranging. However, although practical issues relating to project implementation regularly arise, issues of a more political or economic nature, and their discussion help to build the solidarity and propose the ideas for action to tackle such issues (box 23).

Workshops, seminars or camps

The above three terms cover a wide range of activities which share a number of common characteristics. The terms are somewhat synonymous and can be grouped together as a particular instrument of the methodology of participation. (For reasons of simplicity we shall use the term "workshop" to include each of the three activities.) Workshops, of course, are not uncommon in development practice and are used as a forum for formal training and

---

Box 23. Building a community

Community means primary groups associated because of class or territorial proximity. In these groups the people meet, exchange ideas and support one another. The groups offer their members the possibility to interact, discuss and in fact become communities. The members speak in their own words, using their own terms to express their own ideas and interests. By so doing they eliminate the need for spokesmen with different class and educational backgrounds who have traditionally represented the people. Following from this and because of the focus by the members on their own interests expressed in their own words, the possibility for critical reflection on their environment is encouraged, which in turn may lead to an understanding of the deeper causes of poverty and inequality. In short community means interaction, equality and opportunity within the group and the possibility to grow in a collective consciousness (Bruneau, 1986, p. 117).

---

knowledge transfer; in this approach they are essentially teaching aids and the means by which a new skill or idea can be explained and, it is hoped, accepted by participants. In such workshops the relationship between the "teacher" and the "pupil" is clearly demarcated and is characterised by a transference of knowledge from one to the other. Workshops within a process of participation, however, function on the basis of a different set of premises:

– the rejection of any hierarchical or authoritarian relationship between the teacher/agent and the uneducated or ignorant pupil/person;

– the linking of theory with practice and the relating of the theoretical content of the workshop to the everyday lives of the participants;

– the absence of predetermined answers or pre-established theories which suggest immediate and facile solutions to problems;

– the structuring of the content and the outcomes of the workshops by the participants themselves on the basis of their experience and lessons learnt from that experience.[1]

In some projects workshops appear to achieve a recognisable level of organisation and sophistication and are deliberately orchestrated to achieve a

---

[1] The workshops, seminars and camps are pedagogic tools and in their practice have clearly been influenced by Paulo Freire's ideas on education. In particular, these pedagogic tools are seen as the antithesis to what Freire calls "the banking system of education"; Freire (1972 and 1973). Freire characterised this banking system of education as follows:
The teacher teaches and the students are taught.
The teacher knows everything and the students know nothing.
The teacher talks and the students listen.
The teacher chooses and enforces his choice, and the students comply.
The teacher is the subject of the learning process, and the students are the objects.
See also Institut action culturelle (IDAC): "The workshop as a moment in a process of political education", in K. Bhasin and R Vimala (eds.): *Readings on poverty, politics and development* (Rome, FAO, 1980), pp. 237-242.

---

high level of consciousness; more commonly, however, they are loosely organised, open-ended and essentially geared to arousing interest and establishing some basis for participation.[2] The workshops are basically educational in the broadest sense and seen as an appropriate forum in which adults can explore issues and contribute explanations from their own experiences. While the approach and content may differ in degree, however, there appears to be a common focus in workshop practice. Most workshops seek to combine three elements:

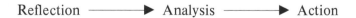

Reflection ⟶ Analysis ⟶ Action

In some workshops this process is followed in the context of a particular tangible activity which the project group is planning to undertake, e.g. access to credit for agricultural productivity; in most, however, the reflection takes place in the social, political and economic context of participants and the rest of the process unfolds accordingly. The purpose of these workshops can be seen in the examples in box 24.

Box 24.   Workshops as an instrument of participation

The Awareness Generation Camps will be a platform for the rural women to come together, exchange their experiences and ideas and, in the process, develop an understanding of the reality and also of ways to tackle their problems and fulfill their needs. The Camps will necessarily be different from formal training programmes in so far as the outsider's role will be mainly restricted to that of an enabler or facilitator. The content of the discussion, which will be the main method of communication, will be left open and finalised on the basis of the local situation (Mathur, 1984, p. 1).

The *Shivir* (workshop) can be viewed as a forum for continuing education. It is not an exclusive closed door activity, but rather an opening out and a sharing of knowledge. It implies an acceptance of different idioms and attitudes, a seeking of their convergence in solving jointly defined or stated problems ... *Shivir* is primarily built around a problem which is a common concern of all the participants at a particular time. It has emerged as an intensive exercise in the village for a period of three to four days. Its interaction aims at systematically understanding the various facets of the problem and arriving at a common perspective (Jain et al., 1988, p. 20).

---

[2] A detailed account of a workshop as an instrument of a process of participation can be found in Centre for Women's Development Studies: *The seeds of change: Role of grass roots rural women's organisations in development* (New Delhi, 1986). This is an extensive account of a workshop held over five days in West Bengal for female grass-roots workers. See also Rahman (undated) and Bhasin (1985).

Most workshops seem to function over a two-to-three day period and the numbers attending can range from 20 to 50. Camps tend to be more substantial activities and can last a week, with up to 100 participants. While the characteristics may vary, there is a common purpose and focus to these workshops; they serve not merely to gain the acquiescence of passive participants but to stimulate, provoke and encourage active participation. Workshops generally function around a number of predetermined themes – *sharing of experiences, approaches to development, analysis of participants' situation* – and these are often mapped out in the form of a programme, but the structures are not rigid and alternatives are permitted. Most importantly, the workshops seek to break the years of silence which have engulfed the lives of many and create an atmosphere in which people feel at ease and are willing to get involved. Workshops also foster solidarity and strengthen group links; the sharing of views develops consensus and eventual commitment to a solution. Most of all, workshops generate a feeling of involvement and a sense that not only is change necessary but also that the people can make it possible. The workshop in a whole variety of guises, and particularly in Asia and Latin America, has become an indispensable instrument for breaking the isolation of the excluded and for building both the structural and psychological basis for future participation (box 25).[3]

Box 25. A women's workshop

In evaluating the experience of this [workshop], it can be said that its main significance was in the fact that it provided a forum for women from different villages to come together, to exchange their experiences and to enjoy their own cultural productions. The women siezed this opportunity for recreation and inspiration with gusto. It was this enthusiasm which encouraged them to demand more such workshops. The experience also taught us that poor peasant women are by no means satisfied with an improvement of their economic situation, but that they also struggle for their human emancipation, for the restoration of their human dignity and creativity. They do not want to be mere objects of development and teaching (Bhasin, 1985, p. 88).

Popular theatre and song

Across the continents there is evidence of an increasing use of different forms of popular theatre and song as instruments of a methodology of

---

[3] An interesting account of the use of the workshop in participatory development in Asia can be found in ILO: *Promoting people's participation and self-reliance* (Geneva, 1988). This is an account not only of a workshop held for project agents but also includes a number of examples of how these agents have used the workshop at local level in their respective countries.

participation. Drama and song, of course, are indigenous to the peoples of these continents and the emerging forms are, in many instances, building upon traditional practices. Popular theatre, folk theatre, visual arts, village drama and folk media are a range of terms which characterise this phenomenon and, particularly since the late 1960s, have been increasingly used as tools to promote development.[4] Popular theatre in a process of participation essentially builds upon the cultural and historical basis of drama and song in people's lives and employs the language and phenomena of these lives. It seeks both to explain current issues and to identify and clarify crucial problems; it is essentially an animated situation and a kind of continuous discussion in action. Kidd (1982) has been one of the more powerful protagonists of the use of theatre to break people's isolation and has argued that it –

> ... provides a means of building consciousness, mobilising people for action, engaging in struggle and reflecting on the struggle. It is the people's medium, drawing on their skills and creativity and expressing their concerns and analysis; as something that people are good at, it reinforces the growth of identity and self-confidence (Kidd, 1982, p. 10).

Popular theatre, however, is not merely an opportunity simply for people to get their grievances or frustrations off their chests: it essentially challenges people to look critically at their situation and to change it. A review of project documentation and literature suggests the following broad uses of popular theatre:

- a way of recovering, reviving and advancing people's own culture and history;
- a forum for popular education, bringing people together and building a spirit of solidarity;
- a medium controlled by the people for expressing their ideas, their views and their concerns in a context where other forms of expression and media are controlled by others;
- an experience of participation and interaction which helps people overcome their fears, and develop their own identity and self-confidence;
- a means of organising and politicising people and of drawing them into people's movements and organisations.

Essentially in the mid-1970s popular theatre changed from being theatre for the people and became theatre by the people, which both changed the nature of the piece of drama and of the role that people played in it. While most projects which use theatre as an instrument of their methodology have a

---

[4]While there are a number of short case studies of popular theatre to be found in project files and other literature, it is important to go back to the earlier debate and examine the central concept of popular theatre as a tool for local development. See, for example, R. Kidd: *People's theatre, adult education and social change in the Third World* (Toronto, International Council for Adult Education/German Foundation for International Development, 1981) for a substantial discussion of the central concept.

cadre of actors or a theatre group to give direction to activities, theatre by the people has people as the performers. This way people have an opportunity to do their own thinking, control their own learning process and base the experience on their own immediate context. Plays, therefore, are not always presented as static, finished products but are often open-ended and left to evolve as people's views emerge.

The people, therefore, are actors and have a direct and active role in the unfolding of the drama. The people also construct the sets and serve as the stage managers; they organise the event, with the support of the theatre group, and this organising develops useful skills. Indeed the process of creating a play is just as useful as the final product and is itself a learning experience. Plays cover a whole range of issues: land rights, access to water, the behaviour of local officials, food prices, input supply, and so on. They do not deal only with the details or symptoms of such issues but more importantly probe for explanations. Similarly, plays have two dimensions; the analysis and explanation of the issue and possible courses of action. One project in the United Republic of Tanzania used drama to highlight relationships between government officials and the people:

> The play involved two Community Development Officers (CDO). The first CDO is domineering and authoritarian. He goes to a community and without listening to their problems, he tells them what projects the Government has decided for them and what they are required to do. The second CDO goes to the community and patiently listens to the various problems people have. He then eventually advises them to call a meeting and discuss the problems they have raised. During the meeting they prioritise their problems and agree what is the most pressing and discuss it in detail. Eventually they agree on what they will do to solve that problem (OXFAM: Tanzania 249).

The method of work is participatory; the plays are often born of discussion and improvisation of situations put forward by the people themselves. Plays are also a unifying force and will often serve as the focus to bring together people within a particular area around a common issue.

Clearly, popular theatre can have a most useful role in developing a process of participation. It can release creative energies and give people a direct involvement in explaining situations and proposing solutions; actions which constitute a major step forward in the lives of many people. If popular theatre, however, is controlled externally and used to try to persuade people to undertake a course of action, it is less successful. The people's direct involvement in the whole process is the key to its authenticity, and this involvement serves to break the barriers of exclusion. Similarly, popular theatre is basically a catalyst; as a mere spectacle its utility in promoting participation is questionable. Essentially it must be seen as an instrument linked both to an organisation and to the development of organisational skills, which jointly will form a solid bedrock for participation. Popular theatre must be linked to action, and this action is a manifestation of participation. Boxes 26 and 27 give some examples of the use of popular theatre and song.

Box 26. Popular theatre as a means of participation

Sistren popular education programme: Jamaica

Sistren's basic objective is to do drama for and with working class communities. Their central focus is the situation of women and the search for solutions to women's problems in the context of the social reality which surrounds them. Through this, Sistren hope to contribute to a process of change which will improve and transform the position of women and create the basis for a more equal and just society.

All the work of Sistren is based on the experience of individual members and the reality they relate to. It is a dialectical process of learning from their experiences and those of the communities in which they work, and of giving back that learning in the form of plays and drama workshops. None of Sistren's major productions has had a previous script. The actual presentation has always been the result of a creative and genuinely collective process of consultation, discussion and rehearsal.

The workshops are researched and prepared before being presented to the target group. Members of the community are interviewed, an appropriate theme is selected and discussed and relevant materials are assembled. To enliven their presentation Sistren make extensive use of audiovisuals and traditional music and dance, and humour is a very important element in their approach.

Overall the plays and workshops aim to stimulate discussions, participation and organisation around the issues with which they deal. In other words Sistren's work aims at social reflection, action and transformation, which is the essence of education (War on Want: Jamaica 003).

Laedza Batanani: Botswana

Laedza Batanani was started by a group of adult educators and extension workers in northern Botswana in 1974. It developed out of their frustrations with their work, their feelings of inadequacy in dealing with the severe problems faced by the rural poor – poverty, unemployment, poor health, community and family disintegration. They realised that they could make very little impact on agriculture or health or community development without starting to analyse the larger social forces controlling their situation. They found it more and more difficult to accept the élitist nature of their work – for example, servicing the needs of wealthier farmers or exploiting the labour of poor people in self-reliance projects – and recognised that real solutions required the mobilisation and active participation of the whole community. They felt isolated and largely ineffective working on their own and saw the importance of combining forces with extension workers from other departments. Finally they started to see the contradiction between their role at the bottom of a hierarchical organisation with its own messages and services and their role as a servant of a local community which had its own concerns and priorities.

Socio-drama mixed with discussion and collective action seemed to provide the beginnings of an answer. At the least the drama dealt with the initial problem of getting people to come to meetings. Its liveliness attracted people and held their attention and this made it possible for other things to happen. It provided a means for expression of feelings and analysis about major problems in the community. It also produced a mirror of the community as the focus for discussion and a stimulus to take a more critical look at the situation (Kidd, 1979, pp. 5-6).

Box 27.   Song as a means of participation

We had observed the great role that songs played in the organisation of work in the fields and as a means of collective expression after work. There were two kinds of songs; their own traditional ballads which they sang during their work and on festive occasions, and songs introduced by the organisers which were expressions of social criticism and of the aspirations of the poor. At the weekend camp we discovered that all the women had learnt these songs and now they presented them as one of their cultural contributions. The response to the new songs showed not only the importance of songs as a powerful means of communication, mobilisation and organisation of illiterate women generally, but also that the people were clearly able to differentiate between songs with an abstract or superficial analysis of their situation, and those which expressed it in concrete terms (Bhasin, 1985, pp. 86-87).

Other instruments

Although the above are the more widely used instruments employed, the practice reveals a range of other less common and usually more localised instruments.

Bible circles

Given the widespread involvement of the Christian Churches in development at the grass-roots level and, in Latin America in particular, the emergence of a theology closely associated with participation as an act of liberation, it is not surprising to find Bible study as a means of furthering people's awareness and involvement. The study of the Bible is seen as an instrument of liberation in that the people reflect upon their common experiences and unite and organise around issues of common concern. Bible circles question injustices, seek biblical guidance and support for tackling these injustices and help form the basis of community groups:

> Up until October the groups used to meet to discuss the weekly bulletin and for Bible readings. In these discussions we try to understand the word of the Lord in our everyday lives from a historical and sociological perspective. We note that some groups spontaneously can make this connection, others find it more difficult (OXFAM: Brazil 223).

The different Christian Churches have both a major influence and role in movements which seek to break barriers of silence and build structures for more effective participation. The use of the study of the Bible to raise consciousness and build solidarity is common practice, particularly in Latin America.[5]

Small group media

On a more sophisticated level, there is a range of what we might call "small group media", as opposed to mass media, which are used as instruments to promote involvement. These include video, puppetry, sound slide productions and photographs; inevitably they are more expensive and in most projects their use is dependent upon external support. Collectively, they constitute potentially the most powerful of instruments available but, because of their cost and the particular equipment and skills they require, their influence is currently limited largely to urban areas. Essentially these instruments are based on popular culture, and the everyday realities and problems of people's lives are used to provoke discussion and reaction:

> The sound slide production understandably captured the hearts of the fishermen for they could understand very deeply a production which was produced by themselves with technical assistance. Heartwarming, the sound slide was a tool for discussion among fishermen which ended with a challenge on what fishermen should do given the situation being projected. The level of consciousness having been raised, they have become more interested in rural development programmes ... (ILO, 1988, p. 1).

Undoubtedly as resources reach previously excluded areas, the use of small group media will become more common; certainly there is evidence to attest to its potentially powerful impact in breaking the reserve and isolation fundamental to beginning a process of participation.[6]

Public meetings and campaigns

These more mass-based instruments are less concerned with the detail or characteristics of particular groups or locations but seek to promote consciousness and involvement on a broader level. In the health field in

[5] Much of the writing on the theology of liberation is in either Portuguese or Spanish; a useful text in English, for example, is L. Boff and C. Boff: *Salvation and liberation: In search of a balance between faith and politics* (New York, Orbis, 1984); see also R. Dickinson: *To set at liberty the oppressed* (Geneva, World Council of Churches, 1978). For a fascinating description of the theology in practice see P. Berryman: *The religious roots of rebellion* (London, SCM Press, 1984); T.C. Bruneau: "The Catholic Church and basic Christian communities", in D.M. Levine (ed.): *Religion and political conflict in Latin America* (Chapel Hill, University of North Carolina Press, 1986).

[6] See, for example, G. Bessette and D. Tighe: "The integration of video in development projects", in *Media in Education and Development* (Basingstoke, Hampshire), June 1988, pp. 44-47; M. Pathak and A. Shah: "The effectiveness of puppetry in the education of rural adult women", in *Indian Journal of Adult Education* (New Delhi), Vol. 45, No. 6, 1984; J. Havet: "Cartoons: A neglected source of insight into international development", in *Development Dialogue* (Uppsala), 1987, No. 2, pp. 128-148.

particular, campaigns are a common way of provoking interest in a health issue on a wide scale and of seeking people's involvement in possible solutions. The public meeting is a mass version of the group discussion and aims essentially to unite a broader body of people in a common cause:

> These public meetings, without stages, platforms, chairs or loudspeakers, started at 8 p.m. and went on till way past midnight. They were attended by hundreds of coolie men, women and children. In ten days we had kindled the same craving for human dignity and basic rights in over 3,000 coolies from 52 villages. We offered no concrete solutions. We did not alleviate their sufferings in any way. We gave them hope and an assurance of support. A feeling of warmth, trust, respect and deep affection spontaneously blossomed. Each subsequent meeting was more intense than the earlier, each declaration of solidarity more powerful (NOVIB: India 85-146).

Mass-based instruments are used to try to make a widespread, immediate and, it is hoped, powerful impact upon a body of people about a particular issue. Midgeley et al. (1986), for example, shows the effectiveness of a nation-wide schistosomiasis campaign in China in generating widespread local concern and involvement in tackling the disease. Inevitably such campaigns create an immediate response and generate awareness of the issue; it is less clear how sustained their impact is given the lack of follow-up or the more detailed concern for people's involvement.

Other less proven instruments found in the practice include the use of pamphlets or other written materials, the radio, local bureaucratic edicts (*actas* in Latin America) and television. While several of these have been evaluated for their usefulness in getting people involved in established development programmes, there is less evidence of their effectiveness for promoting authentic people's participation.

It is on the question of relevant instruments of a methodology of participation that current project practice is both widely underdeveloped but locally both imaginative and innovative in places. The case studies in Chapter 3 confirm this situation with a range of examples from projects seeking consciously to develop appropriate instruments (Ghana, Nepal, Philippines) to others where this detailed concern is clearly lacking (Lesotho, Mexico). Appropriate instruments are fundamental to a methodology of participation and this brief review has helped to highlight a number of issues:

- A methodology of participation needs support from appropriate instruments. It is not enough merely to set up a committee or form a group of local people; there is a need for greater detail and the elaboration of more sensitive and particular means of promoting this participation.

- Appropriate instruments need to be innovative and imaginative. Participation is a unique and complex process and demands detailed and imaginative attention; it is folly to sit back and simply hope that it will occur.

- Instruments of a methodology of participation are mutually supportive and not exclusive. Probably a mix of instruments will be appropriate in any given context.

- Project staff will need at least to be made aware, if not prepared to implement, the above kinds of instruments. They demand a particular approach to relating to people at the project level and particular skills of communication. Equally, the allocation of staff resources to develop these instruments will need to be considered; such instruments will not emerge on their own but only as a result of the effort put into their development by project staff.

- Time must be allowed within the framework of a project for appropriate instruments both to be developed and also to run their course. None of the instruments examined above suggests a one-off approach, but rather a carefully thought-out methodology which is intended to develop a solid base for participation and not merely a temporary gesture.

Instruments of a methodology of participation are subtle and powerful matters and need to be approached with the same level of commitment as, for example, the development of a new crop technology or health practice. They must be seen as important to the methodology and must receive the corresponding degree both of support and resources.

Training in the methodology of participation

A final issue concerns the training that agents who will work with the methodology will require. In the first instance, perhaps, the notion of "training" is inappropriate since it tends to denote a formal exercise of knowledge transfer in preparation for a predetermined task. Verhagen (1987), for example, comments that training practice in development is still largely paternalistic and curative in nature, with a veneration of modern, technical and specialised knowledge; this classical training, he affirms, does not encourage the kind of creative thinking important in a process of participation. Conventional development project practice does not prepare project staff to work with a process of participation. We have seen in the case studies evidence of field agents who have plunged into implementing a strategy of participation with little more to support them than their own intuition, commitment and insight. Where some supposed training in participation has taken place in such projects, this invariably has consisted of briefings upon project procedures, lectures on participation as a broad strategy and information on how project reporting should be undertaken. It is still fair to say that the overwhelmingly majority of development projects which seek to promote participation do not give priority to training staff in appropriate methodologies but assume that a commitment to participation and the setting up of a committee or other representative body will be sufficient. There is little evidence, therefore, that conventional development projects have really taken this issue on board and this is largely due to their perception of what participation is all about and their reliance upon project benefits as the basic instrument of any participation that occurs.[7]

However, encouraged by the pioneering work of Bhasin (1976, 1979, 1985) and, more lately, by practitioners such as Tandon (1987) and Tilakaratna (1987), there is evidence that the training of agents at the project level in terms of participation is now being re-examined. When we talk of "project agents" we are referring to a very broad category of practitioners, ranging from agents working within Ministries or other bureaucracies down to district-, block- or parish-level field staff who are supporting groups of people in a process of participation. Our concern here is with the external agent who is supporting the process and the training that he or she might require in order better to undertake this task. We are not concerned here with the substantial area of the training of rural people. Similarly, we need to distinguish between training in participation and participatory training. The latter is a technique and approach to training which is relevant across the broad spectrum of training activities;[8] our concern is with the former which considers how best an external agent might be trained in order to work with a process of participation. DELTA in Kenya and PIDA in Sri Lanka are two of the more prominent examples of this new approach to training (boxes 28 and 29). In broad terms project agents need to be trained not only in the objectives of the process of participation but also in the practical skill of intervention in order to stimulate people's involvement and collective action. Technical competence alone is not adequate; a broader perspective is required if the agent is truly to enter the people's world and begin to break down their isolation:

> For a development worker engaged in delivering a programme, the focus of training has to be the social, cultural, political and economic reality of the rural area. He has technical competence. He needs to understand the system in which he is applying his technical competence. He has to be sensitised to that system. The dynamics of poverty and underdevelopment need to be understood; the cultural rituals and mores to be studied; the nature of the rural people has to be perceived; the local political structure and social groups and cleavages have to be carefully analysed (Tandon, 1987, p. 5).

[7] A classical example of this is the FAO's training manual for group promotors in its People's Participation Programme. The manual is detailed but almost exclusively concerned with administrative procedures and the duties of group promotors in relation to input provision, group organisation and project reports. See FAO: *Training of group promotors in field projects of the People's Participation Programme* (Rome, 1983).

[8] "Participatory training" has emerged as a supposed antidote to the more teacher dominated approach to training. See, for example, Society for Participatory Research in Asia: *Participatory training for rural development* (New Delhi, 1987). Undoubtedly the most influential writer in the field of training to promote participation has been Khamla Bhasin; her study, *Breaking barriers: A South Asian experience of training for participatory development* (Rome, FAO, 1983), is still a basic text and has been translated into several languages.

Box 28. PIDA: Sri Lanka

PIDA (Participatory Institute for Development Alternatives) is a non-governmental action research organisation established by a group of people who have been involved for several years in the study and setting up of grass-roots activities in Sri Lanka. Its general objectives are to initiate and participate in development action aimed at changing the process of development in favour of the economically and socially disadvantaged groups, to support and strengthen people's organisations emerging out of such development action, and to organise training in catalytic skills for participatory, self-reliant development processes. All PIDA workers have gone through a process of sensitisation (a participatory "training" process) which involved living with communities of the rural poor, direct exposures to the reality of village situations, continual praxis of action followed by reflection, comparison and analysis of each other's experiences, and group learning. Their role is essentially a catalytic one of stimulating the people to initiate development actions according to their own collectively deliberated priorities aimed at self-reliance (Bhasin, 1985, p. 120).

The above represents the broad spirit implicit in the training of agents for participation. It recognises the utility of technical competence, but it deliberately de-emphasises it in favour of an understanding of the dynamics of the context. People do or do not participate not only as a result of the sensitivity of the intervention but also as a function of cultural, economic and political factors. These must form the basis of any training if the agent is to proceed. A review of project files and other literature suggests that the following are the more common issues concerning the training of agents to support a process of participation:

- The basic approach of the training should be not to transmit information but to assist the trainees to learn to think for themselves and be aware of the complexities of intervention.

- Time must be made available for this training to take place and it must be seen as a distinct and discrete part of the agent's overall preparation.

- The emphasis should be upon training through experience and the sharing of practice rather than formal classroom activities.

- The training should emphasise the qualities and characteristics of agents as more important than knowledge or particular skills.

- The training itself should be participatory in the sense that, as they build up their understanding, agents should become actively involved in structuring the training and not merely be compliant trainees.

- The content of the training should concentrate upon techniques and knowledge appropriate at the local level and relevant to the context in which agents will work. There should also be at least a balance in the content

Box 29. DELTA training programme, Kenya

DELTA is a part of the Development Education Programme (DEP) and both are also parts of the Catholic Church's wider approach to rural development in Kenya. It is designed to provide leadership training to people involved in church-based development, and the basis of a methodology for their intervention at village level. The training methodology is one which is designed to fulfil this particular purpose. The implementation at local level is strongly affected by what happens on the training courses, but is none the less autonomous, and not necessarily dependent on any part of the DEP. DELTA training is based upon five elements, which are incorporated into the training process. The programme is described as following a five-stream approach; the streams are seen as tributaries which together form a big river. They are the main elements of the DELTA method. These five elements are:

■ **Conscientisation: The psycho-social method**

The main pedagogic technique of DELTA involves an adapted version of Paulo Freire's methodology of conscientisation, adjusted to the needs of rural Kenyans. This has been named the psycho-social method (PSM), or problem-posing approach. It involves the change agent providing a framework in which the participants are active and creative, raising and tackling wide-ranging questions and controlling the process themselves. The methodology of PSM is very similar to that of Freire, involving the preparation of problem-posing materials for discussion within a learning group and explicitly rejecting the "banking approach" to education. The generative themes that are used are established beforehand using formal research to discover what topics are of common concern amongst the people in question.

■ **Human relations training**

Dialogue in a close, active group is a critical element of the methodology. DELTA recognises that the necessary skills to facilitate this do not always emerge in a group and aims, therefore, to contribute training to achieve better group dynamics. For this it is necessary to create a learning environment, in which everybody feels a part of the group and is active in and committed to decisions, conflict can be handled and resolved, and participatory evaluation and feedback processes are the norm. Such programmes are often seen as middle class or self-indulgent, or as a distraction from the real activities of the group. DELTA, however, sees them as essential in the formation of a successful group.

■ **Organisational development**

The third stream in the DELTA programme is the importance of organisational development, and in particular an American model called "provolutionary development". The idea behind this model is that organisations should have a strong vision to guide them, and clear goals towards which they are moving. These are seen to link very strongly with the level of commitment and unity within the group.

■ **Social analysis**

The analysis of the world is an important part of any Freirian methodology. In the DELTA methodology, there are five "schemas" which together form the basis of this analysis. They are as follows:

Economic reality   Religious reality
Social reality   Group psychology
Political reality

The analysis of these different realities arises from the PSM generative themes, which we have mentioned already. Defining the important sectors of reality, and setting out to analyse them through the three stages of observation, classification and inter-relation are ways of facilitating and advancing the participatory process. The series of schemas also helps in the complex process of analysing a local situation which is influenced by complex international systems which are difficult to conceptualise and analyse. The DELTA methodology emphasises the need to start "where people are"; in other words, to work incrementally towards increasing levels of awareness.

■ **Christian concept of transformation**

The DELTA programme is run through the Catholic Church in Kenya, but is often oecumenical in terms of the participant's denomination. The training programmes and other activities are based around parishes and dioceses. The philosophy of DELTA is that Christians have a responsibility to bring about the transformation of society, and to struggle for the liberation of the poorest. This commitment is part of the wider trend towards liberation theology. It also represents another link between DELTA, in Kenya, and non-governmental activities in Latin America (Hope and Timmel, 1986, Vols. 1-3).

---

between analytical and qualitative skills as opposed to the detail of specific knowledge.

■   The training should be a continuous feature of the work of an agent with periodic sessions to review practice and adjust accordingly.[9]

Interestingly, it would appear from the practice that the very notion of formal training is de-emphasised and the term "preparation" might be more appropriate. Certainly there is no suggestion of the training serving as any kind of test or examination in which an agent either fails or succeeds. Implicit in the practice is the emphasis upon selection. It is not a question of selecting and then training in the hope that the agent will succeed; success is built into selection, which is rigorous and ideologically oriented, and is then followed by a period of preparation before the agent is allowed to intervene alone to support the process. This emphasis upon selection is a radical departure from conventional practice which selects agents on the basis of predetermined qualifications and then seeks to train the agent for project practice. With a process of participation,

---

[9] See ILO: *Promoting people's participation...*, op. cit., for what workshop participants in Asia felt should be the key aspects of the training of external project agents.

---

the emphasis upon selection ensures agents with the appropriate ideological background and personal qualities which provide a solid foundation upon which the techniques of intervention can be built.

It is very difficult in fact to identify in the practice clearly visible training exercises in which agents are prepared to work with a methodology of participation. Assuming that the first wave of agents experimented with and developed an understanding of the methodology, this knowledge is now invariably handed on to other agents as a result of working alongside the more experienced agents. If, however, we do talk in terms of training, it would appear to have two distinct phases:

- a formally structured course in which trainee agents explore and analyse various dimensions of the national and local context in which they will be operating and, to a lesser extent, group dynamics or techniques of group organisation;
- direct experience and training in the methodology by working at the project level with other agents.

There are numerous examples of the above kind of formally structured course, particularly from the Indian subcontinent (see box 30 for one such example), and a noticeable similarity in course contents. Courses range from one week to up to three or four months, with the latter kind of course usually being given by an agency specialising in the training of project staff. The courses fulfil a fundamental requirement for work with a process of participation, which is that participation is not merely an issue of information or technological transfer but inextricably bound up with the forces which influence the local context. Similarly, people's participation cannot be developed if the agent takes a superior and "modern" attitude to the people involved. In terms of skills, most courses emphasise analytical and group development skills as crucial to working with the methodology and behavioural skills in terms of the ability to relate to and work with local people. Finally, skills of building and linking up groups of people are also included as important in creating a broader dynamic of participation. Two examples of courses which have emphasised these skills are given in box 31.

The above examples contrast starkly with the more conventional in-service training programmes for professional agents joining a development programme or project. They represent a radical departure from the notion of training in the context of development as a process of technological transfer. Clearly, also, it is training within the context of a methodology of participation as a process of building a basis for continued involvement. The analysis and sensitivity demanded of the agent are consistent with seeing people as equals and the scope of the ILO example in particular reflects a coherent methodology for the promotion of authentic participation. The point to bear in mind is that the above do not necessarily represent the content of formally structured

---

Box 30.   Development and liberation: A training programme for activists and development workers, Bangalore, India

Phase I: Reflection and analysis of work experience

- Sharing and reflection on participants' work situations, experiences, ideas and expectations.
- Identifying problem areas.
- A critical analysis of issues and problems the participants have dealt with.

Phase II: Reflection on the underlying basis of social action

Moving into deeper reflection processes which incorporate the following:

- An awareness of the causes of underdevelopment with specific reference to the Indian situation.
- Structural analysis of Indian society with particular reference to the impact of socio-economic and ideological forces in the process of development.
- Critical analysis of the agrarian relations existing in India with a focus on land distribution, ownership, and the links between productivity and wages.
- Progressive and neo-Gandhian insights and experiences within social theory so as to arrive at critical understanding of the community organisation process.
- A critique of the approaches to mass education.
- Analysis of the emerging insights and understanding concerning women.
- Cultural implications of development strategies.
- An analysis of caste and communalism and the problems they pose in field situations.

Phase III: Organisational theories, practical skills and action plans

Here we return to the practical problems of strategising and implementation of programmes:

- An exposure to meaningful field programmes.
- An intensive learning programme in the field related to community health.
- Rediscovering and building upon the latent knowledge of people in the fields of agriculture, technology and other relevant skills.
- Developing critical understanding of community action strategies and tactics which lead to participatory people's associations.
- Educational approaches with particular emphasis on non-formal education, within the field of community organisation.
- Role of Legal Aid Cells whereby the oppressed are made aware of their rights in society and provided with access to constitutional justice.
- Reflection on the creative development of women's organisations in the process of social action.
- Role of youth organisations in providing new leadership patterns.
- A critical examination of the role of socio-economic programmes.
- Importance of group dynamics and democratic leadership in the process of development.
- Preparation of action plans (CAFOD: 1988).

Box 31. Training courses emphasising group development skills

■ Social analysis: analysis of micro-level situations within a broader social context.

■ Behavioural skills: development of a subject-to-subject relationship with the people, a relationship of equals.

■ Animation skills: stimulating and assisting social analysis by the people helping them develop their intellectual capacities.

■ Training of internal animators: identification and training of confidence. Potential internal animators from among the people as group dynamics evolve.

■ Knowledge of facilitation: knowledge of government structures, policies, procedures, institutions and other social mechanisms of relevance to grass-roots action. (ILO, 1987, pp. 3-4)

(United Nations, ESCAP, 1985, p. 116)

■ Modes of entry into villages.

■ Process of identifying target groups.

■ Methodology of interacting with them and conducting group discussions.

■ Methods of winning people's confidence.

■ Role playing and group dynamics.

■ Methods of group organising.

(United Nations, ESCAP, 1985, p. 116)

---

courses in a classroom situation. Instead they are the themes which the agent's training includes; some will more appropriately be studied or examined in the context of the practice whereby agents build up both their skills and knowledge with experience. Since the themes of the training are so tied up with practice, it is often the more experienced agents who take responsibility for the training, and thus invaluable knowledge and experience is passed on directly. Training sessions also usually take place at the project level and thus provide a learning scenario which is both concrete and ongoing.

Skilled activists and project agents are the key to the successful implementation of a methodology of participation. While personal commitment and correct ideological perspective are important, they are inadequate for effectively developing the methodology at the project level. The ability to analyse existing experience and qualitatively to develop a process of participation is vital to ensure that the process takes hold. The practice to date suggests that projects rely far too heavily upon commitment and other personal qualities and that specific training is either perfunctory or non-existent. Where some period of training occurs, it appears that those projects are more effective in developing a base for participation; where it does not, it is often difficult to believe that this base will be created. In most sectoral projects there is little, if any, concern for overt training in a methodology of participation, with the result that participation is inevitably directly related to project benefits and continuity; if both these fail, active participation is negligible. It is in the NGO sector, and particularly in Asia and Latin America, that projects are more concerned with training their agents and are experimenting with content, approaches and styles. There is, however, much for us still to learn about how best to prepare an agent to promote a process of participation effectively.

Concluding comments

This chapter has tried to extract the essence of a methodology of participation from a wide range of practice. As such, therefore, it should not be read or used as a model methodology, but more as a guide and framework for project practice. This is an important point to make since it is impossible to talk of a methodology of participation as one would, for example, of a field demonstration, a poster campaign or a farmers' training programme. Such methodologies are proven and function within agreed parameters and check-lists or guides exist to explain their use. A methodology of participation is a broad framework for action which practice suggests occurs in a series of stages. It is different from conventional project methodology in a number of important ways; it is less constrained by time, it is less concerned with immediate quantitative impact, it is less ready to tell people what to do and it is less committed to a predetermined line of action. Indeed it constitutes a radical departure from conventional project methodology and as such demands qualities, skills and resources that are not in abundance.

It would be wrong, however, to conclude that this emerging methodology of participation has taken a firm hold on project practice. As Paul (1987) concluded, the methodology of participation is linked to its interpretation. Projects which view participation in a more limited manner and restrict it largely to participation in project benefits or periodic consultations will, correspondingly, employ equally limited methodologies in its promotion. Time and resources are of the essence and results are demanded; there is, therefore, often great pressure not to be too ambitious in terms of people's participation. The focus in this chapter, however, has been upon those projects which see participation in a different light and which are prepared to commit the time and resources to its development. In these projects we can say that a distinctive methodology of participation is emerging and is increasing in influence. It has to be noted, however, that this distinctive methodology currently flourishes more in projects supported by NGOs and that both government and international aid agency supported projects have yet in general to make the breakthrough to the more detailed and subtle methodologies demanded of an authentic process of participation. Furthermore, this emerging methodology is to date more common among projects in Asia and Latin America than in Africa. The reasons for this are probably complex and certainly political; whatever the explanation, African projects in general appear to lag behind in terms of experimentation with methodologies of participation.

The clear lesson that emerges from this chapter is that a methodology of participation is not a one-off affair, but a continuous unfolding of practice through a series of stages until a state of authentic participation is achieved. The process of participation must be understood in methodological terms and not seen as something that can be simply announced. Time, resources, skills and imagination are fundamental ingredients; commitment is admirable but not enough. Indeed, Tilakaratna (1987) emphasised that the success of projects which seek to promote participation is closely linked to the preparations that they make to develop an appropriate methodology. The issue, therefore, is how conventional project practice can be changed to encourage the wider influence of these emerging methodologies. Realistically it might prove an impossible task. This chapter has shown that we are talking about a new genre of project methodology, more subtle, more demanding and more time-consuming than conventional methodologies. These emerging methodologies must not compromise and tack to the prevailing winds; it is conventional practice which must adjust. Certainly the changes required are radical and far-reaching, but they must surely be an agreeable price to pay for the establishing of an authentic base for people's participation in development activities. At the very least, development projects need to examine their present approaches and begin to experiment in the light of methodologies beginning to emerge in the practice.

6

Evaluating participation

Development is a multivariate quantitative and qualitative change. While scientific judgements about development need to be reasoned, cardinal quantification has often served as a fetish that detached from rather than helped evaluate the more essential qualitative attributes (Haque et. al., 1977, p. 15).

Since "participation" has become an accepted and recognisable objective in development programmes and projects, the issue of its evaluation has come into question. Evaluation is an important component of the project cycle and there is a vast supporting literature, both theoretical and applied, which covers the range of sectors and different types of projects. While we can date the emerging concern for participation in development to the mid-1970s, interest in the evaluation of participation is a more recent phenomenon. Inevitably as agencies have increased support for participation and as it has begun to be implemented, so a concern for evaluation has emerged. It must be said, however, that this concern has yet to translate itself into a substantial body of literature; the truth of the matter is that both conceptually and methodologically the evaluation of participation is still in its relative infancy. In 1980 Lassen commented upon the paucity of "practical guide-lines" on how to evaluate participation; in 1989 the situation is better but we still lack substantial authoritative insights into this complex issue. Indeed some authors (Rahman, 1983; Rifkin et al., 1988) have questioned whether it is at all possible to think of developing an analytical framework to evaluate "participation" in development projects; more generally, however, a variety of projects have begun to tackle the issue and to experiment with different ways of doing this. Before exploring some of the issues involved, however, a number of important points need to be made:

- The parameters and the content of any evaluation of participation will necessarily be linked to the operational understanding of participation. On the one hand, if this understanding is limited to the notion of economic benefits derived from successful projects, physical attendance at project activities or extended project coverage, then the evaluation will probably be largely quantitative. On the other hand, if the operational understanding is more closely linked to participation as a process with a series of qualitative objects, then the evaluation will demand an alternative form.

■ In this respect, it cannot be assumed that the more commonly used quantitative, linear approach to evaluation will be appropriate to the evaluation of participation. While clearly there will be a quantitative dimension to participation, there will also be a qualitative one and this similarly will need to be evaluated. The evaluation of participation, therefore, demands qualitative alternatives to the effort, effect and efficiency criteria of conventional evaluation and, correspondingly, will demand alternative methods of information and data collection and analysis. The evaluation of participation will be concerned with the analysis of a dynamic, qualitative process and not merely the measuring of a static, physical outcome.

■ The evaluation of participation in development projects is not necessarily the same as "participatory evaluation". Much literature reduces the debate on how to evaluate participation by describing techniques of participatory evaluation. But the difference is clear and uncontestable; the evaluation of participation refers to the evaluation of a specific objective or outcome of a development project, whereas "participatory evaluation" is a technique which is widely applicable in evaluation practice. Participatory evaluation may well be a principal technique in the evaluation of participation but it is not a substitute for the evaluation of the process itself.

■ Furthermore, the evaluation of "participation in development" is not the same as the evaluation of "participatory development". In each of these alternatives the focus is at opposite extremes. Although both are relevant dimensions, the evaluation of participation is more than merely assessing the "participatory" nature of conventional development practice. If the issue were merely to do with quantifying results and assessing returns on project investments in participation, then conventional techniques would theoretically suffice. Participation, however, is a much broader process and presents us initially with a series of conceptual challenges.

In comparison with the quite substantial literature available on the economic and quantitative evaluation of rural development projects, the material on qualitative processes such as participation is extremely limited. However, now that it appears that participation as a strategy of rural development has achieved some credibility, there is an increasing urgency to be able to evaluate its outcome. Agencies' project files attest to this increasing concern and suggest that it is apposite to tackle this issue now.[1] However, this concern has come up against a basic problem. Paul (1987), for example, suggested that it was not an easy task to evaluate the outcome of participation in relation to its objectives. Howes (1984) came to a similar conclusion and argued

---

[1] See, for example, G. de Crombrugghe, M. Hawes and M. Nieuwkerk: *An evaluation of CEC small development projects* (Brussels, EEC, 1985). See also the study by H. Gezelius and D. Millwood: *NGOs in development and participation in practice*, Working Paper 3 (Stockholm, University of Stockholm, 1988). Covering EEC and NGO projects, both studies attest to the increasing concern to be able to evaluate a process of participation.

that the more conventional uni-directional causality model of evaluation might not be sufficient to analyse and explain closely the outcomes of projects whose objectives are broader and more process related. Indeed, a central problem is how to disentangle the process of participation from project structure and factors which influence the functioning of this structure. Furthermore, there is the problem of identifying and explaining the project's influence, as opposed to that of other social and political forces, on the process of evaluation. When we see participation as merely contributing to or receiving the benefits of a development project, then these problems become more manageable; when, however, we see it in a wider sense, both the conceptual and practical aspects of its evaluation appear formidable. It is, as Charlick (1984) suggests, a "complex task" which threatens to be unworkable.

Conceptualising the issue

Essentially the question that we have to ask is what forms of evaluation would be more appropriate to understand the outcome of "participation" in development projects. In the light of the points made above, there will be in one sense two broad outcomes of "participation" which could serve as the foci for evaluation:

- the quantitative and more tangible or physical outcomes which will be readily visible and which will be susceptible to statistical measurement; this is a relevant dimension of participation and could be more easily evaluated by existing techniques;

- outcomes more related to participation as a qualitative process of change. These outcomes might be less visible and they will certainly be less tangible and will demand particular techniques in their evaluation.

In terms of the quantitative outcomes of participation, there would appear to be adequate techniques available to evaluate these. Where participation is defined in terms of direct contributions to projects, sharing in the economic benefits or physical involvement in project organisation or decision-making procedures, evaluation of participation draws upon the enormous body of literature and practice already available.[2] In this respect "participation" is seen as a tangible objective which can be measured as an outcome at the time of project evaluation. Certainly the evidence suggests that, where projects have this understanding of "participation", participation is evaluated as part of and in the same way as other project objectives.

[2] Two relatively brief but comprehensive and readable texts which pull together both the theory and practice of the dominant quantitative evaluation paradigm are D.J. Casley and D.A. Lury: *Handbook on monitoring and evaluation of agricultural and rural development projects* (Washington, DC, World Bank, 1981); and United Nations: *Guiding principles for the design and use of monitoring and evaluation in rural development programmes and projects* (Rome, International Fund for Agricultural Development, 1984).

Participation as a qualitative process, however, presents us with more difficult conceptual problems. Here we are dealing with forms of change which have characteristics and properties not necessarily amenable to quantitative techniques. Furthermore such techniques, if used, would probably only capture one dimension rather than the variable dimensions of the change occurring. Attempts to evaluate processes in development in recent years have often focused, for example, upon the analysis of social aspects of development projects. American researchers in the early 1970s spearheaded both the thinking and the practice in this field.[3] *Social cost-benefit analysis* has also emerged as part of this line of inquiry and is now a widely recognised aspect of evaluation studies.[4] *Social impact analysis* similarly is a technique advocated for understanding and evaluating the social effects of development projects.[5] The notion of "impact" suggests a straightforward, one-directional causality resulting from the project and can potentially ignore the fact that the project may be in reality no more than one factor influencing a process of participation. Finally, we have the broad notion of *social indicators*, which are suggested as a means of understanding the effects, other than the strictly economic effects, of development projects.[6]

The above forms of understanding and evaluation of the social effects or processes of development projects are useful in conceptualising the issue of the evaluation of participation. It must be said, however, that while they provide us with some insights, as approaches they are closely allied to the widely recognised techniques of evaluating the material or tangible effects of development projects. These approaches similarly seek to measure and to give a numerical value to the supposed social outcomes of a project. This, of course, is entirely valid but it could be argued that it results in an incomplete view of the "social outcome". Indeed the literature on the above approaches interprets social development largely in terms of improved health, welfare and education facilities, for example, and as such explains development in quantitative terms.

The issue, therefore, is how to understand and evaluate such non-material and non-directly production related objectives of rural development projects such as "participation". Conventional evaluation is dominated

---

[3] An earlier standard text was T. Tripodi et al.: *Social program evaluation* (Ann Arbor, University of Michigan, 1971); more recently, see D. Conyers: *An introduction to social planning in the Third World* (Chichester, John Wiley, 1982), and H. Hardiman and J. Midgeley: *The social dimensions of development* (Chichester, John Wiley, 1982) for discussions on the issue of the evaluation of a more traditional form of social development.

[4] For a succinct account of social cost-benefit analysis see A.K.T. Sadik: "A note on some practical limitations of social cost-benefit analysis measures", in *World Development*, Vol. 6, No. 2, 1978, pp. 221-225.

[5] See, for example, FAO: *Social impact analysis* (Rome, 1981); also J. Ingersoll: *Social analysis of development projects* (Washington, DC, USAID, 1977).

[6] C.A. Mills: *On social indicators and development* (Geneva, United Nations University, 1980); also D. McGranahan et al.: *Methodological problems in selection and analysis of socio-economic development indicators* (Geneva, UNRISD, 1985).

by a concern to measure; but how can we "measure" qualitative change? Imboden (1979) highlighted this dilemma when she suggested that there were certain dimensions of development projects which were not amenable to measurement in quantifiable terms. Concepts such as "participation" are difficult to define solely in specific, quantifiable terms. Unlike, for example, a credit programme to finance the purchase of fertiliser, which we can judge in terms of the take-up of credit, the magnitude of fertiliser application or the eventual level of crop production, a process of participation might not follow such a predictable path. Participation is not only difficult to characterise, but it is equally difficult at the beginning of a project to predict what its outcome or effect might be. For example, a wider range of rural development projects have as an objective: "... to bring about the more effective participation of the people/the rural poor/the project beneficiaries".

Beforehand, however, it will be difficult to spell out precisely how this participation might manifest itself and what its eventual nature might be.

We need an approach to evaluation, therefore, which is not based exclusively on the measurement of material, but which is able also to explain what happens in a rural development project that seeks to promote participation. Participation, like poverty, is an abstract concept and, although we can attribute material or productive characteristics to the process involved, such characteristics are inadequate as the only means of explaining the many potential dimensions of participation. In other words, in dealing with "participation", we are not only concerned with results which are quantitative but more importantly with processes which are qualitative. Participation is a phenomenon which occurs over time and cannot be measured simply by a single "snap-shot" form of exercise. Participation as a process unfolds throughout the life of a project and, it is hoped, continues when the project formally ceases, and it has a range of characteristics and properties. The evaluation of participation, therefore, will involve a number of quantifiable aspects; it will also involve a less predictable number of qualitative aspects (see the example in box 32).

The search for a qualitative approach to the evaluation of participation in rural development projects is only just beginning. Authors such as Weiss and Rein (1970), Parlett and Hamilton (1972), Cohen and Uphoff (1977), Richards (1985), Patton (1987), Oakley (1988b) and Damadoram (1988) have provided some of the building blocks but the evidence suggests that to date their inquiries have had little impact. Essentially we are talking about two complementary but distinct approaches to evaluation which can be summarised as follows:

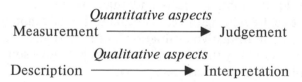

Quantitative aspects
Measurement ⟶ Judgement

Qualitative aspects
Description ⟶ Interpretation

Box 32. Quantitative and qualitative evaluation of participation

When the entire programmes' emphasis is on material development, quantitative analysis is primary. But when the emphasis of development efforts is on the growth of people and their organisation, qualitative analysis assumes more importance. Because material development and the development of people's consciousness and their organisation does (and must) go together, quantitative and qualitative analysis cannot be exclusive of each other. Some groups take an extreme position and reject all quantitative data and measurement of material development. They talk only of intangibles like consciousness-raising, increasing the level of awareness, etc. We felt a need to have a good synthesis of evaluating tangibles and intangibles, quantitative and qualitative results. If one is working with the really poor their material conditions have to be improved fast (mainly of course through their own efforts). The poor are not going to be interested in consciousness-raising for its own sake. All consciousness-raising must lead to an improvement in their material conditions and vice versa. In fact this dichotomy between organisational work and programmes for economic development is false and misleading. Groups primarily doing organisational work also improve the economic status of the poor at least as much, if not more, as the so-called projects for income generation do. Organisations like Bhoomi Sena, Shramik Sangathana and CROSS have led to tremendous economic benefits for the poor through their struggles for recovering alienated lands, higher wages, employment opportunities, lowering interest rates, fighting corruption, reducing the power of middlemen, etc. The poor's economic position can be improved by removing scarcity and exploitation and, if these two tasks go on simultaneously, it is of course ideal (K. Bhasin, 1985, p. 12).

Qualitative evaluation, therefore, is more concerned with describing the characteristics and properties of a process like participation over a period of time and then with interpreting the data and information available in order to make statements concerning the nature and extent of the participation which has occurred. How this might be done we shall examine later. The central importance of the evaluation of the qualitative aspects of participation was underlined by the United Nations ACC Task Force on Rural Development which, in its study on monitoring and evaluation (Oakley, 1988b), argued that participation could not be "squeezed into a set of numbers", but that descriptive statements should be prepared with indications of the changes which have occurred. The nature of qualitative evaluation, therefore, is different from that of quantitative evaluation and it demands different indicators, different methods of collection and different analysis. It has implications for the practice of evaluation in development projects and suggests the need to broaden the basis of this practice. Reviewing the conceptualisation of qualitative evaluation in these studies (or "illuminative evaluation", as Parlett and Hamilton call it), we can note a number of key themes which may help to give some shape to our understanding of this complex issue:

(1) Qualitative evaluation is naturalistic in the sense that the evaluator does not attempt to manipulate the programme or its participants for the purposes of the evaluation. Naturalistic inquiry studies processes as they occur and not on the basis of a pre-planned experiment. As a social development process unfolds, a naturalistic approach would be sensitive to changes in direction, unexpected outcomes and differential impact. Since naturalistic inquiry is not locked into searching only for predetermined and expected outcomes, it is able to identify and describe what actually happens as a result of a project.

(2) Similarly, it is heuristic in that the evaluation approach is subject to continuous redefinition as our knowledge of the project and its outcomes increases. Qualitative evaluation does not restrict itself to preformulated questions or lines of inquiry; rather it evolves, by observable changes being followed up and new questions coming to the fore. The evaluation starts with intensive familiarisation and develops the exercise as a series of stages, thus building up a comprehensive understanding of the activities being evaluated.

(3) Qualitative evaluation is holistic in that the evaluation exercise sees the programme as a working whole which needs to be both understood and analysed from many different perspectives. This holistic approach ensures that detailed attention is given to the different dimensions of a development project: context, participants, inter-relationships with other projects, activities, and so on.

(4) It employs inductive analysis in the sense that the evaluator seeks to understand the outcome of a development project without imposing predetermined expectations. This inductive approach begins with specific observations and builds towards general patterns of project outcome; the evaluator gathers qualitative data on programme outcome through direct observation of programme activities and in-depth interviews with participants, without being limited to stated, predetermined evaluation goals. The approach also is essentially interpretive, built up through description of the significant facts, figures and characteristics of the project which are an accurate reflection of its overall complexity. This continuous interpretation provides the basic material which forms the basis of the project's evaluation.

(5) Qualitative evaluation, by its very nature, implies a continuous and close contact with the participants of a programme in their own environment. The qualitative approach emphasises the importance of getting close to project participants in order more authentically to understand their realities and the details of their everyday life. The evaluator intensifies this close contact through physical proximity for an extended period of time as well as developing a closeness resulting from the shared evaluation experience. Qualitative evaluation demands participation and commitment of the evaluator and discourages detachment and distance, characteristics of other approaches to evaluation.

Qualitative evaluation is based on the assumption that projects are dynamic and evolving and not necessarily following a predetermined direction. The approach, therefore, can be responsive to innovative projects and, more importantly, to objectives which are not easily measurable. The approach of qualitative evaluation draws considerably upon the "phenomenology" school of social inquiry. Emphasis is put upon the identification of key phenomena within any given context and on the systematic recording and interpretation of activities and changes around these phenomena. Qualitative evaluation also redefines the nature and activities of the evaluator by linking him or her both ideologically and physically with project activities and by stressing that evaluation studies should inform, add to understanding and be responsive and readable and not merely destined for academic journals.

Before we examine methodologically the evaluation of participation, we conclude by suggesting a number of key principles which should guide this qualitative exercise. These principles are based upon a review of the albeit limited practice to date, but collectively they provide a basis for the implementation of this type of evaluation:

Qualitative as well as quantitative:	Both dimensions of participation must be included in the evaluation in order for the outcome to be fully understood
Dynamic as opposed to static:	The evaluation of participation demands that the entire process over a period of time be evaluated and not merely a limited snap-shot. Conventional *ex post facto* evaluation, therefore, will not be adequate
Central importance of monitoring:	The evaluation of a process of participation is impossible without relevant and continual monitoring. Indeed monitoring is the key to the whole exercise and the only means by which the qualitative descriptions can be obtained to explain the process which has occurred
Participatory evaluation:	In the entire evaluation process, the rural people involved in the project have a part to play. It is not a question of an external evaluator solely determining the project outcome; the rural people themselves will also have a voice.

On the basis of the above principles and the conceptualisation of evaluation discussed above, we have now to consider how we might evaluate a process of participation. We need to consider, therefore, what indicators we could use to understand this process and how such indicators could be used to collect relevant data and information.

Indicators of participation

Since so much of the literature sees the evaluation of participation largely in terms of the practice of participatory development, our knowledge of appropriate indicators of the process is rather limited. Indeed in the past four or five years few, if any, substantial works have emerged. Haque's (1977) work over a decade ago was the first major attempt to formulate an evaluation design appropriate to a process of participation; subsequently the works of Huizer (1983) and Oakley (1988) took the issue a stage further and laid a useful foundation which, however, has yet to be really built upon. In fact, it must be stated that few development agencies appear to be actively concerned with the issue. While there is a widespread support for the notion of participation, this has not been translated into effort to develop operational indicators or guides as to how this participation might be evaluated. In the past UNRISD has researched the issue of field-level indicators of social development in which "participation" is subsumed; currently the FAO is vigorously experimenting with several approaches to the monitoring and evaluation of its People's Participation Project; but the United Nations Panel on Monitoring and Evaluation paid only scant attention to indicators of participation in its publication *Guiding principles for the design and use of M&E in rural development programmes and projects* (1984).

An indicator is the means by which the outcome of a project can be understood and, in one form or another, measured or explained. Indicators of a project's outcome, therefore, should accurately reflect the changes which have taken place; they should be able to be identified and monitored or observed; they should be intelligible and unambiguous in the sense that they do not cause confusion; and they should not involve costly operations in collection and recording. In terms of relevant indicators of a process of participation in a general sense, a number of authors have put forward ideas. At the beginning of the debate Hamilton (1978) suggested that we should identify the "critical traits" of the process and use them as broad indicators; Lassen (1980) referred to "vital signs" of participation which should serve as a framework for evaluation; Charlick (1984) proposed that the "what", "how" and "where" of participation should be the basis of its evaluation; finally, Rifkin, Muller and Bichmann (1988) have developed a broad continuum of participation from wider to narrower and see these two ends of the continuum as two extreme indicators. All of these researchers are essentially grappling with an issue in which currently we have insufficient empirical evidence to substantiate our hypotheses. It is within the context of this statement that suggestions on relevant indicators of a process of participation should be considered. Furthermore, it should be noted that there are no model lists nor authoritative guide-lines of indicators of participation.

Quantitative indicators

The literature is stronger on quantitative indicators of participation than of qualitative indicators. Already different sets of lists do exist which provide a framework for the evaluation of participation in quantitative terms. The following is a composite list of quantitative indicators drawn from a number of sources.[7]

Economic indicators: The measurable economic benefits of a project, by the use of commonly employed quantitative techniques

Who is participating in the project's benefits; an analysis of those sections of the rural population who have directly benefited and a quantitative assessment of this benefit on their lives and their future ability to sustain the level of activities

Organisational indicators: Percentage of rural adults within a project area who have some knowledge of the existence of the project organisation

Percentage of rural adults within a project area who are formal members of the organisation

Frequency of attendance at project organisation meetings

Changing size of membership over project period

Participation in project activities: Number of project groups or associations of project groups formed

Number and attendance rates at project group meetings

Number of members actively involved in project group meetings

Total work-days contributed by members to project activities

Number of project group members who acquire positions in other formal organisations

Development momentum: Number of project members aware of and in contact with development agencies' services

Number of project members who receive some kind of formal training from the project

[7] Haque et al. (1977); Huizer (1983); United Nations (1984); A. Stephens (1988); and Oakley (1988b).

Number of links established with similar project groups

Internal sustainability, or the ability of the project group to maintain its own development momentum

It should be noted that the above criteria represent aggregate numbers of rural people; by differentiating between different recognisable groups or strata, more detailed information could be obtained.

Few would argue that quantitative indicators alone are adequate to evaluate fully a process of participation; indeed Rugh (1986), for example, comments that they are "relevant, appropriate but limited"; Cohen and Uphoff (1977) similarly recognise the need for a broader and not solely a quantitative dimension. The use of such quantitative indicators is, however, a good way to start. If nothing else they provide a solid framework for at least understanding one dimension of the process. It is not enough, however, merely to aggregate the economic returns from a project, divide by the number of participants and pronounce a global index of participation; more critical will be who participates and the relationship between the aggregate figures and different project groups. Similarly, while the strong relationship between organisation and participation inevitably leads to organisational indicators, participation in organisations is not a static or one-dimensional activity. But the commonest indicators currently used are those related to participation in project activities, and thus practice is a reflection of the economic pressures to "cost" participation and to relate those costs to expected benefits. In all of this we can clearly see that there is a major dimension missing; this dimension involves the quality of the participation or the human and behavioural aspects of the process of participation.

Qualitative indicators

The qualitative indicators of a process of participation are directly related to the rural people involved in the project, and particularly to the changes which occur in the nature, growth and behaviour of the project "group" as a result of the project activities. We have already seen in Chapter 4 the kinds of objectives relating to participation which projects establish and we can judge from these the difficulties involved. Werner and Bower (1982) and Feuerstein (1986) both similarly emphasised the relationship between qualitative indicators of participation and behavioural changes in the project group and argued that, although they present difficulties, they could be ignored. The central difficulty is how to select relevant indicators. What particular factors, phenomena or features can we choose which will authentically represent the qualitative process of participation? In an earlier study Oakley and Winder (1981) approached this by comparing the characteristics of a project group, as explained by project staff, before a process of participation with those after a period of time (see box 33). This exercise identified a number of key indicators and served as a basis for further work by Oakley (1985) in which he suggested three broad areas of qualitative indicators of participation:

Organisational growth: Internal structuring of project group

Allocation of specific roles to group members

Emerging leadership structure

Formalisation of group structure

Group behaviour: Changing nature of involvement of project group members

Emerging sense of collective will and solidarity

Involvement in group discussions and decisions

Ability to analyse and explain issues and problems

Group self-reliance: Increasing ability of project group to propose and to consider courses of action

Group members' knowledge and understanding of government policies and programmes

Changing relationship of group with project staff/ group facilitator

Formalisation of independent identity of the group

Independent action undertaken by the group

It is, of course, one thing to present a list of indicators as above; the next and more difficult task is to determine how these indicators might be observed and recorded. How, for example, do we observe and make a judgement on "... an emerging sense of collective will and solidarity"? This is a very real problem and to date little research has been carried out at project level to yield any clues. Essentially, we need to give some form or substance to these indicators, to relate them to some observable activity within the project so that we can observe them in action. Since qualitative indicators manifest themselves over time, we cannot simply tick them off but we must monitor them accordingly. Monitoring, therefore, has emerged as the key to the evaluation of participation and certainly as the only way to ensure a continual supply of relevant data and information.

Monitoring indicators of participation

The evaluation of participation involves careful monitoring, over an extended period of time, and the collection of data and observable phenomena related to both the quantitative and qualitative indicators (box 33 gives an example of such indicators). In terms of the quantitative indicators, this

---

Box 33.   Group characteristics before a ~~of participation~~

Before

- Individualism: lack of collective action
- Lack of critical analysis and inability to explain c
- Economic and political dependence on others
- Lack of confidence
- Lack of any form of organisation
- Suspicion, isolation and fear of discussion

After

- Group cohesion and sense of solidarity
- Internal group structure and element of self-management
- Increasing ability to analyse and discuss critically
- Collective activities
- Ability to deal with and relate to officials
- Interest in linking with other groups (Oakley and Winder, 1981)

Indicators of community participation

- The existence of already organised community groups
- The number of community groups and organisations involved in health promotion before versus after new health promotion activities are introduced
- The community's receptivity to and responsibility for solving or preventing its own health problems
- The number of existing community-based health activities and projects before versus after contact with the formal health system
- Demonstrated willingness to commit community human, material and financial resources to support a [community health worker] who would provide services specifically for that community
- An increase or decrease in the extent of coverage of health services (Rice and Boylan, undated, pp. 7-8)

---

monitoring presents us with fewer problems; indeed it could be argued that these indicators present us with the first level of participation and that projects could begin this complex task with them. The qualitative indicators, on the other hand, are much more problematic. In the first instance we need to identify a series of phenomena which will illustrate the qualitative indicators. Although we might accept, for example, that an "… emerging sense of collective will" would be an indicator that the project was beginning to build up a base from which people could participate, how could we identify and observe this? It is not like a plant whose growth we could easily observe; it is an intangible process which could be observed by means of key phenomena which will characterise

or example, if we were to observe over time the internal
f a project group, we might note certain phenomena in relation to
which might illustrate whether "… an emerging sense of collective
s developing.

Since we have already suggested that the evaluation of the qualitative
ocess of participation would be based on description and analysis, we will
need to monitor and to observe and record, on a regular and continual basis, this
qualitative process unfolding. To do this we will need to structure our observing
and recording around a series of predetermined aspects of the project. In this
respect Oakley (1988) has suggested four aspects of a project which, if monitored
continually, should provide us with relevant information and data for both
quantitative and qualitative indicators:

Project or group activities: Economic or other production activities

Physical or construction work

Collective project group work

Project group internal structuring

Changes in project group behaviour: Nature of project group meetings

Levels of explanation and discussion

People's involvement in project group discussions

Incidence of consensus and disagreement

Emerging patterns of leadership

Group action and articulation: Independent action by project group

Levels and nature of contact with outside officials

Levels and nature of contact with other project groups or organisations

Project-group relationship: Nature of initial relationship

Building up of the project group

Nature of changes in relationship between project and group

Project withdrawal

The above four aspects are not presented sequentially, nor is it intended
that they should all be monitored simultaneously. Furthermore, not all might be
relevant to the project being monitored. Instead they constitute a framework
and an indication to projects of the nature of the tasks involved. The two common
steps in the process, however, which will be applicable to all projects, are:

- the identification of the indicators to be used to reflect the process of
  participation being monitored;
- the determining of the broad aspects of the project which will be monitored.

This exercise must be particular to each individual project since there are few universal truths in a process of participation. Here we show one way of sketching out this exercise and is meant to serve as an example for the individual exercises which will need to be done for each project.

The range of examples presented on the previous pages are meant to serve as a resource in determining how best a process of participation might be evaluated in a particular project. They are not presented as universally applicable models, but more as food for thought in a difficult conceptual and practical task. All of them concentrate upon the central issue of indicators and are quite different in the way in which they seek to value or rank order these indicators. Finsterbusch and Van Wicklin (1987) and Shrimpton (1989) add numerical value to this ranking (box 34 and table 3). Rifkin et al. (1988) (box 34) employ the same approach but are able diagrammatically to evaluate performance of the indicators in a relative manner. All the examples concentrate upon identifying the indicators and evaluating their performance; the next important task is how these indicators might be evaluated and the information and data gathered and interpreted.

Box 34. Examples of designs and indicators for the evaluation of a process of participation

		Value score 1-7	Confidence score 1-5
A. Participation questionnaire for evaluation code sheet			
(1)	Beneficiaries' role in the planning phase		
	(a) degree of participation in original idea	☐	☐
	(b) degree of participation in project planning	☐	☐
	(c) beneficiary commitment to project	☐	☐
(2)	Beneficiaries' role in implementation phase		
	(a) degree of financial contribution	☐	☐
	(b) degree of participation in implementation	☐	☐
	(c) degree of indigenous knowledge used vs. dependency on outside experts	☐	☐
	(d) degree of organisation of beneficiaries	☐	☐
	(e) extent to which organisation is theirs vs. engineered by others	☐	☐
	(f) democracy and equality in organisation	☐	☐
	(g) extent to which beneficiaries redesign project	☐	☐
(3)	Beneficiaries' role in maintenance phase		
	(a) degree of participation in maintenance	☐	☐
	(b) degree of indigenous knowledge used vs. dependency on outside experts (after project is completed)	☐	☐
	(c) degree of local vs. outside ownership and control of facilities and organisations	☐	☐

	Value score 1-7	Confidence score 1-5
(4) Project linkages to beneficiaries		
(a) adequacy of communication from project team	☐	☐
(b) degree to which project increased beneficiary capacity	☐	☐

Note: Each project is scored on a seven-point scale from 1 = exceptionally low to 7 = exceptionally high. The coder's confidence in this judgement is registered in the second score on a five-point scale from 1 = very little confidence and very strong doubts to 5 = great confidence and very little doubt. (Finsterbusch and Van Wicklin, 1987, p. 10).

B. Analytical framework for the evaluation of participation

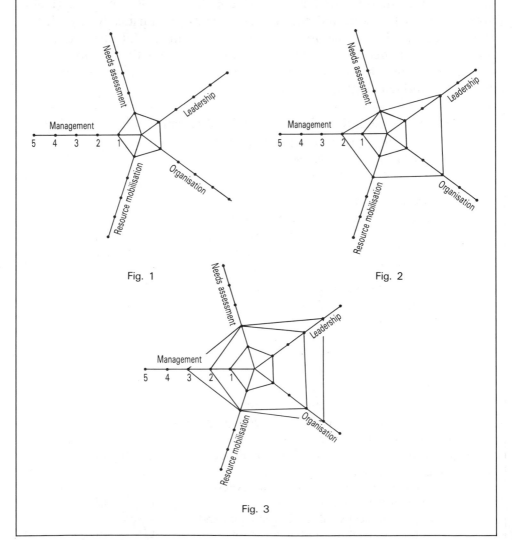

Fig. 1

Fig. 2

Fig. 3

Collecting information and data

The next stage is to consider how we might collect information and data based on the above broad framework for the evaluation of participation. In this respect we shall concentrate upon the qualitative aspects of participation; there are already ample guides on methods for the collection of quantitative data on project performance.[8] The qualitative aspects of participation present us with the much more difficult task of information and data collection. As we have seen, the approach to qualitative evaluation is one of

Description ──────────▶ Interpretation

in terms of a selected number of aspects of a project, and the continuous recording and observing of these aspects over time. To date little work has been done on this aspect of the evaluation process: Oakley's (1985) work is the more substantial, whilst Carr et al. (1984), Gianotten (1986), Simmonds (1987) and Rifkin et al. (1988) have also all, to a varying extent, examined methods for qualitative information and data collection. While it is not yet possible to talk in terms of a "monitoring system" for qualitative evaluation, a review of these different works suggests a number of guiding principles which should influence the monitoring process:

- the monitoring process should be a participatory exercise in which both project staff and the rural people have equal roles;
- the approach of the monitoring should be simple but effective, with the emphasis upon the continuous monitoring of a limited amount of information and data (which can be steadily increased) rather than a grandiose exercise which is both complex and inoperable;
- the approach must similarly take note of the time required and, given the considerable demands on both staff and rural people, it should be realistic in the demands it makes;
- the monitoring process must be a continuous exercise, built into the routine of the project and with a recognised place in work patterns, and not a periodic and frantic response to sudden dearths of information and data.

The above are suggested as important principles to guide the information and data collection process. They are not presented as a universal model but should be examined in the context of the project to be monitored and adapted accordingly. Collectively, however, they do imply that the monitoring of the qualitative process of participation needs careful thought and cannot be approached in the manner of the more common belated evaluation mission.

---

[8] See, for example, E. Clayton and F. Petry: *Monitoring systems for agricultural and rural development projects* (Rome, FAO, 1981) for a comprehensive account of different monitoring systems for quantitative data for project evaluation.

In terms of the specific methods to be employed, there is as yet little substantial field evidence of tested and proven methods in this exercise. In the first instance there is the issue of a base-line survey. Such surveys are, of course, common in development practice but do present problems in terms of the qualitative aspects of a project. In this respect we need to think in terms of some kind of project group profile, or a description of the qualitative characteristics of a group before a project begins, as can be seen in the previous section. This group profile will provide a framework for the qualitative indicators and will be the critical first methodological step. Indeed, if some sort of initial qualitative group profile is not undertaken, it is difficult to imagine how an evaluation process could be established. More specifically, some experimentation has begun on how to collect the information and data required. This experimentation has suggested the following forms of collection:

Questionnaire: The use of a structured questionnaire will certainly be relevant to the quantitative aspects of participation. In terms of the qualitative aspects, a questionnaire could be used to verify the magnitude of particular changes which are beginning to emerge. For example, the continuous monitoring might detect the emergence of a sense of solidarity in the project groups and a sample questionnaire could be used to check this. In the use of such questionnaires, the emphasis must be put on open-ended questions which will provide the narrative and description vital to the qualitative evaluation process.

Records and reports: These records and reports, which will provide the continuous account of events as they unfold, will be the basic methodological tools. They will take two forms: an individual group record, which is a kind of log-book in which a continual record of group activities, decisions and membership are kept; and a diary, which is a continual account of the unfolding of a process of participation.[9]

Group discussion: Active participation in group discussions and activities of a process of participation. Hence these discussions and activities will be central to generating the information and data required. Such discussions can also be used for seeking the collective views of the project group in terms of how they see the qualitative changes occurring.

Key informants: This technique is well tried in conventional research methodology and it is suggested that, in a process of participation, key informants can often be a source of useful insights or can raise unexpected

---

[9] See Huizer, op. cit., for an account of the use of individual group records for the FAO People's Participation Programme. The use of a diary as a means of keeping a continuous record of project and group development is an emerging phenomenon; one of the most complete diaries kept by a project was the Sherpur Journal, which is a fascinating account of the unfolding of a process of participation on a project in northern India. The project was supported by OXFAM. Another example is the diary kept by a female animator working with fisherwomen in North-East Brazil and which is referred to in Oakley (1981).

issues. Such key informants could include staff not directly involved with the project groups, influential local people who may have observed the project's progress or key members of the groups themselves who have the confidence of others and could represent their views and feelings.

Field workshops: Huizer (1983) has developed the idea of an annual field workshop as an important means of reviewing overall the nature of the participation which has occurred in a project. Such workshops give the opportunity for both project staff and group members to come together to review collectively the information and data collected over the year.

The essential principles to adopt in this process of information and data collection are those of experimentation and continuity. There are no universal models for the qualitative evaluation of participation, but only a range of options and techniques. The above list is a review of these and is presented for adaptation to the particular characteristics of the project concerned. The issue of continuity, however, is universal since without it the necessary information and data will never be collected and the process of participation will never be understood.

A further issue related to the information and data collected concerns storage. As information and data are collected, they will need to be stored in a way which makes both access and retrieval easy. In this respect there are no fixed models or mechanisms on how best to store this qualitative material. A study by Oakley (1985) examined this issue and suggested a system for storing information and data. This system is outlined in box 35 and explains in detail both the different stages of storing and the procedures involved. Oakley's system is presented as an example and as an indication of the steps to be taken. An appropriate system for the storing of information and data is vital in the process of evaluation, but any system must be developed on the basis of existing resources and project requirements.

Interpreting the information and data

Interpretation is the final stage in the evaluation of a process of participation. Here again we shall concentrate upon the qualitative since the statistical interpretation of the quantitative information and data presents us with fewer problems.[10] This latter data will present us with one dimension of the participation which has occurred; but it will be equally important to understand the other dimensions. The interpretation of this qualitative information and data, however, presents a number of problems. First, the subjective nature of the recording and observation will need to be taken into account; second, the

[10] See, for example, N. Imboden: *Setting up a monitoring and evaluation system for social programmes* (Paris, OECD, 1979).

Box 35. Storing the information and data collected while monitoring a process of participation

- Give each project group a number
- Establish an individual record card system by number for each group
- Record on this card system, on a monthly basis, the following information:
  - the number of group members/by sex
  - group meetings/dates
  - attendance at group meetings, etc.
- Establish a general filing system for each group
- Within the general filing system of each group establish an individual filing system for each aspect. These different aspects could be marked, for example, as follows:
- A – Project/group activities
- B – Changes in group behaviour
- C – Action/articulation
- D – Project/group relationship
- Information on the different aspects should be stored monthly, and on a separate sheet of paper, as follows:
  A.1.1 (first month), A.1.2 (second month), etc.
  B.1.1 (first month), B.1.2 (second month), etc.
- At the beginning of the second year of monitoring, the information can be stored thus:
  A.2.1/A.2.2/A.2.3, etc.
  B.2.1/B/2/2/B.2.3, etc.
- In order to have some continuity in recording and development of observations, only one member of the project staff should have responsibility for recording the information in any one group filing system. Probably each staff member will have responsibility for the filing systems of a number of project groups

(Oakley, 1985, pp. 60-61)

---

differing levels of ability of project staff will influence the quality of the material obtained; and third, participation can be a slow process with the result that some indicators may unfold equally slowly and hence observations may lack substance. Finally, the critical importance of a base-line survey or group profile must be re-emphasised since without some kind of initial statement, it will be impossible to interpret outcomes in relation to the previous situation.

When undertaken, the interpretation should be done with as much rigour as possible. It should be a participatory exercise and should involve both staff and project group members; it should also be done on a regular basis, e.g. every three months, so that a steady profile can be built up; and, where possible, verbal interpretation should be translated into some kind of diagrammatic form.

The important thing is to ensure that the interpretation does not become merely an ad hoc exercise, with consequent lack of structure and authenticity, but is conducted on as "scientific" a basis as possible. It is equally important not to spend countless hours on unstructured and endless discussion, but to structure and control a limited exercise which allows all those involved to contribute to the interpretation. The most difficult task will be to structure the qualitative material in a way that more tangibly allows us to see what the material means in terms of a process of participation. In this respect the importance of some form of visual or diagrammatic presentation must be underlined. Haque's (1977) pioneering conceptualisation has led to several further experiments and suggestions such as the following:

(1) *Indicators-phenomena chart:* If, for example, we determine that "increasing confidence" could be an indicator of participation, then we could identify those phenomena of project activities (e.g. increasing ability to take initiatives) which would reflect this "increasing confidence". These phenomena then become the basis of regular, monthly records and also help us to build up a visual and composite picture of the phenomena associated with a particular indicator.

(2) *Phenomena recording form:* As a support to (1) above, we could devise a form on which observations relating to particular phenomena were systematically recorded. As these observations were built up, it might be possible at a later date to produce a check-list which could note the presence of particular phenomena over a period of time and thus provide the continuous evidence upon which to base the interpretation.

(3) *Case study:* While monitoring will take place across the project groups, it would be useful to undertake a more detailed case study and analysis of one or a small number of groups. If we concentrated upon acquiring a detailed knowledge of the process of participation of a particular group, even though the context might vary, we could use the experience to understand better what might be happening with the other groups. Certainly a detailed understanding of one group would help with interpreting the process as it occurs with other groups.

A vital part of the interpretation overall, however, is the explanation of the emerging process of participation. In this respect we can imagine "participation" as a series of phases and structure the interpretation around these phases. Galjart and Buijs (1982), for example, suggest four principal stages of a process of participation:

■ Promotion
■ First action phase

- Construction phase
- Consolidation phase[11]

A further example is given in box 36.

**Box 36. Framework for interpreting information and data
of a process of participation**

Phases of project group participation	Indicators
Initial phase	Building confidence
	Establishing rapport
	Loosely structured meetings
Intermediate phase	Continuous project group structuring
	Solidarity
	Active internal participation
Principal phase	Structured organisation
	Formalisation
	Independent action
	External contacts

(Oakley, 1985, p. 68)

Since participation evolves over time, interpretation would be helped if it were undertaken within the framework of some expected structure of the process. Again there are no universal models in this respect, other than a suggestion that such a framework can be used to place all the material gathered in the monitoring exercise within some overall, coherent process. Table 3 presents an example of such a framework for judging participation in primary health care and nutrition projects. The important thing is to work on the assumption of this kind of framework and to develop it from the beginning of the monitoring exercise.

---

[11] See also, for example, J. Migdal: *Peasants, politics and revolution* (Princeton, University of Princeton Press, 1978). Migdal distinguished between four distinct phases of a process of peasant participation: passive, active, communal and class. In the late 1970s he concluded that most peasants in the Third World were in the initial (passive) phase of participation, yet some had experienced the latter (class) phase of participation in terms of their involvement on the national political stage, i.e. Mexico from 1911 to 1918 and Cuba from 1956 onwards.

Table 3. An analytical framework for judging community participation aspects of primary health-care and nutrition projects

Indicator	Ranking				
	1. Nothing/narrow	2. Restricted/small	3. Mean/fair	4. Open/good	5. Wide/excellent
Needs assessment/action choice	None	Done by outsiders with no VHC involvement	Assessment by outsiders and discussed with VHC whose interests are considered	Community does assessment and outsider helps in analysis and action choice	Community does assessment/analyses/action choice
Organisation	VHC imposed with no activity, or no community organisational support	VHC imposed, but some activity, or limited community organisation links	VHC imposed, but became very active	Active co-operation with other community organisations	Existing community organisations involved in controlling activities
Leadership	One-sided organisational support dominated by élite or health staff	CW working independent of social interest groups or community support structure	Organisational support functioning under leadership of independent CW	VHC or organisational support active. taking initiative together with CW	Organisational support fully represents variety of interests in community and controls CW
Training	Little or no training of CW or in unfamiliar language	Lengthy preservice training of CW in remote institution with no in-service training	Preservice CW training in local institution with little in-service training	Short local preservice CW training followed by regular in-service training by outsiders	Short local CW pre-service training, plus regular in-service training through supportive local supervisor/trainers
Resource mobilisation	No resource contribution by community. No fees for services. CW externally financed	Fees for services, no fund-raising. VHC has no control over money collected. CW externally paid	Community fund-raising and fees paid but no VHC control of expenditure. CW voluntary	Occasional community fund-raising, but no fees, and VHC controls allocation of money. CW voluntary	VHC raises funds, collects fees and controls allocation of money, pays CW

Table 3 (continued)

Indicator	Ranking				
	1. Nothing/narrow	2. Restricted/small	3. Mean/fair	4. Open/good	5. Wide/excellent
Management	Induced by health staff. CW only supervised by health staff	CW manages independently with some involvement of VHC. Supervision by health staff	VHC self-managed without control of CW activities	VHC self-managed and involved in supervision of CW	CW responsible to and actively supervised by VHC
Orientation of actions	No clear objectives, no targeting. Curative only	Process-oriented objectives, but no targeting. More curative than preventive	Impact-oriented objectives, but no targeting. More curative than preventive	Impact-oriented objectives, VHW interventions targeted to at-risk groups. More curative than preventive	Impact-oriented objectives, CW interventions targeted to at-risk groups. Preventive and curative
Monitoring evaluation/ information exchange	No IS, or information used locally. Nobody aware of problem dimension or programme progress	Information sent to outsiders who are aware of problem dimension and programme progress, but not fed back to VHC	IS used for routine daily activities/decision-making by CW who is aware of dimension of process and programme progress	VHC receives information necessary for decision-making from CW. VHC aware of problems, programme progress/ benefits	VHC disseminates information so that community is aware of problems, programme progress/ benefits

VHC = Village Health Committee; CW = Community worker; IS = Information system.

(Shrimpton, 1989, p. 7.)

Participatory evaluation

Given the qualitative nature of a process of participation, its evaluation demands that local people should be directly involved. In this respect it could be argued that the technique of participatory evaluation would be appropriate to the evaluation of participation. We have, however, already cautioned that both concepts are not the same; the evaluation of participation is the evaluation of a discrete process, while participatory evaluation is a form or technique of evaluation which is relevant in evaluation exercises across the sectors in rural development. Furthermore, participatory evaluation as a technique is often examined in the literature within the overall concept of participatory action research. Research and evaluation are both essentially supportive dimensions of development project practice, and indeed are at different ends of the project continuum. They are commonly lumped together in examinations of key participatory aspects of project practice. Rahman (1982), Hatch (1983) and Fernandez and Tandon (1986), for example, review both concepts together and effectively argue that they are dimensions of the same process.

Participatory evaluation is, therefore, a relevant technique in the evaluation of participation. In practice it is also often referred to as self-evaluation, which emphasises evaluation not only as a learning process but also as a vital dynamic in the overall process of participation. Where the local people are involved in discussion, debate, analysis and interpretation of project activities, they come to share a common perspective and a shared commitment to action, and this can transform a loose group of individuals into a cohesive and effective project group. In a broader sense, participatory evaluation methodologically is entirely consistent with the whole process of participation in development; given the general thrust of people-centred, bottom-up development, it makes sense to ensure that the process of evaluation has similar characteristics and meanings. In this sense it would be a contradiction to have people-centred, bottom-up processes of development evaluated by externally commissioned and designed initiatives. In their study on participatory evaluation, Choudhary and Tandon (1988) characterised the central concept as follows:

> The central characteristic of participatory evaluation is that people involved in a given development programme or organisation, both as implementors and as beneficiaries, start participating in and take charge of the evaluation efforts.
>
> The control over the process of evaluation remains in the hands of those who are developing and implementing and benefiting from the programmes. Thus, the evaluation serves the interest of furthering the benefits and improving the programmes and organisations involved in development at the base, and not those who are intending to control it from the top. In a way, participatory evaluation is an attempt at redefining and reaffirming development as a "bottom-up", "people-centred", "people-controlled" process and not a technocratic, top-down intervention. It is this thrust that provides the distinctive meaning to participatory evaluation methodology (Choudhary and Tandon, 1988, p. 8).

Participatory evaluation, therefore, is concerned with the assessment of project outcomes; it seeks to assess the impact of a project (e.g. in terms of participation), to analyse the underlying assumptions upon which the project is based, to consider the relevance of the project activities in the socio-political context and to judge the manner in which these activities have been carried out. Its focus, therefore, is at the project level and entails the active and direct involvement of local people along with field staff. This focus is a critical element of participatory evaluation since it helps shift the whole emphasis of the evaluation exercise away from an external bureaucracy and down to the grassroots level. Indeed it could be argued that participatory evaluation has its own distinctive style and that the basis of its approach is radically different from conventional evaluation practice. For example, the Centre for Rural Health and Social Education in Tamil Nadu, India, suggested the following as the basic premises of participatory evaluation:

- The actual work carried out by a group of people in the context of socio-economic, political and cultural realities, spread over a long period of time, cannot be evaluated by a team of evaluators, however competent the evaluators may be, by merely spending a week or ten days at the project area.

- Even though the impact of the programme may have far-reaching social and political implications, it is none the less difficult to establish cause-effect relationships since social change is a complex phenomenon.

- Evaluation is a continuous process and the outcome of the evaluation cannot be dissociated from the process of evaluation. Therefore, if the outcome is viewed independently and is not related to the process itself, then it may not be a fruitful exercise.

- Evaluation is effective and useful only when the people concerned themselves carry out this exercise against a set of objective criteria; and the exercise is preferably facilitated by an outsider in whom the project staff have confidence.

- Evaluation is a process which benefits the evaluators as much as it is helpful to the project people.

- Evaluation should be delinked from funding to widen its scope and to eliminate a sense of fear usually associated with evaluations.

- Evaluators should clearly state their role in this exercise at the very beginning in order to overcome role ambiguity. For example, it would be helpful if the evaluators, through their spoken words and actions, communicated that they were performing a facilitative role rather than an investigative role.

- Evaluation should follow a participatory model if it is to be productive not only at the level of the highest officials but also down to the core staff of the organisation.

- Evaluators should share at the very beginning the methodology and the tools to be used for the evaluation, and the project staff should be convinced of the objectivity of the tools and should be inclined to use them.
- Lastly and most importantly, at the very outset the objectives of the evaluation should be clearly spelt out.

Hatch (1983) similarly examines the basis of the practice of participatory evaluation and suggests that issues such as community ownership of the instruments of evaluation, simplicity of language used, regular and systematic application and allowing evaluation to evolve are essential principles of this practice.

Equally importantly, most commentators see participatory evaluation not as a one-off limited exercise but as a continuous process which unfolds in a series of stages. Too often evaluation becomes a snap-shot exercise conducted by people not directly related to the project and in which the local people are seen as the objects of the evaluation exercise. Participatory evaluation not only sees people as subjects of the exercise but sees the evaluation occurring over a period of time. Feuerstein (1986), Choudhary and Tandon (1988) and Egger (1988a), for example, have all suggested a series of stages in participatory evaluation in which the local people play a central role. The illustrative examples in box 37 clearly show the process nature of participatory evaluation and also how the local people are closely involved at all stages. The examples complement each other: Choudhary and Tandon sketch out these stages in a broad manner, while Feuerstein presents the detail of actions at each stage. Both examples support the general focus of the evaluation of participation, that is the notion of an unfolding exercise and the critical stages of identifying the key parameters and the collection and interpretation of data. They similarly suggest the importance both of allocating time to evaluation and also of a systematic approach which seeks to follow the stages outlined.

Box 37. Stages of a process of participatory evaluation

(1) All those involved in a programme need to decide jointly to use a participatory approach

(2) Next, they need to decide exactly what the objectives of the evaluation are. This is often harder than they think it will be

(3) When they have reached agreement on the evaluation objectives, it is time to elect a small group of "evaluation co-ordinators" to plan carefully and organise all the details of the evaluation

(4) Now is also the time to decide what methods will be best for attaining the evaluation objectives. The choice of method, such as analysis of programme records or use of a questionnaire, will also be influenced by the capabilities of the people involved, and by how much time and how many resources are available for evaluation

---

(5)   As these decisions are made, the written evaluation plan is formed. This plan shows why, how, when and where the evaluation will take place, and who will be involved

(6)   Next the evaluation methods must be prepared and tested (for example, a questionnaire or a weighing scale may be needed). Selected programme participants will also need basic explanation of and training in interviewing, completing written or oral questionnaires, conducting various kinds of checks or examinations, etc. All programme participants will need explanations of the objectives and general methods to be used in the evaluation. The more they understand, the more they can participate in the entire evaluation process, wherever and whenever requested by the evaluation co-ordinators

(7)   Having prepared and tested the evaluation methods, the next step is to use them to collect the facts and information required for the evaluation

(8)   Then the information and data are analysed by the programme participants. The major part of this work will probably be done by the evaluation co-ordinators

(9)   The results of the analysis (or the evaluation findings) are then prepared in written, oral or visual form. There are different ways of reporting and presenting the evaluation findings to different groups connected with the programme. For example, a Ministry (or programme funders) will usually need a written evaluation report but community-level participants will be better able to share results if they are presented as charts or pictures, or if they are presented during discussion meetings

(10) Programme participants then need to decide exactly how the evaluation results will be used, and how such results can help to improve the performance and effectiveness of the programme (Feuerstein, 1986, pp. x-ix)

Setting objectives: Frames of reference ↓	First stage: Discussion of evaluation objectives
Identifying parameters and information needed ↓	Second stage: Collection of data between the animators and local population
Identifying sources of information ↓	Third stage: Discussion of particular aspects of the project with the people
Developing methods to obtain that information and data collection ↓	Fourth stage: Interpretation of results
Analysing the data ↓	Fifth stage: Discussion of results by the people
Creating future scenarios ↓	Sixth stage: Synthesis and agreement
Evolving action plans	
(Choudhary and Tandon, 1988, pp. 16-18)	(Egger, 1988a, p. 15)

Within the framework of the stages outlined above, there have recently appeared a number of more detailed guides or manuals which explain graphically how participatory evaluation should be implemented at the project level. These fall into two categories; those aimed at project staff and those directed at project participants themselves. For example, the FAO has pioneered the preparation of such manuals for its People's Participation Project, and those written by Huizer (1983), Oakley (1985), Brown (1986) and Stephens (1988) already assist project staff in evaluation. The most complete manual is the one prepared by Feuerstein (1986), which offers detail of each stage of the evaluation process and is essentially directed at project-level workers. Feuerstein's work relies much on diagrams and illustrations and on detailed and easily intelligible guide-lines across the whole evaluation process. Such manuals are extremely useful and all underline the systematic nature of participatory evaluation. In relation to the evaluation of participation, the main criticism that we could make of such manuals, however, is their emphasis upon quantification and the ways in which they seek to encapsulate project activities within controllable parameters. Such manuals are invaluable in participatory evaluation; they should be used more cautiously in the evaluation of participation.

Concluding comments

It would be wrong to conclude that conceptually, and particularly methodologically, rural development projects are currently grappling vigorously with the issue of the evaluation of participation. In comparison with statements of support for participation and efforts to develop its methodology, its evaluation has yet to substantially take off. Too often in the literature and project documentation there is a yawning gap; at the most there is reference to quantitative aspects or to participatory evaluation. However, some experimentation is under way and we await results from, for example, the FAO's trials with its People's Participation Project. In the meantime we can make a few observations concerning the implications of the evaluation of participation for project practice:

(1) The evaluation of participation in rural development projects is a central part of the project dynamic and not an occasional or separate activity. To be successful it must be built into the whole project process and not merely be resorted to when particular judgements concerning performance are required.

(2) To evaluate participation implies a broadening of the whole evaluation concept. Quantification and controlled measurement are not enough; the demands of the qualitative dimensions of participation will push the evaluation exercise into uncharted areas and, in terms of time, resources and methodologies, a project must be ready for this.

(3) The evaluation of participation, since it is a process which essentially seeks to understand how people are faring as a result of a development project, implies that people will be centre-stage. The evaluation dynamic will be internal and suggests a wholly different style of relationships between the people and project staff.

There is much to be done. None the less, the evaluation of participation challenges the professional evaluator to rethink practice and procedures and to suggest ways in which we might better understand such qualitative processes of rural development.

7

Conclusion

The development community has reached the point where participation must be demythologised. It is a development strategy which has been alternatively undervalued and over-sold (Bamberger, 1986, p. 144).

How true is Bamberger's statement? There can be no sure response since all statements about "participation" are predicated upon their ideological content. Undoubtedly as we enter the 1990s "participation" still holds a central position in both development thinking and practice; it also continues to be an issue of much controversy. There have been few, if any, development strategies in the past that have provoked such divergent debate; "participation" simply means different things to different people. It is not just that there are shades of disagreement over particular aspects of interpretation or implementation, but that there are clearly fundamentally opposed views as to what participation means in practice. The curious paradox is that on paper at least there is a fairly broad consensus around the concept of people's participation in development, the arguments for it, its importance and its key parameters, e.g. situation analysis, decision-making, implementation and evaluation; the fundamental divisions appear when the concept is put into practice. There are indeed two worlds of practice and it is increasingly difficult to see how the two could even meet. It is equally curious to see participation holding the central ground in two such divergent schools of thought and practice, which makes its study somewhat schizophrenic and certainly challenging.

This study has deliberately taken the "project" as its focus for an examination of the practice of participation. There are many who will argue that this is too narrow a focus and that, in any case, projects operate within a wider cultural, social, economic and political context from which it is impossible to divorce project practice. This is quite true, but it could be equally impossible to encompass within the scope of one study the whole matrix of vertical and horizontal forces which might potentially influence this practice. Such a monumental study would be beyond the grasp of most authors. This wider debate concerning participation in development projects, therefore, must be acknowledged and must stand as a caveat to all statements regarding the efficacy or otherwise of such projects. The influence of these contextual issues raises the question of whether in practice people's participation in development can only be meaningful and authentic after a period of structural change during which the basis of the conditions for this participation must be established. In other words, can we talk meaningfully of people's participation in development if the forces which have caused their exclusion are not initially confronted? How effective will all these development projects be in promoting people's participation where the change is limited to the immediate project environment but where the larger social and political context remains unchanged? Some argue that this broader contextual change is a prerequisite to authentic participation; others that only the emerging and growing dynamic of a process of participation can bring about the contextual change. Both approaches have their advocates, but the weight of the practice lies in the latter.

In terms of this practice one conclusion must be that a process of participation is not a science. Some project staff clearly recognise this and are prepared to operate within the demands of a potentially complex process whose direction is not predeterminable and whose progress cannot be assumed; they see participation as a qualitative change that cannot necessarily be predicted and they accordingly adjust both their style of work and expectations. More commonly, however, projects dominated by staff with scientific or technical backgrounds approach participation in the same manner as they approach other project inputs. Participation is seen as something which is controllable, manageable and able to be planned according to the project timetable. Project files bear witness to the exasperation, which at times culminates in indifference and hostility, that results from efforts to treat participation in this manner. This exasperation is often felt in terms of replicability and the at times anxious search to find a model of participation which can be replicated elsewhere. There is, of course, a coherence, a structure and even a discipline to a process of participation, but these can only be understood through the people involved. Nobody really knows what an authentic process of people's participation is, but many are experimenting. What can be said, however, is that it is radically different from conventional project practice; it is a complex process involving cultural, psychological, social and political factors and there are no universal models or guide-lines. Experimentation is the order of the day; structured but sensitive, manageable and yet not controlled. The project agent who seeks to encapsulate this complex process within the confines of some limited check-list of actions will only succeed in counting heads!

At the heart of attempts to disentangle the practice of participation is the distinction which must be drawn between participatory development and participation in development. The crux to understanding the practice lies in this distinction. Participatory development essentially means conventional project practice in a more participatory and sensitive manner. There are, of course, variations along a continuum; at one extreme there is rigid, conventional practice which, as a sop to participation, introduces elements of discussion or predetermined organisation into the project (e.g. Lesotho case study); at the other extreme there are genuine efforts to alter this practice more radically and openly encourage people's participation (e.g. Nepal and the United Republic of Tanzania case studies). Whatever the location along the continuum, participation is essentially introduced within the predetermined project framework; the differences reflect the degree of tinkering with this framework. Participation in development, on the other hand, is a very different concept. Here the understanding of participation is derived from the characteristics of the rural poor's livelihoods; dependence, submission, limited access to resources, and so on. Participation in development concerns efforts to change these characteristics and to bring the vast majority within the ambit of local and national development initiatives. Somewhat incongruously the project has become the vehicle for this more qualitative process (e.g. Bangladesh, Peru and the Philippines case studies). A seminar at the Institute of Development Studies, University of Sussex, suggested that participatory development was essentially top-down participation, while participation in development was bottom-up participation. The two are necessarily mutually exclusive since they lead to distinct styles of practice. Furthermore, the former appears more dominant in terms of resources available and studies which have been widely disseminated; the latter, however, is now quite widespread and increasing in influence.

A major issue in the practice of participation, whatever its intrinsic nature and focus, concerns the development agency which works with or supports the process. Simply put, the question is asked whether government or NGO development agencies are "better" or "equally good" at promoting participation. There is, of course, no clear-cut answer since it all depends upon what one understands by "participation". However, there is no doubt that imaginary lines are being drawn. Governments generally look with suspicion upon projects which genuinely seek to promote people's participation in development, with all the challenges and potential conflicts with vested interests which that implies; equally some NGOs react strongly to development initiatives which, in the guise of participatory development, continue to control people's lives. A clear-cut distinction between the two imaginary lines can be seen in the language used to describe participation. Reading project files is like moving from one world to another; the terms used are often similar ("involvement", "decision-making", "access", "empowerment") but it is quite clear that there are two worlds of interpretation. It is wrong, of course, to caricature the entire practice of participation in this way, and yet it is relevant in order to convey how this practice has been interpreted so radically differently by development projects.

It is very difficult to avoid the conclusion that in general government-supported projects which supposedly seek to promote people's participation are not successful in developing an authentic base for sustained local involvement. This is not to suggest that all governments are either unwilling or even hostile to the notion of greater people's participation; indeed, most are signatories to several international declarations which openly support this greater participation. The main reasons for this limited government success would appear to be twofold. First, government's understanding of participation is generally limited and seen as management within the demands of project development. Government projects inevitably talk of "beneficiaries", suggesting that to benefit is to participate; or else they detail the ways in which local people can participate by collaborating with project activities in the form of labour or materials. Government-supported projects often see participation as building up the economic base of some in the expectation that benefits will diffuse into the wider local community; accordingly much of the dynamic is dependent upon external injections of material support. Second, inflexible, unimaginative and often cumbersome project procedures frustrate many government projects' efforts to develop local participation. There is a formidable rigidity to many of these projects, with firm professional control, clearly laid down timetables and strict financial management; which all adds up to an environment which is hardly conducive to the qualitative and indeterminable demands of a process of participation. MacDonald's (1989) apt study presents a scenario of project practice in which it is difficult to imagine participation emerging. However, it would be wrong to conclude that all governments are opposed to the idea of people's participation; Rahman's (1985) review of the ILO-supported Participation of the Rural Poor programme, for example, concluded that –

> ... all governments are not monolithic organisations firmly wedded to the principle of "development from above", but that refreshingly imaginative quarters exist within some government bureaucracies either to initiate or support action from below which challenges this principle. However it may be, the nature of the work concerned unquestionably makes government agencies typically unsuitable to handle (participation) on a significant and sustained scale (Rahman, 1985, pp. 17-18).

Rahman's comment is probably quite accurate and it certainly raises the question of whether it is realistic to think in terms of turning this dominant practice around by such things as cajoling or training or whether this will only happen as a result of increased pressure from below.

On the other hand, it is difficult to come emphatically to the conclusion that NGOs are the best agencies to support a process of participation. Such ambivalence is largely due to the very broad church of NGOs, which makes generalised statements impossible. However if we characterise NGO-supported projects as usually more flexible, less constrained by time, more ideologically committed to people's involvement and more willing to experiment, then we could argue that such projects would be more conducive to promoting participation. A major failing of NGO projects, however, is their lack of attention to the detail of participation, their emphasis upon commitment rather than proven ability and their increasing reluctance to evaluate. It is a curious situation that, despite their widely acknowledged support of bottom-up processes, few NGO-supported project files capture the essence or the detail of participation, and there appears little concern to understand its methodology, its tactics or its processes. The strength of NGO projects is their overt support for bottom-up development, which is reflected in their style, their language and their solidarity; their weakness lies essentially in not capitalising more systematically upon these strengths and building up our knowledge and understanding of this complex process. Notwithstanding these failures, however, we must conclude that at this moment many NGOs (e.g. PIDER, Sri Lanka; ORAP, Zimbabwe; FASE, Brazil), with their ideological perspective and intrinsic commitment to bottom-up development, have had a major influence upon both thinking and practice of this form of development and have been responsible for developing the basis for sustained people's participation in their countries.

Perhaps the major issue which emerges from this study concerns the relationship between the "project", as a basic instrument of rural development, and a process of participation. In other words, can a process which seeks to tackle basic psychological, cultural and political aspects of people's exclusion and build an authentic basis for their participation really be encapsulated within the framework of a development project? The evidence suggests that the response would be negative. Essentially, participation has been incorporated into the existing project framework; we have seen the sectoral examples of this in Chapter 2. Participation, however, demands a distinctive strategy and methodology and these are difficult to implement within the conventional project framework. Inevitably the predetermined objectives and the administrative and bureaucratic project demands frustrate the whole process. Participation stutters, does not flourish, or even dies in projects unless certain principles are followed: the case studies from Ghana, Lesotho, Mexico and the United Republic of Tanzania attest to the tremendous energies needed just to support the project framework, which results in diluted effort and energy to sustain the process of participation. In such projects participation is linked too closely to the performance of the "delivery system" and, if this fails, then the whole dynamic is lost.

People's participation is essentially to do with economic and political relationships within the wider society; it is not just a matter of involvement in project activities. Development projects need to recognise this wider dimension, to support and facilitate it and not restrict it within their own functional and geographical limits. Development projects are in fact awesome responsibilities and their bureaucratic artificiality is so demanding of time and energy that complex processes such as participation go by the board. Also, projects mean money and the inevitable pressure to commit funds; participation, on the other hand, is often limited and not resource intensive, and is therefore unable to use substantial funds. Projects which support participation fall into two broad types:

-   projects which are essentially a contractual arrangement between the development agency and the local people, where the basis and terms of participation are clearly spelt out;
-   projects which are essentially a general vehicle of support for a wider process and which are used to provide timely resources and advice to activities which people undertake within this wider process.

In the former the participation can be tangible and economically productive but it is subject to the vagaries of project behaviour and is often transient in nature. In the latter the participation can be slow to mature and can be subject to many hostile forces, but if it takes hold it sets down deeper roots. Perhaps the solution, as Verhagen (1985) suggests, is to eschew the development project in favour of the development programme; but that is another debate.

This study has also revealed the paucity of understanding of a process of participation, particularly in terms of its methodology and evaluation, currently prevalent in many development projects. While the examples given in Chapters 5 and 6 represent a rich vein of current practice, they are the exception and not the rule. While we may have widespread commitment, this has yet to be translated into the practice of many thousands of development projects. There are two important points to be made here. First, there would appear to be a fairly widespread lack of concern, or interest in, the detail of the practice of participation; projects may stress it in their strategy and objectives, but reporting still tends to concentrate upon the inevitable bureaucratic nightmares and available data on project performance and impact. It is difficult to avoid the conclusion that many development projects espouse participation in name alone, and are less concerned with the detail of its implementation. Given the normal staffing characteristics of development projects this is not surprising; what is surprising, however, is the apparent lack of concern of many NGOs to understand better the complex process with which they are dealing. Second, inevitably the question is now being asked about how we might turn around current project practice and introduce an element of participation. Indeed, what impetus currently exists is in that direction. The answer goes back to the distinction between participatory development and participation in development. With the former, a turn-around might be possible given massive resources, professional readjustment and a realignment of the project framework; with the latter, the project is increasingly looking an inappropriate instrument.

A final comment must stress the remarkable paradox in which this study has progressed. Documentation abounds with ringing commitments to the concept of participation; yet despite many imaginative examples, the weight of development projects has altered little. Ten years, of course, is a very short time in development, but there seems little indication that a substantial breakthrough is about to occur. NGOs undoubtedly carry the flag, but frustratingly so many of their initiatives have no more than a local impact. The vast majority of rural people still constitute Freire's (1972) "culture of silence", with no voice, no access and no involvement. The study has tried to detail the imaginative ways in which this silence is being broken; they are encouraging, growing and producing results, but they are still so few. But there will soon be more and eventually the dominant paradigm must succumb to pressures from below.

Bibliography

de Abrew, S. 1988. *Promoting participation and self-reliance among small farmers in Sri Lanka.* London, Methuen.

Annis, S. 1987. "The next World Bank: Facing development from the bottom up", in *Grassroots Development* (Washington, DC, Interamerican Foundation), 11(1).

Apthorpe, R.; Conyers, D. 1982. "Decentralisation, recentralisation and popular participation in developing countries: Towards a framework of analysis", in *Development and Peace* (Budapest, Hungarian Peace Council), Vol. 3, No. 2, pp. 47-60.

Azad, N. 1986. *Empowering women workers: The Working Women's Forum in Indian cities.* Mylapore, Working Women's Forum.

Bagadion, B.; Korten, D. 1985. "Developing irrigators' organisations: A learning process approach", in M. Cernea (ed.): *Sociological variables in rural development.* Oxford, Oxford University Press.

Baldus, R.; Ullrich, G. 1982. *Promotion of self-help organisations of the rural poor in Africa.* Bonn, German Foundation for International Development.

Bamberger, M. (ed.) 1986. *Readings in community participation.* Washington, DC, Economic Development Institute of the World Bank.

Belloncle, G. 1987. *Proposals for a new approach to extension services in Black Africa.* Tours, University of Tours.

Benor, D.; Harrison, J.Q. 1982. *Agricultural extension: The training visit system.* Washington, DC, World Bank.

Berger, P. 1974. *The homeless mind.* London, Penguin.

Bhadwi, A.; Rahman, A. (eds.) 1982. *Studies in rural participation.* New Delhi, Oxford and IBM Publishing

Bhasin, K. 1976. *Participatory training for development.* Rome, FAO.

———. 1979. *Breaking barriers: A South Asian experience of training for participatory development.* Rome, FAO.

———. 1983. *Breaking barriers: A South Asian experience of training for participatory development.* Rome, FAO.

———. 1985. *Towards empowerment.* Rome, FAO.

———; Said Khan, N. 1988. *Grappling with each other: Action theory.* New Delhi, FAO.

———; Vimala, R. (eds.) 1980. *Readings on poverty, politics and development.* Rome, FAO.

Bottrall, A.F. 1981. *Comparative study of the management and organisation of irrigation projects,* World Bank Staff Working Paper No. 468. Washington, DC, World Bank.

Briscoe, J.; de Ferranti, D. 1988. *Water for rural communities: Helping people.* Washington, DC, World Bank.

Brown, C.K. 1986. *Guidelines for the establishment of a participatory management information system for PPP projects.* Rome, FAO.

Bruneau, T.C. 1986. "The Catholic Church and basic Christian communities", in D.M. Levine (ed.): *Religion and political conflict in Latin America.* Chapel Hill, University of North Carolina Press.

Buijs, H.J. 1979. *Access and participation,* ICA Publication No. 33. Leiden, University of Leiden.

———. 1982. "The participation process: When it starts", in Galjart and Buijs, 1982, op. cit.

Carr, M. et al. 1984. *Assessing rural development projects: An approach to evaluation as if people mattered.* Brussels, EEC.

Castillo, C.T. 1983. *How participatory is participatory development: A review of the Philippine experience.* Manila, Philippine Institute for Development Studies.

Centre for Women's Development Studies. 1986. *The seeds of change: Role of grassroots women's organisation in development.* New Delhi.

Cergueira, M.T. 1989. *The role of participation in community nutrition education programmes.* Ithaca, New York, University of Cornell.

Cernea, M. 1985. *Putting people first: Sociological variables in rural development.* Oxford, Oxford University Press.

———. 1987 "Farmer organisation and institution building for sustainable development", in *Regional Development Dialogue* (Nagoya, Japan), Vol. 8, No. 2, Summer, pp. 1-19.

———. 1988. *NGOs and local development,* World Bank Discussion Paper No. 40. Washington, DC, World Bank.

Chambers, R. 1983. *Rural development: Putting the last first.* Harlow, Essex, Longmans.

———. 1988. *Farmer first: A practical paradigm for the third agriculture.* Brighton, Sussex, Institute of Development Studies.

———; Pacey, A.; Thrupp, L.A. 1989. *Farmer first: Farmer innovation and agricultural research.* London, Intermediate Technology Publications.

Chandrasekharan, C. 1985. *Rural participation in forestry activities.* Rome, FAO.

Charlick, R.B. 1984. *Animation rurale revisited.* Ithaca, New York, Centre for International Studies, Cornell University.

Choudhary, A.; Tandon, R. 1988. *Participatory evaluation: Issues and concerns.* New Delhi, Society for Participatory Research in Asia.

Cohen, J.M.; Uphoff, N. 1977. Rural development participation: Concepts and measures for project design implementation and evaluation. Ithaca, New York, Cornell University.

———. 1980. "Participation's place in rural development: Seeking charity through specificity", in *World Development* (Elmsford, New York), Vol. 8, No. 3, Mar., pp. 213-236.

Constantino-David, K. 1983. *Community organisation and people's participation.* Uppsala, Dag Hammarskjöld Centre.

Crombrugghe, M.C. de; Howes, M.; Nieuwkerk, M. 1985. *An evaluation of EEC small development projects.* Brussels, EEC.

Crowley, J. 1987. *Community-based health care programme.* Nairobi, Kenya Catholic Secretariat.

Czech, H. 1987. *Towards a new approach to resource conservation.* Reading, University of Reading. Unpublished dissertation.

Damadoram, K. 1988. *The qualitative evaluation of rural social development.* Reading, University of Reading. Unpublished dissertation.

Dasgupta, S. 1988. *Understanding the tribal dilemma: Tribal women and forest dweller economy.* New Delhi, Indian Social Institute.

de Camino Veloso, R. 1987. *Incentives for community involvement in conservation programmes.* Rome, FAO.

Delion, J. 1986. *Objectives, pedagogy and institution of participation in rural development.* Hawaii, East-West Centre.

Drijver, C.A. 1989. *People's participation in environmental projects in developing countries.* Leiden, University of Leiden.

Economic Commission for Latin America. 1973. "Popular participation in development", in *Community Development Journal* (Oxford), Vol. 8, No. 2, pp. 77-93.

Egger, P. 1988a. *Des initiatives paysannes de developpment en Afrique.* WEP working paper. Geneva, ILO.

———. 1988b. *Participation and the voice of the poor.* Geneva, ILO. Mimeographed.

El Ghonemy, R. 1982. *People's participation in rural development.* Rome, FAO.

———. 1984. *How development strategies benefit the rural poor.* Rome, FAO.

Esman, M. J.; Uphoff, N. T. 1984. *Local organisations; Intermediaries in rural development.* Ithaca, New York, Cornell University Press.

Falconer, J. 1987. Forestry extension: A review of the key issues. London, Overseas Development Institute (ODI).

Fals-Borda, O. 1988. *Knowledge and people's power.* New Delhi, Indian Social Institute.

Farrington, J.; Martin, A. 1987. *Farmer participation in agricultural research: A review of concepts and practices.* London (ODI).

Fernandez, W. (ed.). 1981. *People's participation in development* New Delhi, Institute of Social Studies.

———. 1985. "Development and people's participation", in W. Fernandez (ed.): *Development with people.* New Delhi, Indian Social Institute.

———.; Tandon, R. 1986. *Participatory research and evaluation.* New Delhi, Indian Social Institute.

Feuerstein, M. T. 1986. *Partners in evaluation.* London, Macmillan.

Finsterbusch, K.; van Wicklin, W. A. 1987. "The contribution of beneficiary participation to development project effectiveness", in *Public Administration and Development* (Chichester, John Wiley), Vol. 7, pp. 1-23.

Food and Agriculture Organisation of the United Nations (FAO). 1983. *The training of group promoters in field projects of the People's Participation Programme.* Rome.

———. 1988a. *Participatory monitoring and evaluation: A handbook for training field workers.* Bangkok, Regional Office for Asia and the Pacific.

———. 1988b. *A soil conservation strategy for Africa.* Rome.

Freire, P. 1972. *Cultural action for freedom.* Harmondsworth, Middlesex, Penguin.

———. 1973. *Education: The practice of freedom.* London, Writers and Readers Publishing Cooperative.

Fuglesang, A.; Chandler, D. 1986. *Participation as process: What we can learn from Grameen Bank, Bangladesh.* Oslo, NORAD.

Galjart. B. 1981. "Participatory development projects: Some conclusions from research", in *Sociologia Ruralis* (Assen, Netherlands), Vol. 21, No. 2, pp. 142-159.

———. 1987. "Participatory development projects", in *Netherlands Review of Development Studies* (Amsterdam), No. 1, pp. 55-65.

———; Buijs, D. (eds.). 1982. *Participation of the poor in development.* Leiden, University of Leiden, Institute of Cultural and Social Studies.

Gamser, M. 1987. *Experimenting with different forestry extension methods in the Northern Sudan.* London, ODI.

Gezelius, H. 1989. *Popular participation in development.* Stockholm, University of Stockholm. Unpublished manuscript.

———; Millwood, D. 1988. *NGOs in development and participation in practice: An initial inquiry.* Stockholm, University of Stockholm, Department of Social Anthropology.

Ghai, D. 1984. *Small farmer development programmes. Mid-term evaluation.* Rome, International Fund for Agricultural Development (IFAD).

———. 1985. *An evaluation of the impact of the Grameen Bank Project.* Rome, IFAD.

———. 1988. *Participation in development: Some perspectives from grassroots experiences.* Geneva, United Nations Research Institute for Social Development (UNRISD).

Gianotten, V. 1986. *Methodological notes for evaluation.* Rome, FAO.

Gran, G. 1985. *Development by people.* New York, Praeger.

de Groot, W. T. 1989. *Participation and environmental management: An explanation.* Leiden, University of Leiden.

Guiza, E. C. undated. *People's self-review: A case experience on participation evaluation.* Manila, Process. Mimeographed.

Hall, A. 1981 "Irrigation in the Brazilian North-East: Anti-drought or anti-peasant", in S. Michell (ed.): *The logic of poverty: The case of the Brazilian North-East.* London, Routledge and Kegan Paul.

Hamilton, D. 1978. *Beyond the numbers game*. Berkeley, California, McCatchan.

Haque, W. et al. 1977. "Towards a theory of rural development", in *Development Dialogue* (Uppsala) No. 2, pp. 7-137.

Hatch, J. 1983. *A manual for participatory evaluation in community-based enterprises*. New York, Technoserve Inc.

Healey, K. 1988. "A recipe for sweet success: Consensus and self-reliance in Alto Beni", in *Grassroots Development* (Washington, DC, Inter-American Foundation), 12(1), pp. 32-41.

Hedenguist, J.H. 1989. *Popular participation in rural development: The Masare Project in Zimbabwe*, Working Paper 5. Stockholm, University of Stockholm, Department of Social Anthropology.

Hope, A.; Timmel, S. 1984. *Training for transformation*. Zimbabwe, Mambo Press. 3 vols.

Howes, M. 1984. *An evaluation of the Sri Lankan National Freedom From Hunger Campaign Board Small Tank Renovation and Rural Development Project*. Brussels, EEC.

Huizer, G. 1983. *Guiding principles for people's participation projects*. Rome, FAO.

Hunter, G. 1981. *A hard look at directing benefits to the rural poor and at participation*. London, ODI.

Illich, I. 1969. *Celebration of awareness*. Harmondsworth, Middlesex, Penguin.

Imboden, N. 1979. *Setting up a monitoring and evaluation system for social programmes*. Paris, OECD.

International Labour Office (ILO). 1982. *The struggle toward self-reliance of organised resettled women in the Philippines*. WEP working paper. Geneva.

———. 1984. *Group-based savings and credit for the rural poor*. Geneva.

———. 1985. *Differentiation among the rural poor and its bearing on solidarity and organisational development*. WEP working paper. Geneva.

———. 1987. *Conception of a programme of training for the promotion of participation in rural development*. Geneva. Mimeographed.

———. 1988. *Promoting people's participation and self-reliance*. Geneva. Mimeographed.

Jain, S. et al. 1988. *Exploring possibilities: A review of the women's development programme: Rajasthan*. Jaipur, Institute of Development Studies.

Jiggins, J.; Roling, N. (eds.). 1982. *The role of extension in people's participation in rural development*. Rome, FAO.

Khan, N.S.; Bhasin, K. 1986. *Sharing one earth*. Rome, FAO.

Kidd, R. 1979 "Liberation or domestication: Popular theatre and non-formal education in Africa", in *Educational Broadcasting International* (Basingstoke, Hampshire), Mar. pp. 3-9.

———. 1982. *The popular performing arts: Non-formal education and social change in the Third World*. The Hague, Centre for the Study of Education in Developing Countries.

Korten, D. 1980. "Community organisation and rural development: A learning process approach", in *Public Administration Review* (Lahore), Sep.-Oct., pp. 493-503.

———; Alfonso, F. (eds.) 1981. *Bureaucracy and the poor: Closing the gap*. Manila, Asian Institute of Management.

Kronkenburg, J.B.M. 1986. *Empowerment of the poor*. Amsterdam, Royal Dutch Tropical Institute.

Lassen, C.A. 1980. *Reaching the assetless rural poor*, Monograph Series 11, New Delhi, Indian Social Institute.

Leconte, B.J. 1986. *Project aid: Limitations and alternatives*. Paris, OECD.

Lele, U. 1975. *The design of rural development: Lessons from Africa*. Baltimore, Johns Hopkins University Press.

Levi, Y.; Litwin, H. 1986. *Community and cooperatives in participatory development*. London, Gower.

Lubett, R. 1987. *Non-government organisations as agents of empowerment*. Reading, University of Reading. Unpublished dissertation.

MacDonald, A. 1989. *Nowhere to go but down: Peasant farming and the international development game*. London, Unwin and Hyman.

MacDonald, J. 1989. *The education of health professions for CIH*. Geneva, World Health Organization (WHO). SHS/SG 89.4.

Mahoney, D. 1987. *Forestry extension training in Somalia.* London, ODI.

Marques, S.A. 1988. *UNIFEM and NGOs*, Occasional Paper No. 2. New York, UNIFEM.

Mathur, A. 1984. *Women's Development Programme: Rajasthan.* Government of Rajasthan.

Mazumdar, V. 1986. *Rural workers organise for women's empowerment.* New Delhi, Centre for Women's Development Studies.

Midgeley, J. 1987. "Popular participation, statism and development", in *Journal of Social Development in Africa* (Harare), Vol. 2, No. 1, pp. 5-15.

———. et al. 1986. *Community participation, social development and the State.* London, Methuen.

Millward, B.; Gezelius, H. 1988. *Good aid: A study of quality in small projects.* Stockholm, Swedish International Agency.

Morss, E.R. et al. 1976. *Strategies for small farmer development.* Boulder, Colorado, Westview Press. 2 vols.

Noppen, D.; Fugelsang M. 1988. *The Coop Members Participation Programme: CMPP*, Paper No. 4. Stockholm, University of Stockholm, Department of Social Anthropology.

Nyerere, J. 1968. *Freedom and socialism.* Dar es Salaam, Oxford University Press.

Oakley, P. 1981 "Fisherwomen and group development in North-East Brazil", in *Year Book of Agricultural Cooperation.* Oxford, Plunkett Foundation.

———. 1985. *A manual for the monitoring and evaluation of the PPP.* Rome, FAO.

———. 1987a. *Strengthening participation in rural development.* New Delhi, Participatory Research Institute for Asia.

———. 1987b. *People's participation in conservation: A review.* Lesotho, Southern African Development Co-ordination Conference.

———. (ed.). 1988a. *Proceedings of the International Symposium on the Challenge of Rural Poverty: How to meet it, Feldafing, January 1987.* Rome, FAO and Feldafing, DSE.

———. 1988b. *The monitoring and evaluation of participation in rural development.* Rome, FAO.

———. 1988c. "Extension and technological transfer: The need for an alternative", in *Hortscience* (Alexandria, Virginia, American Society for Horticultural Science), 23(1).

———. 1989. *Community involvement in health development: An examination of the critical issues.* Geneva, WHO.

———; Winder, D. 1981. "The concept and practice of rural social development", in *Manchester Papers on Development* (Manchester, University of Manchester), No. 1, May, "Studies in rural development", pp. 1-71.

———; Marsden, D. 1984. *Approaches to participation in rural development.* Geneva, ILO.

Omvedt, G. 1986. *Women in popular movements: India and Thailand.* Geneva, UNRISD.

Padron, M. 1982. *NGDOs and grass-roots development: Limits and possibilities.* The Hague, Institute of Social Studies.

Paredes, J. 1987. "Participatory research for social change in Bolivia", in *Ideas and action* (Rome, FAO), No. 176.

Parlett, M.; Hamilton, D. 1972. *Evaluation as illumination.* Edinburgh, University of Edinburgh.

Patil, R.K. 1987. *Economics of farmer participation in irrigation management.* London, ODI.

Patton, M.Q. 1987. *How to use qualitative methods in evaluation.* Beverly Hills, California, Sage Publications.

Paul, S. 1987. *Community participation in development projects*, Discussion Paper No. 6. Washington, DC, World Bank.

Pearse, A.; Stiefel, M. 1979. *Inquiry into participation.* Geneva, UNRISD.

Pradhan, P. 1979. "Baglung suspension bridges: Outcome of People's Participation in Nepal", in *Rural Development Participation Review* (Ithaca, Cornell University), Vol. 1, No. 1, pp. 13-14.

Racelis, M. 1988. *Health: A basic government development in Africa.* Geneva, WHO; 88/7.

Rahman, Md.A. undated. *Catalytic action to promote participatory rural development.* Geneva, ILO. Mimeographed.

———. 1981. *Bhoomi Sena.* Geneva, ILO.

———. 1982. *The theory and practice of participatory action research.* WEP working paper. Geneva, ILO.

Rahman, Md. A. 1983. *SARILAKAS grass-roots participation in the Philippines*. WEP working paper. Geneva, ILO.

———. 1984a. *NGO work of organising the rural poor*. WEP working paper. Geneva, ILO. Mimeographed.

———. 1984b. *Participatory organisation of the rural poor*. Geneva, ILO. Mimeographed.

———. 1984c. *Grass-roots participation and self-reliance*. New Delhi, Oxford and IBH Publishing Co.

———. 1985. *Participation of the rural poor in development*. Geneva, ILO. Mimeographed.

———. 1987a. *Further interaction with grass-roots organising works*. Geneva, ILO. Mimeographed.

———. 1987b. *The concept of community participation through family units*. Geneva, ILO. Mimeographed.

———. 1987c. *Theoretical and methodological questions in the promotion of people's participation in rural development*. Geneva, ILO. Mimeographed.

———. 1989. *Glimpses of the other Africa*. WEP working paper. Geneva, ILO.

Ratnapala, N.; Ariyaratne, A.T. (eds.) undated. *Collected works*. Colombo, Sarodaya Research Institute, Vol. 1.

Rice, M.; Boylan, K. undated. *Indicators of health promotion and education*. Washington, DC, Pan-American Health Organization (PAHO).

Rice, M.; Poganin, J.M. (eds.). 1988. *Social participation in local health services*. Washington, DC, PAHO.

Richards, M. 1985. *The evaluation of cultural action*. London, Macmillan.

Richards, P. 1985. *Indigenous agricultural revolution*. London, Hutchinson.

Rieger, H.C. 1976. *Himalayan ecosystem research mission: India report*. Heidelberg, Heidelberg University, South Asia Institute.

Rifkin, S. et al. 1988. "Primary health care: On measuring participation", in *Social Science and Medicine* (Elmsford, New York), Vol. 6, No. 9, pp. 931-940.

Rogers, A. 1988. *Making aid invisible; Development as seen by an adult educator*, Reading Rural Development Communication No. 23. Reading, University of Reading.

Roling, N. 1985. *Five essentials for the creation of active utiliser systems*. Amsterdam, Royal Tropical Institute.

———. 1987. "Extension and the development of human resources: The other tradition in extension education", in G.E. Jones (ed.): *Investing in rural extension: Strategies and goals*. New York and London, Elsevier.

———; Jiggins, J. 1982. *The role of extension in people's participation in rural development*. Rome, FAO.

Rudguist, A. 1988. *Consultations as a means of promoting popular participation*. Stockholm, University of Stockholm, Department of Social Anthropology.

Rugh, J. 1986. *Self-evaluation: Ideas for participatory evaluation of rural community development projects*. Oklahoma, World Neighbours.

Russell, J. 1985. "Farmer participation and the village extension worker", in M. Cernea (ed.): *Agricultural extension: The T & V System*. Washington, DC, World Bank.

Sanders, D.W. 1988. *Environmental degradation and socio-economic impacts: Past, present and future approaches to soil conservation*. Rome, FAO.

Schumacher, E.F. 1973. *Small is beautiful*. London, Abacus.

Sen, D.; Das, P.K. 1987. *The management of people's participation in community forestry: Some issues*. London, ODI.

Sethi, H. 1987. *Refocussing praxis*. New Delhi, Setu-Lokayan.

Shah, P.; Weir, A. 1987. *Approaches to social forestry in Western India: Some aspects of NGO experience*. London, ODI.

Sharma, M.; Oakley, P. 1988. *People's participation in rural Nepal: Case studies*. Kathmandu, APROSC/FAO.

Shepherd, A.; El Neima, A.A. 1983. *Popular participation in decentralised water supply planning*. Birmingham, University of Birmingham, Institute of Local Government Studies.

Shepherd, G. 1986. *Forest policies forest politics*. London, ODI.

Shrimpton, R. 1989. *Community participation in food and nutrition programmes: An analysis of recent government experiences*. Ithaca, New York, Cornell University.

de Silva, G.V.S. et al. 1983. *Cadre creation and action research in self-reliant rural development*. Geneva, ILO.

Simmonds, S. 1987. "Evaluation at the local level; The roles of outsider and the community", in *Health Policy and Planning* (Oxford), 2(4), pp. 309-332.

Stephens, A. 1988. *Participatory monitoring and evaluation*. Bangkok, FAO, Regional Office for Asia and the Pacific.

Stinson, W. 1987. *Creating sustainable community health projects: The PRICON experience*. Maryland, Centre for Human Services.

Swanson, E. (ed.). 1984. *Agricultural extension manual*. Rome, FAO.

Talagune, A.B. 1985. *Operational aspects of the change agents programme*. Colombo, Ministry of Rural Development.

Tandon, R. (ed.). 1987. *Participatory training for rural development*. New Delhi, Society for Participatory Research in Asia.

Therkildsen, O. 1986. "Participation in rural water supply: Experiences from a Dutch-funded project in Tanzania", in Bamberger, 1986, op. cit.

Thomas, B.P. 1985. *Politics, participation and poverty: Development through self-help in Kenya*. Boulder, Colorado, Westview Press.

Tilakaratna, S. 1985. *The animator in participatory rural development: Some experiences from Sri Lanka*. Geneva, ILO.

———. 1987. *The animator in participatory rural development*. Geneva, ILO.

Tinklenberg, L. 1988. *Health indicators as a tool for community participation in program planning*. Manchester, University of Manchester. Unpublished dissertation.

Tola, A. 1986. "Who is concerned", in *Splash* (Maseru, Southern Africa Development Coordination Council), Vol. 2, No. 1, pp. 2-4.

Tsiane, B.D.; Youngman, F. (eds.). 1985. *The theory and practice of people's participation in rural development*. Botswana, Ministry of Finance and Development Planning.

Ullrich, G. (ed.). 1982. *Promotion of self-help organisations of the rural poor in Africa*. Bonn, German Foundation for International Development.

Unia, P. 1988. *Some action group strategies for OXFAM in the Indian sub-continent*. Oxford, OXFAM.

United Nations. 1984. *Guiding principles for the design and use of M & E in rural development programmes and projects*. Rome, FAO, ACC Task Force.

———. 1985a. *UN Development Fund for Women. Developing cooperation with women; The experiences and future direction of the Fund*. New York.

———. 1985b. Poverty, productivity and participation. Bangkok, ESCAP.

———. 1987. *Popular participation policies as methods for advancing social integration*. New York.

University of Wageningen. 1978. *The small farmer and development cooperation*. The Netherlands, International Agricultural Centre.

Uphoff, N. 1981. *Farmers' participation in project formulation, design and operation*. Washington, DC, USAID.

———. 1985. *Optimum participation in irrigation management: Issues and evidence from Sri Lanka*. Ithaca, New York, Cornell University.

———. 1986a. *Improving international irrigation management with farmer participation: Getting the process right*. London, Westview Press.

———. 1986b. "Approaches to participation in agriculture and rural development", in M. Bamberger (ed.): *Readings in community participation* (Washington, DC, Economic Development Institute of the World Bank).

———. 1987. "Activating community capacity for water management in Sri Lanka", in D.C. Korten: *Community management: Asian experience*. West Hartford, Kumarian Press.

———. 1988a. "Assisted self-reliance: Working with rather than for the poor", in J. Lewis (ed.). *Strengthening the poor*. New Brunswick, Transaction Books.

Uphoff, N. 1988b. "Participatory evaluation of farmer organisations' capacity for development tasks", in *Agricultural Administration and Extension*, No. 30.

van Heck, B. 1983. *The training of group promoters in field projects*. Rome, FAO.

van Wijk-Sijbesma, C. 1979. *Participation and education in community water supply and sanitation programmes*. The Hague, International Reference Centre for Community Water Supply.

Vergara, N. et al. 1986. *Social forestry research issues*. London, ODI.

Verhagen, K. 1985. *The promotion of small farmer cooperative action and organisation*. Amsterdam, Royal Tropical Institute.

———. 1987a. *Self-help promotion: A challenge to the NGO community*. Netherlands, CEBEMO/ Royal Tropical Institute.

———. 1987b. *Introduction to the leading themes of the experts' consultation on the promotion of autonomous development*. Netherlands, Oegstgeest, CEBEMO.

de Vos, P. 1987. *Community participation and local management of primary health care*. Amsterdam, Royal Tropical Institute. Unpublished thesis.

Waddinba, J. 1979. Some participation aspects of programmes to involve the poor in development. Geneva, UNRISD.

Weiss, R.; Rein, M. 1970. "The evaluation of broad aim programs: Experimental design, its difficulties and an alternative", in *Administrative Science Quarterly* (Ithaca, New York), Vol. 15, No. 1, Mar., pp. 97-109.

Werner, D. 1988a. "Empowerment and health", in *Contact* (Geneva, World Council of Churches), No. 102, pp. 1-9.

———. 1988b. "Public health, poverty and empowerment – A challenge", in *IFDA Dossier* (Nyon), No. 165, May/June, pp. 3-10.

Werner, D.; Bower, B. 1982. *Helping health workers learn: A book of methods, aids and ideas for instructors at the village level*. Palo Alto, Hesperian Foundation.

White, A. 1981. Community participation in water and sanitation. The Hague, International Reference Centre for Community Water Supply and Sanitation.

Whyte, A. 1983. *Guidelines for planning community participation in water supply and sanitation projects*. Toronto, University of Toronto, Institute for Environmental Studies.

World Bank. 1975. *Annual Report*. Washington, DC.

———. 1988. Rural development: *World Bank experience*. Washington, DC.

World Council of Churches. 1981. *People's participation and movements*. Geneva, Vols. 1-3.

World Health Organization. 1987. *Report of the interregional meeting on strengthening district health systems based on primary health care*. Geneva. DHS 87.13.

World Resources Institute. 1987. *The Tropical Forestry Action Plan*. New York.